Y0-DNG-219

HC 59.7 C653

3 0050 00124 5256

CAL-STATE UNIVERSITY, HAYWARD
LIBRARY

Economic Development and Econ

Economic Development and Economic Growth

Edited with an Introduction by

James V. Cornehls

A NEW YORK TIMES BOOK

Quadrangle Books

CHICAGO

HC
59.7
C653

ECONOMIC DEVELOPMENT AND ECONOMIC GROWTH. Copyright ©
1972 by The New York Times Company. All rights reserved,
including the right to reproduce this book or portions
thereof in any form. For information, address: Quadrangle
Books, Inc., 12 East Delaware Place, Chicago 60611.
Manufactured in the United States of America. Published
simultaneously in Canada by Burns and MacEachern Ltd.,
Toronto.

Library of Congress Catalog Card Number: 77-130379
SBN Cloth 8129-0215-7
SBN Paper 8129-6179-X

The publishers are grateful to the contributors herein
for permission to reprint their articles.

CAL-STATE UNIVERSITY, HAYWARD
LIBRARY

To the memory of Ben Seligman

Contents

3. What Is Being Done, and How Well Is It Succeeding?

4. How Can We Help . . . and Not Help?

5. Prospects for the Future

Economic Development and Economic Growth

Introduction

ON MAY 31, 1970, a violent earthquake shook the Andes Mountains in South America, obliterating several Peruvian towns and villages and severely damaging many others. Thousands were injured, and an estimated thirty to fifty thousand were killed. News of the disaster was relayed instantly around the world. Soon after, filmed reports depicted the terrible sight of tons of earth sliding down mountainsides to engulf entire villages.

The world responded immediately and generously, both through its governments and through the efforts of private citizens. Within days, a dozen governments and the United Nations had announced plans to provide relief. The President of the United States ordered tons of medical and other supplies rushed into the area, and announced a $10 million U.S. grant. Mrs. Nixon flew to Lima carrying the donations of thousands of Americans, and accompanied Peru's first lady on a survey mission to confirm United States concern and interest. Not to be outdone, the Soviet Union announced its own plans for a massive airlift of aid, including sixty-five cargo planes and a complete field hospital. The Peruvian government mobilized the country and rushed supplies and thousands of medical and technical personnel into quake-stricken areas to combat starvation and disease. The urgency of the response and the impressive technical display in mobilizing resources to meet this widely publicized disaster undoubtedly saved thousands of lives. Perhaps even more significant, the entire effort was accomplished with apparent ease.

On precisely the same day, May 31, 1970, but with considerably less fanfare, some fifteen thousand other persons throughout the world died from starvation and malnutrition-induced illness. With the exception of relatives and close friends, virtually no one noticed. It is a common occurrence—it takes place quietly, it happens every day. Each year millions starve throughout the world, while uncounted additional millions suffer the ravages of shortened life expectancy due to malnutrition and disease. Because these deaths are not really newsworthy and because they take place in such widely separated parts of the globe, the same sense of urgency does not apply to what amounts to a *daily* disaster. This book is about those other unnoticed deaths, about the billion or so other people—roughly a third of the world's population—who struggle daily for a meager existence filled with hunger, illness, and despair. They make up most of the population in the world's economically underdeveloped countries. Many of them are themselves on the edge of becoming one of the daily fifteen thousand.

Both the disasters related above are tragic. But an earthquake is a natural disaster which ordinarily cannot be predicted or averted, while we know that tomorrow another fifteen thousand will starve. And we know that, technically, at least, the potential to prevent further deaths, as in Peru, is available in these other cases. Why then do these potentially preventable deaths continue almost unabated? Why is there not an equally massive response to this daily disaster? These questions form part of a much broader range of issues and questions which have to do with economic underdevelopment: Why do so many starve and suffer debilitating diseases in some parts of the world and not in others? How can we account for the tremendous disparities in income and wealth among nations? Why have some countries led in the development of scientific and technical progress while others have languished? Why have the technical achievements of the richer countries not been readily transferred to poor countries? What have the developed countries done to foster economic progress in the poorer countries, or to retard it?

Our attempt to shed light on these and associated questions will begin with a brief examination of how interest in economic underdevelopment has grown; some observations on United States and world aid to underdeveloped countries; and some evidence about the time-horizon for economic development. Next we will explore the full meaning of economic underdevelopment, examining its principal characteristics and some of the major obstacles to economic progress. Finally, we will consider economic development as a process which involves both technical and cultural factors.

Among the inhabitants of the developed countries, widespread public interest in the economic development of the so-called "third world" countries is comparatively recent. World poverty was "discovered" by the wealthier peoples of the world only shortly after World War II. Poverty for others was an accepted fact of life until recent times, even in the United States. Not until 1960 did the United Nations initiate its Decade of Development; not until 1961 did President John F. Kennedy inaugurate the Alliance for Progress; and not until 1959 was the first modern, comprehensive textbook about economic development published.

After World War II our awareness of and interest in the underdeveloped nations grew quickly. A variety of factors contributed to this change of attitude. Principal among these without doubt was the Cold War. The struggle for spheres of influence between East and West turned attention to the underdeveloped—and, by implication, undercommitted—nations. The game of economic assistance landed squarely in the forefront of international diplomacy.

Some of the more clever and cynical leaders of the less developed countries were quick to grasp the possibilities in this new situation. They more or less skillfully played both sides against each other in the hope of obtaining a greater share of international aid for their own countries, and not infrequently for themselves personally. In a few instances, the military hardware given as "aid" was used to put down popular political movements in underdeveloped countries, movements which might have led to useful reforms.

A second important factor in the increased interest in underdeveloped countries was the post–World War II growth in world communications. The world's poor were given increased visibility, and the same network of communications provided the poor with an increased awareness of their own plight: they were now able to compare their way of life with that of others. A logical outgrowth of this phenomenon was a demand among the poor that something be done to lessen their suffering—what has since been called "the revolution of rising expectations."

A final element in the increased awareness of underdevelopment was the population explosion. The booming rate of world population growth elicited constant fears of famine and an even further lowering of living standards for much of the world over the next few decades. The serious threats of an overcrowded globe and severe ecological imbalance helped stimulate interest in economic development, precisely because economic development has generally been accompanied by falling birthrates.

In the United States these early signs of interest in the economically underdeveloped world led to the inauguration in 1949 of a modest aid program known as "Point Four." American foreign aid grew slowly throughout the fifties and peaked in the early sixties at about $3.6 billion. Since then it has fallen to around $2 billion. It would be nice to believe that American aid was prompted solely by humanitarian motives, that it represented a sacrifice, and that it had a great impact on the economic well-being of the world's poor. But none of these was true. A substantial proportion of United States assistance was—and is—of the military variety and is prompted by fear of communism. And while $3.6 billion certainly represented a substantial amount of money, it nevertheless represented only a tiny fraction (less than three-fourths of 1 per cent) of our gross national product. More important, it was far from enough, even when combined with aid from other nations, to make more than a small dent in the monumental needs of the underdeveloped countries. There were also unfortunate side effects.

Americans are a generally optimistic people, somewhat obsessed with the idea of getting things done in a hurry. They can become frustrated when faced with complex and time-consuming problems. Economic underdevelopment proved to be one such intractable problem, and Americans became disappointed that the time-table for economic development as they perceived it was so slow. There was a feeling that all our aid should have produced more immediate and tangible results. If it did not, it must have been wasted.

The United States was not alone in providing aid. Other nations assisted in varying amounts, though during the peak period of the early 1960's aid from all contributing countries was never much more than $6 billion. Given the scope of world economic underdevelopment, that level of economic assistance was little more than a drop in the bucket. At its maximum, it provided roughly $3 a year per person to underdeveloped populations. In India, American aid amounted to about $2 a year per person. By way of contrast, in 1964 the United States was spending as much on space research as it was on its total aid program. Committing ourselves to just 1 per cent of our annual output for aid (as tiny Holland does) would result in a fourfold increase in our aid program, but even so it is obvious that American resources cannot buy economic development for everyone. The major effort must come from the resources of the less developed countries themselves. Still, assistance from the world's developed nations can be of immense importance when used selectively and wisely, as Barbara Ward and Senator J. W. Fulbright suggest in Part 4.

We have expected too much from our aid. Economic development, as we now know, is a time consuming and complex process. And while dreams may sometimes drive men to great achievements, to suggest miracles that do not materialize can bring serious consequences. The Alliance for Progress may have been one such case. With the infusion of $10 billion in United States aid, a matching amount from other sources, and a great deal of dedication, officials were enthusiastic about achieving a dramatic turn-around in Latin America in the short span of ten years. Many Latin Americans, and North Americans, too, were sadly disappointed by the results of the Alliance. This is not meant to disparage cooperative efforts but simply to note that some hard realities will delay significant progress in third-world economic development.

One of these realities involves nothing more than some historical perspective on the development process. The United States, with abundant and rich natural resources, a small population relative to land area, and an early start in industrialization, required three-quarters of a century to become a large-scale manufacturer. The Soviet Union, able to borrow the most advanced machine technology from the rest of the world, needed forty years to become an industrial power. Many countries throughout the world simply lack sufficient natural resources and size to become important industrial nations. Given the best of circumstances, half a century seems like an optimistic estimate for much progress to be made in most nations.

Another hard reality is that economic underdevelopment is always a characterization relative to some other, more developed area or country. The developed countries will not stand still. Relative underdevelopment is likely to get a good deal worse before it gets better, as income per person continues to grow year after year in the developed nations. A simple illustration may clarify this not so obvious point.

In 1964 (the last year for which there are comprehensive and reasonably accurate data) per capita output in the United States was $3,242 while the corresponding figure for Peru stood at $209. In recent years the average annual rate of growth of the U.S. gross national product has been around 5 per cent. If we assume a set of highly favorable conditions for Peruvians—say, an annual growth rate double that of the United States and, even more important, a population growth rate no greater than in the U.S. —by the year 2000 per capita output in Peru would be $3,337. But it would be $13,304 in the United States. The problem is, of course, the different size of the base from which we begin. The yearly increase in the U.S. gross national product is now around $40 billion. Peru would be growing at a much faster rate and would eventually overtake the United States if these favorable conditions remained constant indefinitely. But it would not be within most of our lifetimes.

In fact, the above assumptions are completely unrealistic. The population is increasing at a much more rapid rate in Peru, and in underdeveloped countries generally, than it is in industrial nations. Historically, it has been virtually impossible for any country to maintain a growth rate as high as 10 per cent per year for any sustained period. The overwhelming evidence is that in the foreseeable future the gap between poor and rich nations is likely to get much wider than our optimistic example would suggest. The recent annual rate of growth of income in the more advanced countries has averaged 4.4 per cent as compared with 4.7 per cent for the less developed nations. This gives the under-developed areas a slight edge. But at the same time, population growth in the advanced countries has been only 1.3 per cent per year, while population growth was almost twice as rapid—2.4 per cent—in the less developed countries. When population growth is considered, the rate of growth of income *per person* has been much more rapid in the developed countries than in the underdeveloped areas.

Soon we shall make a national commitment in the United States to eradicate the worst forms of domestic poverty through a guaranteed minimum income. The program will cost from $9 to $20 billion annually, depending upon the details of final legislation. Few seriously doubt the wisdom or necessity of such a program in the United States, yet our contribution toward less-ening a far more massive and debilitating international poverty is at present far less ambitious. And a strong downward trend has characterized our aid in recent years. We cannot eradicate world poverty with our aid, but we can help to arrest the current trend toward a widening gap between the developed and underde-veloped worlds.

What Is Economic Underdevelopment?

In a very important sense, economic underdevelopment is poverty on a massive scale, a kind of poverty with which few people in the Western world are acquainted. Poverty in the United States became an important public issue in the early 1960's. The revelation that substantial numbers of Americans suffered real economic hardship in the most affluent nation in the world rightly aroused public indignation. Some areas of the United States, indeed, would qualify as underdeveloped areas under general international standards now employed. But the cut-off line for domestic poverty in the United States is currently defined as about $3,500 annually for a family of four, or a per capita figure of a little under $900 per year. Poverty is, of course, a relative phenomenon. No one would question that existing on

$900 per year is difficult in a society such as the United States. But poverty, as defined in the United States, would be affluence for hundreds of millions in underdeveloped countries. The economic deprivation of nearly half the world's population is much more intense than our own domestic poverty; it is virtually beyond the comprehension of most Americans who have not witnessed it directly.

Income per person is perhaps the most widely used criterion for determining whether a country is considered developed or underdeveloped. While income per person in some areas is less than $100 (India, Uganda, and China, for example), countries are usually classified as underdeveloped if their per capita incomes are less than $500 per year. This limit includes most of Latin America, all of Africa and Asia, with the exception of Japan, all of the Middle East except Israel, several of the communist bloc nations, and a few European countries.

The distribution of income is also important. In oil-rich Kuwait, for example, per capita income is quite high, but little of it filters down to the people. The same is true in Venezuela, where income per capita is higher than in Argentina but where about one-third of the people are undernourished. Indeed, a fairly common feature of many underdeveloped countries is the presence of greater income inequality than is found in developed areas. Great contrasts of wealth and squalor tend to exist side by side. In many capital cities in Latin America, only a few city blocks separate the most opulent residential sections and the most hideous slums. Unlike the United States, Latin America still has too much poverty to hide.

Per capita income thus cannot serve as the sole measure of economic development, though it will often serve as a rough first approximation. It should, whenever possible, be qualified. Perhaps the most useful qualification would be to define any country as underdeveloped where more than half the population lives in poverty, and where poverty is defined as a level of living which barely covers the minimal essentials of food, clothing, and shelter for the maintenance of health (a higher standard than is currently the lot of well over half the world's population). Robert Heilbroner, in a now classic example from his book *The Great Ascent,* has conjured up a striking portrait of what the cold figure "less than $100 a year" means in terms of human suffering. He takes a fairly typical American family, living in a small suburban house on a moderate income of $8,000 to $9,000, and transports the family to an underdeveloped setting.

First, the family's home is stripped of all furniture, leaving only old blankets, a kitchen table, and a wooden chair. Only one change of the oldest and most ragged clothing is retained, and only the father is allowed to have shoes. The entire kitchen is emptied with the exception of a few moldy potatoes for the evening meal, a little flour, sugar and salt, and a few onions and dried beans. Everything else is removed, including canned goods, crackers, and sweets.

Once all the bathroom fixtures have been removed, all utilities, including running water, are similarly disposed of. But that is not all; the house itself is removed, and the entire family moves into the one-room tool shed standing behind the house. They are fortunate, for in many other countries not even this modest shelter is available. Hundreds of thousands simply live in the streets, sleeping in doorways or on sidewalks.

Before we are finished, our American family's standards must be reduced even further. The entire area where they live must be converted into a slum where other families live in nearby shacks and raw sewage runs through the streets. They must live without communications except for an occasional radio. All public services must be removed, including fire and mail services. Hospitals are taken from the immediate area, and only a clinic, staffed by a midwife, is to be found within ten miles. The children have a two-room school three miles away, but only half of them may attend.

Finally, each member of the family exists on a low protein diet of 1,700 to 1,900 calories, insufficient to replace the calories used by his living cells, so that his body steadily deteriorates, shortening his life span by as much as thirty years. The father produces less than $300 worth of crops yearly. Two-fifths of this is taken by his landlord and the local moneylender. Then, and only then, can our American family be classified along with the world's underdeveloped peoples.

Like the tragic story related by Peggy and Pierre Streit in Part 1, this picture of economic underdevelopment provides the human dimension necessary to appreciate the despair faced by so many, and perhaps to create the sense of urgency which must prevail if there is to be a successful assault on world poverty. But while such a sketch is important, it is not enough to know that few Asians have radios or nearby hospitals and are hungry. We must also examine the most important characteristics of economic backwardness which stand as obstacles to development.

Agriculture

A dominant feature of economic underdevelopment is a heavy reliance on agriculture as the mainstay of economic activity. In the large majority of underdeveloped countries, anywhere from 50 to 85 per cent of the working population engages in agriculture. Two factors account for this. First, most people in underdeveloped countries work to eat; if they do not grow their own food, they go hungry. Second, productivity is so low in agriculture that it requires a large proportion of the work force just to supply the nation's basic food requirements. Even with such a large part of their work force engaged in food production, many poor countries still are large importers of food. India and China are the best-known examples. India has received tons of surplus food grains from the United States, while China in past years has imported wheat from Canada. We tend to think of developed nations not as agricultural producers but as industrial centers. Yet agriculture is generally far more productive in developed countries than in the underdeveloped areas. This productivity differential of output per worker is also true in terms of crop yields. In poorer countries the most rudimentary techniques are employed; little use is made of such improvements as tractors, pesticides, and improved seed varieties. Low levels of technical knowledge and restrictive systems of land ownership and use, including sharecropping, impede the adoption of better production techniques.

With such a large part of the labor force engaged in agriculture, it is surprising to learn that many workers in underdeveloped areas are unemployed much of the time, and only partially employed at other times. In part this is the nature of agricultural employment, which tends to be seasonal. And in part it is the result of excessive crowding on the land. At the same time, few practical employment alternatives are available. The failure of the rest of the economy to provide additional sources of employment retards improvements in agriculture at the same time that it wastes human resources.

Industrial Development

In developed countries, industry may account for anywhere from 30 to 45 per cent of the labor force. Hence a corollary to the heavy reliance on agriculture in underdeveloped countries is the absence of employment in industrial or manufacturing activity. In the typical underdeveloped country, the percentage of the labor force in industry may vary from 10 to 20 per cent. Often the countries with the highest percentages are those with important extractive industries (mining and petroleum) which in many instances are controlled by foreign corporations and make only a limited contribution to the local economy.

Industrial jobs are characterized by high output per worker. This is because industry normally makes use of more machinery in combination with labor. Industry in the poorer countries does not put much of the labor force to work in these high-productivity occupations, and so labor contributes far less to total output than in higher-income countries. Here is a key characteristic of poor countries: the relative undernourishment of industrial activity. As we shall see, this situation has important historical roots in the international economic system. The results of heavy dependence on agriculture and single-crop specialization can be seen in the articles by J. Anthony Lukas on India and José Yglesias on Cuba.

Industrialization, especially the growth of manufacturing, is virtually synonymous with economic development. The ability to turn machines and technology to human use in the form of energy and mechanical processes lies at the core of economic progress. It is the key factor in moving labor from low-productivity to high-productivity jobs, both in industry and agriculture. The great productivity of American agriculture has been aided by an almost constant stream of innovations and inventions fostered by the manufacturers of agricultural machinery. Tractors and combines are the extension of industrial machine processes to agriculture.

Unemployment and Dualism

The lack of suitable employment alternatives in industry, and the inability of agriculture to utilize fully the human resources available to it, are associated with two further characteristics of underdeveloped regions: general unemployment, and something economists call "economic dualism."

It seems almost perverse that unemployment should be such a serious problem in poor nations. It is wasteful enough in rich countries to have idle resources in the face of important unmet needs. But in poorer countries, the wholesale waste of available resources compounds the tragedy. And unemployment is generally much more widespread in the underdeveloped countries than in the richer countries.

Unemployment in developed Western countries tends to be associated with the ups and downs of the business cycle, with recessions and depressions. It is partly the result of affluence, as gaps develop between the capacity of the economy to produce and the willingness of consumers and businesses to buy. In underdeveloped areas, where unemployment is much more intractable, the causes appear to be more closely associated with the structure of the economy itself. This involves overreliance on agriculture, uneven development of the various parts of the economic system, and economic dualism.

Dualism refers to a rather pronounced division in the economy. One part, generally small in terms of numbers, is characterized by technologically advanced methods of production. The other part, sometimes referred to as the traditional sector, uses much more primitive techniques. These two parts of the economy often exist side by side, but with practically no interaction and very little understanding between them. The more advanced sector will ordinarily include such activities as mining and petroleum, plantation agriculture, and the finance and service sectors associated with them. This sector of the economy is in many ways similar to the same activities in developed, market-dominated Western nations. A number of the enterprises comprising it may well be foreign owned or controlled, and many of its economic contacts are outside the country. It tends to be internationally oriented. In fact, it may give the impression of being grafted onto the socio-economic base of the country, with little real penetration. Such sectors are sometimes referred to as exclaves, signifying a lack of real connection with the native economic and social structure.

Dualism has a number of unfortunate side effects. It promotes greater inequality in the distribution of income, and the modern sector may aggrandize a disproportionate share of the country's natural resources for its own use. It also generally fails to help modernize the more backward sectors of the local economy, its interests being private and somewhat narrow. Dualism may lead to greater social divisiveness, including a tendency for members of the "modern" or "Western" sector to regard their fellow citizens as inferiors and, in effect, aliens in their own country. Close association with the "Westernized" modern sector promotes values and attitudes similar to those in Western commercial nations. Without drawing any moral conclusions, these may be inappropriate in trying to provide incentive for the vast majority of the populace, which is neither Western-educated nor Western-oriented. The sources of dualism and its perpetuation, which can be likened to a somewhat blind effort to reproduce success Western-style, seem to lie at the very heart of the developmental dilemma.

Population

We have already noted that populations are growing rapidly in most underdeveloped countries. The effect of population expansion can be a mixed blessing. At one end of the scale, countries have attempted to stimulate population growth by subsidizing larger families and by encouraging immigration. The goal is a population large enough to exploit fully the nation's natural resources and to provide for an extensive national market. The United States, Argentina, and Australia are examples of countries which historically have received large numbers of immigrants.

There is, of course, a real sense in which an absolute lack of population can be a contributing factor in nondevelopment. Some parts of the world are not currently overpopulated; a number are virtually uninhabited, though many of these areas are not very hospitable either. Sometimes the case is one of internal mal-distribution of the population (all located along the coast, for example), and a larger population may be actively sought in certain regions. Brazil has in recent years attempted to encourage population expansion in its largely unexploited and uninhabited interior regions. Population densities (inhabitants per square kilometer) vary widely between countries, ranging from one person in Libya to 879 in Bermuda. In general, the more densely populated areas in underdeveloped countries are found in Asia, with Africa and South America considerably less densely popu-lated. But it is also obvious that merely larger populations, with-out regard to their educational characteristics, skills, and age, do not necessarily insure economic development. And the *rate* of population growth is fundamental in analyzing the question of population expansion. As we shall see, the crux of the population issue lies precisely in the areas of rate of increase, age structure, and skill levels.

The higher the rate of population growth, the faster the econ-omy must grow. In several underdeveloped countries, economic conditions have actually been deteriorating rather than improving because the growth rate of output has been less than that of population growth. In many other countries, the rate of increase in per capita income has been only around 1 or 2 per cent per year. Under the best conditions that can be observed currently, simple arithmetic tells us that an increase of 2 per cent per year in a typical country will mean that per capita income will rise from, say, $300 to $306 in one year.

World population is now growing at an unprecedented annual rate, and the vast bulk of this increase is occurring in the under-developed countries. High birthrates, coupled with rapidly falling death rates, are yielding large rates of natural increase. As Pro-fessor Kingsley Davis points out in his analysis of the population explosion (Part 2), the current rate of expansion simply cannot continue indefinitely, or else there will be six billion human beings on the planet by the close of the century and thirteen billion by the year 2050.

Another significant effect of rapid population growth is to produce a population which is on the whole quite young. Almost half the population in less-developed countries is under age twenty, as compared with less than one-third under twenty in developed countries. This means that a larger proportion of the population is not available for work (even if there were jobs available), and hence more persons must be supported by each one who is employed. Add to this the cost of attempting to educate such a young population in order to upgrade skill levels, and the difficulties of the poorer countries are compounded. If present trends continue—and there appears to be no immediate reason to expect any dramatic changes—the situation is likely to get much worse before it improves. The consequences arc not difficult to foresee either: increasing misery and hunger as overcrowding takes place on already worn-out lands. The United Nations Food and Agricultural Organization, along with numerous private scientists, has displayed increasing alarm over these future prospects, as the following passage taken from a United Nations report indicates:

World food supplies must be tripled by the turn of the century if world population, which is expected to double and to exceed 6,000 million by then, is to have enough to eat. At present it is estimated that 300 to 500 million people out of 3,000 million in the world are underfed and that up to one half of the world population—perhaps even more —suffer from hunger or malnutrition.

It is against this grim background that the Freedom from Hunger Campaign launched by the Food and Agriculture Organization of the United Nations (FAO) needs to be viewed. The magnitude of the problem and the continuing inadequacy of food production in the "hungry regions" of the world present a challenge to all who think in terms of a better and peaceful world. Such a world is impossible in the present circumstances.

A massive attack is needed just to prevent world hunger, to say nothing of promoting rapid and sustained economic development. An optimist nowadays is turning out to be one who thinks that success is merely the prevention of further deterioration in living standards in poor countries.

The great surge in population in the underdeveloped countries has come about primarily as the result of a dramatic decrease in death rates through the application of modern scientific methods, while birthrates have remained more or less constant. Little success has been achieved up to now in lowering birthrates. We are faced with a real ethical paradox. What is the value of prolonging human life through medical and scientific achievements if the prospect for that life is increasing misery?

Education and Skills

One of the major differences between poor and rich countries, and one of the greatest obstacles to rapid economic development, is the difference in the education and skill-level of the populations. The ability of a country to use modern technology effectively in agriculture, industry, and even in the process of governing itself, is severely hampered by the lack of skilled labor and the scientific and technical personnel needed to implement new programs. The great success of the Marshall Plan (the post–World War II United States assistance program for the reconstruction of Europe) in helping rebuild Europe's war-ravaged economy, was made possible by the existence of a skilled population, well-educated and supported by social institutions conducive to economic growth.

In the rich countries, the illiteracy rate is generally less than 5 per cent for the population over the age of fifteen years. Comparable figures for illiteracy in underdeveloped countries range from 34 per cent to 80 per cent illiterate. The inability to comprehend simple written instructions is an enormous impediment to improving methods in everything from the operation of simple machinery to agriculture and local public hygiene. Alan Howard, in his analysis of Guatemala's adult literacy campaign (in Part 3), examines some other, more subtle values of literacy, and tries to weigh the successes and failures of investing millions of dollars in a program with a drop-out rate of more than 90 per cent. Others argue that the most serious obstacle in developing nations is the shortage of technical personnel of middle-level education, scientists of all sorts, and managerial personnel. They believe the returns from educational investment are greater in these areas than in education for literacy. The needs are so great it is difficult to know where to begin. Underdeveloped countries must cope with so many problems that the choice of priorities becomes the thorniest problem of all.

Resource Base, Size, and Specialization

A shortage of natural resources can be a factor in economic development. Not all countries are equally endowed with natural resources, to be sure, but this in itself is no excuse for not taking advantage of whatever is available. Tiny Switzerland stands as a monumentally successful example for any country with limited natural resources, though Switzerland could hardly aspire to become one of the world's industrial giants.

The boundaries of many countries were established for political reasons, and with little regard for their economic potential and viability as self-contained economic units. Recently we have seen what is perhaps the last modern example of this process, in Africa, where bloody struggles have marked the political fragmentation of nations. Africa, as noted by Chester Bowles in an article in Part 2, enjoys a favorable natural resource base, as do many parts of Latin America. But the advantage of such resources may be lost with excessive and uneconomic fragmentation. Where fragmentation has long ago taken place, as in Latin America and Europe, we find efforts under way to circumvent the limiting effects of small national markets, nondiversified natural resource bases, and the resultant loss of economies of size. The European Common Market and the Latin American and Central American Free Trade Associations are market-extending devices, with much broader long-range political implications for coordinated industrial development and regional economic planning. Their ultimate aim is to eliminate the ill effects of uneconomic fragmentation of nation states.

The size of a country and its limited natural resource base can be impediments to development. Barring some form of economic cooperation or consolidation, such as a federation of states willing to relinquish certain political prerogatives, about the only avenue open to a poor, small country is to specialize in several products and trade with other countries for those goods it cannot produce as efficiently. One of the oldest theories of international economic relations held that industrial nations should supply industrial products to the rest of the world, while nations with food and raw materials should stick to their primary economic activities and trade with the industrial nations for manufactured goods. In this way, it was alleged, the benefits of worldwide international specialization would be realized by all countries, and presumably all would be well off.

This theory of international specialization was partly a rationalization for the imperialistic methods of the newly industrialized nations during the eighteenth and nineteenth centuries. Colonies were established throughout what is now the underdeveloped world to control the sources of raw materials used in the factories of the industrial nations, and supposedly to provide captive markets for the manufactures of the mother country. There is little evidence that the other part of the process was ever successful—the inhabitants of the colonies remained too poor to buy many of the industrial nation's products.

With the passage of time many realized that the industrial countries got much richer much faster than their partners in the specialization process. This was because there were much greater limits on the potential of raw materials and agricultural production in the absence of a balanced economic system. The industrial nations became more efficient not only in their own specialties but in the specialties of the nonindustrial nations as well, because the technology of industrialization spilled over into agricultural and raw materials production. The whole concept of specialization was a static argument when applied too narrowly. The essence of economic development is transformation of the economic system, and the development of new products and new activities. (Japan is now more efficient in the production of steel than the United States.)

Savings, Capital Accumulation, and Income Distribution

Probably the most overworked theme in explaining why poor nations have so much difficulty in growing is a supposed shortage of savings, which, in turn, is supposed to explain why they are unable to accumulate large quantities of capital. A casual inspection of any industrial country will reveal that an extraordinary amount of physical capital (machinery and tools) is available for the use of each worker. In manufacturing in the United States, somewhere on the order of $20,000 worth of capital is employed per worker (for machines, tools, and so forth). The effect of this is, of course, to make American workers extraordinarily productive. How the accumulation of capital came to pass and how the same process can be made to work in the underdeveloped countries is a major concern.

Traditional notions of economic development argued that capital accumulation took place as individuals sacrificed current consumption, causing a corresponding increase in the supply of savings. Further, since the rich (especially hard-working capitalists) were the only members of society capable of sacrificing their own current standard of living—and with sufficient foresight to do so—in order to save, the process seemed to argue for an unequal distribution of income. Unequal distribution presumably allowed these few citizens to provide for the future of the nation. This whole notion was probably just a rationalization for the unequal distribution of income. But to the extent that it was a useful way of looking at matters, it was more relevant to a situation of fully employed resources than to one in which resources were idle or underutilized.

Waiting on prior savings to put idle resources to work has not proved successful in the past. So instead of waiting for the theory to come true, perhaps we should re-examine it to determine if it is valid. One clue in unraveling the mystery is the fact that a good deal of saving goes on in most underdeveloped countries. Another is that the distribution of income is much more lopsided in underdeveloped countries than in the industrial nations where a great deal of capital formation takes place. In fact, there would appear to be a higher correlation between capital formation and *equal* distribution of incomes than the reverse.

One of the reasons for underutilized resources in the underdeveloped countries is the lack of a broadly based market and consumers with sufficient income to buy goods. This is partly the result of low incomes in general, but it is also specifically related to the unequal distribution of purchasing power. Putting these underutilized resources to work seems to have been hampered by the belief that it was necessary to wait for an accumulation of savings. In fact, capital is made from natural resources—human labor, raw materials, equipment, and technical know-how. If these resources are available and currently underutilized, it makes no sense to wait for an accumulation of savings to put them to work. The resources will pay for themselves through the creation of a new capital asset, because the new capital will contribute to the growth of the economy. Multiplied by many such instances, real growth in income pays for itself. More equitable distribution of incomes in underdeveloped countries and the improvement of mass purchasing power will probably go a lot further toward promoting economic development than trying to coax out more savings through higher profits and greater inequality in the distribution of income.

Economic Development as Process

The systematic development and application of scientific and technological processes stands out as the fundamental driving force behind economic development. Science and technology develop with an inner logic of their own, building directly on past achievements. The extent to which their potential is utilized depends on a variety of forces associated with man's social and economic organization. Curiously, there is no guarantee that the opportunities available through improved knowledge and skills will be put to use for society's benefit. The world abounds in tragic examples of the failure to take advantage of better ways of doing things because of cultural and social barriers erected by the institutional organization of societies. Institutions—that is, conventional ways of doing things—tend to favor the status quo and resist change.

Such resistance to change is not unique to the underdeveloped countries, though it would seem more prevalent there than in other places. In the United States, for example, the technical capabilities to eliminate poverty and provide adequate medical care for all persons are available. Yet we remain amazingly reluctant to employ them. Such new policies and techniques clash with strongly entrenched beliefs that the poor are somehow responsible for their own poverty and with the medical profession's extraordinary ability to convince legislators that full medical protection represents some vague threat to the system of private medical care.

Similar examples can be drawn from underdeveloped countries. One common example of an institutional barrier to economic progress in many underdeveloped countries is the prevailing system of land use and land ownership, and the corresponding attitudes of landowners. Changes in land tenure and land use, which would encourage technical progress in agriculture, have been prevented wherever a powerful landed class has controlled the government. Great tracts of land have been left virtually idle or grossly underutilized while thousands of hungry peasants willing to work the land have remained unemployed. Primarily interested in land only as a mark of social position, these landowners have been generally content with stable rents from their properties. They have also benefited by an abundant and hence cheap supply of rural labor, and thus have had no incentive to introduce machinery or other measures to increase productivity. Put more baldly, maintaining social position and a certain way of life has depended on keeping the lower classes in their places, usually hungry and submissive.

Rigid caste systems, social classes, and pronounced ethnic divisions are examples of social institutions which may impede necessary changes and hence economic progress. The lack of upward social mobility effectively limits opportunities for large groups of people while simultaneously robbing the nation of potential talent. This means there will be a perennial class or group of underdeveloped citizens who cannot contribute much to the economic welfare of the society, and who are a continual drag on development. The institutional barriers to economic development are far more formidable than a lack of natural resources or a weak industrial base. With institutional modifications, the chain of industrial development already realized in the developed countries can be set in motion.

One must be careful, however, to avoid the conclusion that underdeveloped countries, to be successful, must faithfully imitate the attitudes, values, religious persuasions, and economic and political systems of Western nations. There are many ways of organizing an economic system, each of which can effectively realize the advantages of modern science and technology. In fact, one of the problems already identified in a number of underdeveloped countries, economic dualism, is at least partly a reflection of the attempt to mirror too faithfully the institutional organization of Western market economies. As a result, the so-called modern sector remains isolated; it does not penetrate beyond the small enclave of Western-oriented and often Western-educated personnel who manage and control it. Its methods and values are not widely appreciated, understood, or adaptable in the more traditional sectors of the economy.

Like the industrialized nations, the underdeveloped world enjoys a remarkable cultural diversity. The institutional basis of economic systems is just as variable. No single strategy of economic development—that is, a particular set of principles or policies—can be expected to have equal relevance in all places. There are, however, at least two common ingredients which underlie all successful cases of sustained economic progress. The first is industrial development, which fosters processes and methods that promote pragmatic solutions to problems. The second is a willingness to experiment, to depart from conventional ways of doing things; in short, a healthy disregard of tradition for tradition's sake. This does not imply cultural anarchy, but it does suggest the need to make man the master of his own forms of social organization.

Social institutions and cultural diversity are with us to stay. Institutions and regularized patterns of social behavior insure order and organization in the world. But we need to rid ourselves of the notion, perpetuated by the long-standing ideological struggle between East and West, that there are only two institutional alternatives for mobilizing an economy—the free-market system or communist-style central control. One of the chief difficulties faced by leaders of underdeveloped nations is to identify that set of institutions most likely to promote rapid and orderly progress. That this implies some fundamental changes cannot be denied. And it is a job which cannot be done by outsiders; it is ultimately the responsibility of the peoples of the developing countries themselves. Our role is to make available to anyone who wants it all of our technical know-how, and to offer as much economic assistance as we possibly can.

Part 1

WHAT IT IS LIKE
TO BE POOR

THE ARTICLES IN this section illustrate one common theme: the utter desperation and hopelessness which everywhere accompany extremes of poverty. The human spirit is fragile. Severe deprivation breeds resignation and a sense of futility. As the article by the Streits illustrates, even the will to ask that a simple admissions fee be waived is beyond the comprehension of the "Mahmads" of the world. They have learned the lesson of their poverty all too well: this is a harsh world where the rules of survival prevail and where no one can expect special favors. In the slums of Latin America's shantytowns, the dignity of the family and social life is pitilessly crushed beneath the weight of overcrowding, hunger, and filth. Why do they come to the city? Are conditions so much worse elsewhere? As Sam Schulman points out, few rural migrants find opportunities in the city. They come because they are being pushed off the land, and the city offers one possibility which is utterly lacking in the village—hope. No matter how remote the possibilities, everyone knows of someone who hit it big. That is why lotteries are so popular among Latin America's poor. Only two things are certain about life in the village—hunger and lethargy.

For Want of $3.94

by Peggy and Pierre Streit

SHIRAZ, IRAN

TODAY THE SURGERY is finished and Mahmad lies on his hospital bed staring at the ceiling, his thick, peasant hands slack at his sides. Next to him, sitting in rigid silence is his wife, her faded garments a blur of color against the antiseptic walls. About them flows the casual urgency of hospital life, a life far removed from the soil and the sky, from the acrid odor of dust, from the long shadows of a depleted sun setting over a brown plain—from the life that Mahmad has always known.

For Mahmad all that is familiar and secure lies in his village, a primitive agglomeration of mud huts fifty miles distant. He was born in this village (he isn't sure when), he was married there, and for at least thirty years one day has routinely followed another, each devoted to the incalculable, all-absorbing trivia of a simple life.

He has plowed the hard brown earth in the spring, he has sown the rice, he has helped to irrigate the fields; and in the fall he has harvested the crop, collecting his small percentage of it from the man who owns the earth he tills—his landlord. He has drunk his tea and eaten his bread and gossiped with his neighbors; and, if life had no more to offer, at least he could hope that it had no less.

Mahmad remembers now, as he lies in his bed, that it was

From the *New York Times Magazine,* April 30, 1961, copyright © 1961 by The New York Times Company.

fall. The leaves of the poplars were yellow and the harvest was gathered, piled on the ground in a huge golden heap. On a night like hundreds before it, he and his villager friends set off for the fields—a quiet, companionable little group that would pass the long night guarding the grain from the maraudings of men and of animals.

Out along their familiar way they went, and gradually Mahmad realized that the signposts he had known since childhood were all missing—the rocks at the side of the path, the bridge over the stream, the abandoned mud hut at the roadside—all were gone. Suddenly he realized that they were gone because he couldn't see, and a rush of horror engulfed him.

How does a man of the land of Iran guide a plow if he cannot see? How does a man whose vision is gone follow the sheep, seeking out those small, vital spots of green pasturage on a barren landscape? How can a blind man take his place among his fellows, replanting the little shoots of fresh, green rice in new beds? What is there for a sightless man in an Iranian village but to be led about by a small impatient boy or to go to the city to beg?

Mahmad held his hands before his eyes. There, standing in the stillness of the night, he knew that he was blind and he sank to the ground and cried.

Throughout the night he stayed where he fell, his tears finally spending themselves. But when dawn broke he wept afresh, but now with relief and gratitude, for he found that he could distinguish night from day and he knew that he wasn't completely blind. The sight of his right eye was gone but vision remained in the left, and as the day dawned, so did hope.

When the men came back from their vigil in the fields they led Mahmad home to the only man of the village with the knowledge or the power to help him—their landlord. Standing before him, his cap in his hand, his head humbly bowed, as befits an Iranian peasant, Mahmad asked for counsel.

Go to the city, said the landlord. Go to Shiraz. There was a modern hospital, staffed by Iranian and American doctors, and there he might find assistance. And so, next morning, Mahmad and Pari, his wife, set off, riding the fifty miles to the hospital atop a truck loaded with sacks of rice.

Mahmad's case fell to an American neurosurgeon to whom the medical history was urgently clear. The man suffered from a tumor of the brain that had already destroyed the sight of one eye and there was imminent danger that it might rob him of vision in the other. It was probable that an operation would save his life but his sight was suspended between the jumps of the minute hand of a clock; each hour brought Mahmad closer to total irrecoverable blindness.

Immediate surgery was indicated and Mahmad was given a note of admission to the hospital's clinic for indigents, some blocks down the street. At the admissions desk he was asked routinely for 50 toman—$6.57. But Mahmad and Pari didn't have $6.57. Tied in a knot in the end of a scarf was the raggle-taggle end of a few good harvests—a meager collection of coins and bills that represented their total negotiable wealth: $2.63.

Almost surely, had Mahmad protested the demand for the money—had he gone back to his doctor for help, the fee would have been waived. But he didn't protest, for it isn't in the nature of a peasant to dispute the ruling of a superior. He never complained. He never said in desperation, "But I'm going blind, let me in," for he presumed, as any other Iranian peasant would presume, that one doesn't get something for nothing in this world.

Fifty toman was fifty toman and that was that. He was losing his sight? But that was his affair, wasn't it? Didn't everyone have problems? Who was Mahmad? What claim had he on the services of a hospital or a doctor if he couldn't pay the fee?

And because he took for granted that he had none, he turned, unquestioning, from the admitting desk and, led by his wife, groped his halting way back to the street. There they found a truck that carried them back to the anonymity of their distant village.

On their way they nursed a last hope. One of the few times of the year that an Iranian peasant can hope to have cash in his hands is at harvest. When Mahmad and Pari had left their village for the hospital, the gathered crop was on the ground and by right of tradition and custom a fragment of it was Mahmad's—the reward for a year of his work.

The bulk of it, of course, belonged to the landlord—the man

who owned the land Mahmad worked and the cattle Mahmad plowed with and the seed Mahmad sowed and the water Mahmad drank. But a bit of the grain was Mahmad's and if this small fragment could be converted quickly to the $3.94 he needed, the hospital fee could be met.

But when they arrived back at the village they found that in their absence the division of the crop had been made among the peasants and Mahmad's share had found its way into the storeroom of the landlord. When they asked him for it he said, "You have been sick and away from your work during part of the harvest. You can't expect to be paid for something you haven't done, can you?"

Mahmad never protested. He showed no surprise, no resentment; for he knew as well as any other peasant that the man who left his gains unguarded, for whatever reason, stood in danger of losing them.

He knew the rules of survival and he knew they applied to all men—to landlord and peasant alike. This was a pitiless world; a man took what he could get, protected himself as best he could, and one of the best protections on an earth abounding in misery were the blinders a man could don to shut the misery out. Deep in his tough peasant heart Mahmad knew that were he the landlord, he, too, would hold sway with ruthless self-interest. Without demur he turned back to his cottage and his private ordeal.

Mahmad needed $3.94. What of his family and friends and the people who share his life in their hamlet? Why didn't he seek the money from them? But who in a small village would dare part with $3.94 if he had it; for who knew when disaster might strike? How many in Iran, including the landlords, were confident enough of the future, secure enough in the present, to afford that great luxury—generosity?

For fourteen days Mahmad sat in the doorway of his cottage as day by day and hour by hour the sight in his left eye slipped away. Finally, on the fifteenth day, stirred from his apathy by the magnitude of his fear and horror, he went again to the landlord and asked, not for his share of the crop, but merely for $3.94. "I don't have it," said the landlord. "Go to the hospital." And because there was no other hope Mahmad and Pari left once again for the city.

This time, as they groped their way to the out-patient clinic, Mahmad was claimed by one of the hospital attendants, alerted to his disappearance by the deeply perturbed and baffled American neurosurgeon who had been searching and waiting, day after day, to operate. Where had Mahmad been? Why hadn't he come to the clinic as he had been told? Dull and frightened and uncomprehending, he told the simple truth: he had gone to find $3.94.

A week has passed since the tumor was removed from Mahmad's brain. The operation was successful; his life has been saved. But the days and the hours of wasting and waiting have taken their toll and what might have been, had Mahmad's world been different, can never be now. The operation was too late. Mahmad is blind.

What lies before him? No one knows better than the impoverished peasant who lies on a hospital bed and stares at the ceiling with all the desperate intensity of a sightless man—or the stolid woman sitting silently at his side. In another two weeks Mahmad will return to his village and there he will sit, like a lump of clay, for the rest of his life.

Latin-American Shantytown

by Sam Schulman

IN BRAZIL it is called *favella;* in Argentina, *banda de miseria;* in Peru, *barriada.* In Colombia it is *tugurio.* But whatever the name, its characteristics are the same: It is the rudest kind of slum, clustering like a dirty beehive around the edges of any principal city in Latin America.

In the past two decades poor rural people have flocked to the cities, found no opportunities but stayed on in urban fringe shantytowns, squatting squalidly upon the land. In modern Caracas or cosmopolitan Lima, as in tens of other Latin-American cities, a glance at the surrounding hills is a view of misery at its worst. Death is easy and often. Hunger and pain are facts of everyday life.

Traditional living patterns undergo intense strain and often give way in these slums. Living almost like animals, the *tugurio's* residents are overwhelmed by animality. Religion, social control, education, domestic life are warped and disfigured.

For more than nine months my wife and I studied and worked in such a slum—the "Barrio of 65" ("the 65th Street Neighborhood")—a hillside shanty settlement in Bogotá. The barrio clings to the rounded knobs and slopes of the small foothills at the

From the *New York Times Magazine,* January 16, 1966, copyright © 1966 by The New York Times Company.

base of the Andes along the eastern edge of the city. A wide dirt path, an extension of Calle 65 (65th Street), winds through the area and gives it its name. There are about 250 individual dwelling units and about 1,200 residents.

Throughout Latin America, extensions of the central city have been traditional living areas for the poor. Squatting has always been an accepted mode of life, and even at the turn of the century, small isolated squatters' holdings began to spring up around Bogotá. With the beginning of national strife after the assassination of the Liberal party leader, Jorge Elíecer Gaítan, in 1948, thousands ran for safety to Bogotá. The city could not absorb them. It had neither industry nor services to provide places for the illiterate and untrained country people.

They spilled over into the uninhabited or sparsely settled hills bordering Bogotá's poor sections and remained, building hovels. In the lower part of the Barrio of 65, property owners expanded their facilities, adding a few more rooms facing a courtyard, building additional shacks nearby, and renting these out for nominal fees to the newcomers. As the newcomers kept coming, spaces between shacks and more permanent dwellings were filled: a few more scraps of cardboard, a few more rolled-out oil cans, a few slabs of corrugated iron for roofs. These, too, were soon rented.

About four years ago, several of the tenants of the lower barrio, tired of paying rent, began an invasion of a large municipally held hill above them. With the settlement upon the hill a new phase of the barrio's growth began, and, month by month, a few more shacks crept upward. In 1966 they are still creeping.

And they are still creeping up most of the other hills bordering the poor areas of Bogotá. At present, one in every 10 residents of this city of more than 1.7-million lives in a hillside *tugurio*. Seven out of 10 urbanites in Colombia are poor, but the *tugurio* is the worst face of urban poverty.

There is no real water supply in this *tugurio*. Women and children fetch water in old oil or lard cans from a municipal hydrant at the base of a hill. Only a few homes have electricity—illegally secured by tapping the electric company's power line. A few houses have one- or two-burner bottled-gas stoves; most residents cook over small wood fires around each of which are placed three large stones supporting a cooking pot.

The barrio has about 20 latrines. A few belong to special families, and their doors are secured by padlocks. Others are not so exclusive; they belong to groups of people or to compounds. In every case, foul water carrying human excrement floats from under the privies and runs in black rivulets down paths of the barrio. Children play alongside and in the contaminated streams.

It is no surprise that endemic and epidemic diseases run rampant. Children are the chief victims. A measles outbreak may kill large numbers of youngsters. Infant diarrheas, upper respiratory infections, malnutrition also take a high toll.

Diets are typically protein-low, if not completely protein-absent. The average daily fare is built largely around potatoes, rice and a hot drink made from unrefined sugar. When it is possible—and it rarely is—a heavy soup is made from scraps of meat or fish that have been classified as unsalable in local food markets. Perhaps a chicken that has been carefully raised among the children and debris of the barrio is added.

Sheep, hogs, a few cows are seen, but they are usually raised for sale. A burro or two are the prized animals of only a few, and these are used to aid in the dull and heavy tasks associated with slum life—hauling water, firewood, or clothes to be laundered in a ravine a few blocks away.

Living space is extremely limited. In the lower area of the Barrio of 65 a family usually has a single room and a small lean-to for cooking. Houses of the upper barrio are larger. They, too, may consist of only a single room, or the space may be partitioned into several rooms of minimal dimensions. Most of the barrio's residents live close to one another. A child being spanked is heard by 50 neighbors. The total effect is that of masses of tightly packed shacks ringing small common patios. Here clothes are hung to dry, garbage is accumulated, a hog and some chickens are enclosed, and here the children pass most of their day.

A typical house has a low ceiling and a dirt floor. A rustic door or curtain at the entrance shields the residents from wind, rain and passersby. Windows are rare. In this dingy room, a family sleeps, dresses, eats and attends to its personal necessities.

One or two narrow beds—usually handmade cots or their cheap, poorly made commercial equivalents—are placed against the walls. One bed is usually reserved for adults, who often sleep with the youngest child. Other children sometimes crowd five to a bed. More hardy youngsters roll up in blankets and sleep on the earth floor.

A wooden trunk, containing most of the family's possessions, is placed alongside a bed. Atop the trunk is the family's washbasin. A chair or two and a small table may be wedged in among the other things. Clothes, especially "Sunday" clothes, are hung on the wall, the door, the headboard of a bed, or may dangle down from the ceiling. Beneath one of the beds is the dwellers' chamberpot. Profusely ornamenting the walls are religious pictures and a photograph or two: the bride at marriage, the husband doing his stint in military service, the baptism or confirmation of a child.

This can be home for a dozen people. Privacy is unheard of, and all know the extreme intimacies of human contact. Only darkness hides the nakedness of this contact.

The home has no real facility for bathing. And washing is not a cherished custom. Faces and hands of children and adults may be cleaned, hair combed or brushed for receiving visitors, attending mass or going to the local church. But usually the living area smells heavily of continued, unwashed occupation, and is usually in disarray. The chamberpot often is not emptied after each use, but only when it is full. Then it is dumped into one of the few latrines, a drainage gutter or the paths that serve as streets in the barrio. Children grow up with the sounds of sleeping, eating, evacuation and sexual relations—of their own family, and their neighbors—in their ears.

In this setting, traditional norms of family life are challenged. Most of the barrio's residents still have their roots in the country. But Colombia's rural poor still retain their basic peasant dignity. There are free spaces and clean air beyond their shacks; there is a tiny garden growing products for home consumption; there is no sharp comparison between peasant life and the affluence of many others. Close by, perhaps, is the master's fine home, but it is a singular jewellike exception to those of his peasants.

In the city, whole neighborhoods of fine homes and vast numbers of "better" people are only blocks away from the *tugurio*. There is no longer free space and tiny gardens. And the peasant's dignity is buried in urban poverty's abyss.

In such a setting, there is little feeling of community. True, when outside authorities seek to exert control within the barrio, residents may come together in common defense. But generally they are tied only by the bond of misery, and do not help each other.

Violence is common. A weekend seldom passes without some explosive episode. The men, whose chief recreation is playing a rustic pitch-and-toss game called *tejo* and drinking beer, may dispute a point and fall into a drunken fight with fists or knives. A backyard rivalry or sexually based competition among women may result in a stabbing. Habitually, men castigate both their women and their children by beating them, and a mother's reprimand to a child is often a hard slap or a switch across the face or bottom. Brutality is part of life, and is accepted.

Unemployment is another fact of life. Economic need is so great in the barrio that young people try to obtain jobs as soon as they can, if jobs are available. It is easiest for young girls to secure positions as beginners in domestic service: They earn between $3 and $4 a month, and are supplied uniforms, sleeping quarters and food. The relatively few men in the barrio are employed at simple tasks—when they can find work—such as gardening and construction.

But squatters, never an integrated part of the greater community of Bogotá, face the employment dilemma of most other deprived peoples: "Last to be hired, first to go." And unemployment has soared in the city. In late 1965 it amounted to almost 20 per cent of the labor force. Those who have suffered most are the unskilled people of the *tugurios*. Mothers and children are often seen in better neighborhoods begging. Idleness, extreme poverty and need have forced some of the men to become petty sneak thieves; some of the women have turned to prostitution; many of the children have become street gamins.

Unemployment and disrupted family structures go hand in hand. More than half, perhaps as many as two-thirds, of the family units in the barrio are quasi families, lacking a permanent father. A few have no mother or father, and children live with grandparents, aunts, godparents or friends. Abandoned women with children are commonplace. A man feels little obligation to the woman he lives with and seldom participates in guiding the development of children. In an almost totally Roman Catholic country, people of the barrio do not have time, money, or ambition to indulge in the requisites of the church. A "free union," a condoned form of sexual alliance, is the dominant form of marriage in the slums. Partners are married as long as they wish to remain married.

There are, of course, some couples in the barrios who are both legally and religiously married, but they are rare exceptions. Their marriage is not seen as something "better." In the eyes of other residents, they have had "more luck," "more money" or "more pull."

Outside the barrio, however, a religious marriage is thought to have greater prestige and slum couples will invent such an event to keep from being humiliated. In a recent series of interviews, a field worker reviewed the details of their "marriage" with a pair from the barrio, speaking to each member individually. Both said they had been married in the church, but each gave the name of a different church and even a different date for the event.

But any man and woman who live together in the barrio are considered "married," and the woman is addressed as *"Señora."* It is also custom to call an unmarried mother by the same term: She is a *señora,* though she is single. Children born to any "married" couple will bear their father's surname; those born to a single woman will bear hers.

Barrio women have many children. Contraception, even the simplest kind, is not understood. It is not unusual for a married woman to have had 10 or 12 pregnancies. Many babies die at birth. But the death of a child is not a horrible event. There is grief, but also a feeling that the "tiny angel" goes directly to heaven. There is also the feeling the child is fortunate to meet God without having to endure the hardship of adult life. It is a rare family in the barrio that does not have one or more *angelitos.*

Even in homes where the husband or male partner is seldom

present, he is the undisputed source of authority. A husband's needs are met before those of any other member of the family. He eats first, and the best of what little there may be. Children do not disturb him when he is resting. Spending money for beer while his children beg for food is not considered wrong.

Even the health of others is subordinated to his needs. Children are not taken to the local clinic when they are ill because their mothers must spend most of their mornings preparing lunch for working husbands. It would have angered the men if lunch were not brought to the job on time. Women make long treks on foot or in overcrowded buses with freshly cooked food to keep their men in good spirits. A seriously ill child might die for lack of attention on one hand; a woman might face a beating, social castigation and possible desertion on the other.

All important decisions are made by men. The role of a woman is simply caretaker of the home and children. Children are brought up by their mothers and seldom have an adequate example of an adult male on which to orient their lives. When a man is not working, he spends his time with his cronies, not with his youngsters.

Some mothers will lock their children in shacks for hours on end while doing day work. The money earned is quickly given to the husband. One completely happy young man, living in his mother's house with his wife and child, felt extremely fortunate: His mother had a steady job and his wife worked several days a week. He did not work. He would periodically look for a job, but he was not driven to finding work. There was no need to do so while his women were employed.

Family life in a *tugurio* is based upon simple, uncluttered, primitive norms. It reflects the attitude of people who know and expect only harshness. Yet there are few ugly children. They are beautiful, with the smooth skins and large dark eyes of the Colombian mestizo; they are joyful, playing along the dirt paths and in the contaminated waters of the barrio. But life's harshness bends them. Women age while still young, and men are content to be brutes. The barrio, in the end, makes its people as ugly as itself. Families cannot help but mirror the harsh and ugly total social milieu that encompasses them.

Each year, the barrio forces itself more and more on its residents. Few can leave, for there is really no place to go. Gradually fear of the "outside" develops.

In mid-1965 two families were offered the opportunity to leave and start new lives with adequate financial support from an agency of the municipal government. Both refused: the first, because the barrio had always been "home" and its members wanted their roots to be maintained; the second, because of intense fear of all the unknowns of an inimical big city.

The *tugurio* is a deep intellectual and spiritual crevice filled with constant misery and peopled with depressed and passive human lives. Escape is virtually impossible and, when a way out is allowed a select few, they do not understand. They suspect it, and remain in the depths. And the depths will remain for decades. The *tugurio* is firmly rooted in Colombian urban life.

There are some men—their numbers are small, but they are growing—of goodwill and insight who are profoundly disturbed, and passionately concerned with the eradication of these subhuman clusters. Msgr. Ruben Isaza, Bishop Coadjutor of Bogotá, has called them "malignant tumors that have grown upon my city" and, along with others of his countrymen, is working for their displacement and for the betterment of the social and economic factors which have created them. There is much planning, and there are the beginnings of action programs. The Mayor of Bogotá is dedicated to a platform of slum clearance, and has given first priority to the *tugurios*. The Colombian Army has established labor battalions to help construct low-cost homes for *tugurio* inhabitants. The Alliance for Progress has given substantial sums—and will continue to give them—to assist the Colombian Government's urban resettlement agencies in the diminution of the *tugurios*. High-school and university students, religious groups, citizens' organizations, the major newspapers of Bogotá and other cities—all have voiced concern and are urging development programs to remedy a condition which they admit is abhorrent, dangerous and shameful to their national pride.

But the Colombian economy is too weak to support a full-scale "war against poverty." The fight against the *tugurios*, the scores of barrios like the Barrio of 65, moves at a slow pace, and the problem is large—growing a little bit larger every day.

Village of Hunger and Lethargy

by J. Anthony Lukas

BASEHRA, INDIA

THE MONSOON is India's sensuous season. After months of stifling heat, the rains refresh not only the arid land but man's parched spirit. The slow, rhythmic slap of the *tabla* drum and the languorous whine of the eight-string sitar echo in the rain-splashed night. Painters show lovers on a balcony gazing out over the greening landscape as a peacock, its rainbow tail spread wide, struts its monsoon dance. Poets celebrate the mythical chataka bird which lives on raindrops or they sing of monsoon love: "Clouds with lightning/lightning with clouds/branches in blossom/shower in joy/and peacocks loudly chanting/for both of you."

But here on the dun plains of the Ganges basin the monsoon of song and painting is only a gauzy memory. No peacocks or raindrop-eating chatakas here—only the brown sparrow grubbing for dead seeds in the furrow. No lovers on a balcony—only villagers breaking stones in the forest to earn a handful of grain. No *tabla* and no sitar—just the plaintive bleat of the Brahman's conch horn asking the gods for rain.

For, like many villages throughout India, this cluster of mud houses straddling the tar road 30 miles east of Allahabad had vir-

From the *New York Times Magazine,* October 2, 1966, copyright © 1966 by The New York Times Company.

tually no monsoon last year. Instead of the 37 inches of rain which normally fall on this section of Uttar Pradesh state, Basehra got only 11 inches—barely enough to water down the layer of chalky dust which covers the village's narrow, winding paths.

This summer's monsoon has been disappointing too.

A few showers have spread a thin sheen of green across the fields—like one of the translucent chiffon saris which the village women wear on festival days—but, like the torn and spotted cotton petticoat which can be glimpsed beneath the sari, the scorched, cracked earth is plainly visible under the scraggly grass. Every morning a few yellow *kanail* blossoms are scattered on the stone phallus near the two small temples in the center of the village, an offering to the gods for fertility and a good harvest, but by evening, they have already turned brown around the edges.

This is Basehra's testing time. The effects of last year's drought are most severe now, just before the fall harvest, for whatever meager stocks of grain the villagers had accumulated have now been exhausted. Moreover, these weeks will determine the strength of this year's monsoon and the fate of the coming crop.

Basehra's farmers are almost totally dependent on rainfall. There are only four irrigation wells in the village. A canal flows through Basehra's fields, but almost all the village's land is above the canal, and there are no pumps to boost the water up. The villagers squat in their dusty fields and watch their children and the black water buffaloes splashing in the useless water.

Their narrowed eyes as they squint into the dry sky betray their anxiety. "It was bad in 1904, very bad, but this is worse," says Alam Singh, a gnarled farmer with a tangled white beard who, at 80, is the oldest man in the village. "I don't know what we'll do if it gets any worse."

Everyone agrees the past year was "very bad" for Basehra. Officials estimate that the village's total crop of rice, wheat, barley and other food grains was only about 50 tons compared to about 220 tons in a normal year.

However, what this has meant to the people of Basehra is a matter of considerable controversy in neighboring Allahabad, the district headquarters, and in Lucknow, the state capital. Conditions in Basehra became a major issue in state politics last spring when the Samyukta Socialist party (S.S.P.) contended that two persons had died of starvation here. It demanded that Basehra be declared a "famine area."

The Uttar Pradesh Government refused, although conditions here are probably as bad as in many famine areas elsewhere in the country. An official, impatiently brushing lint off his spotless white cotton shirt, insists there have been no starvation deaths in Basehra or anywhere else in the state.

One of those who died in Basehra last February was Bhugani Darzin, the 60-year-old widow of a Moslem tailor. Since her husband's death 25 years ago she had eked out a living repairing the villagers' old clothes. However, when the food shortage became acute last winter there was no work to be found and even handouts were rare. "When we had nothing ourselves, how could we give her anything?" one villager asked. She began to supplement the little grain she got by collecting wild berries in the forest. One day in the forest she collapsed and died.

The other person who died last February was Beni Kushwaha. A 65-year-old landless laborer who worked in other men's fields, Beni suffered from a mild paralysis of the legs for the last five years of his life and took to begging—chiefly in neighboring villages because he could not bear to beg from his friends. One day he collapsed on a begging tour. A passerby carried Beni back to the village. Neighbors say he had no food left in his bag. He died the next morning.

Short of an autopsy, it is difficult to say what Beni and Bhugani died of. Both were elderly derelicts and were undoubtedly suffering from chronic diseases anyway. However, severe malnutrition almost certainly accentuated their already weakened condition and tipped them over the edge.

This is the real danger in Basehra. Many of the village's 850 persons live close to the subsistence level, and the margin has been sharply whittled down during the last few months. There has apparently been an increase in diseases caused by malnutrition, insufficient water and impure food. Night blindness, anemia, rickets and dysentery are rife, and Basehra had five serious cases of typhoid in July and early August. Many of the lower-caste children have bloated bellies, symptomatic of a severe protein deficiency which can cause permanent physical defects. These are danger signals whose real meaning may only be read in months and years to come.

The burden of the drought has fallen largely on those like Beni and Bhugani who have no land. About half of the households in the village are landless, chiefly the lower castes—the Chamars (traditionally leather workers), the Kols (farm laborers), the Lohars (blacksmiths), the Kahars (watermen) and the Khatiks (weavers). The landowners are those of the middle castes, like the Ahirs and the Kushwahas, and the upper castes—the Brahmans, the Kaisthyas and, particularly, the Thakurs.

The Thakurs, a subdivision of the Kshatriya (warrior) caste, gained their predominant position in Basehra because they were relatives of the Rajah of Manda, the Thakur prince who once ruled this area.

In 1951 when the landlord system was abolished, the Rajah's Thakur relatives who had been working his lands were allowed to buy the land outright for a payment of 10 times the annual land revenue. Today 11 villagers—most of them Thakurs—own more than 50 acres each, and together own more than 60 per cent of the land in the village. (These would be considered very large holdings in most regions of India, but most of Basehra's land is rocky, and a farmer needs a relatively large tract to get a good crop even in a good year.)

Dhan Bahadur Singh, a young Thakur with a hooked nose and a scraggly beard, owns 223 acres—the largest tract in the village. Bhagwati Singh, a Thakur with a neat little mustache and coldly penetrating eyes, owns 168 acres. The government has prohibited any landlord from owning more than 80 acres in the Basehra area, but this land reform ceiling is easily circumvented by putting the land in several names.

With the Thakur's control over the land go other kinds of dominance. Like all Indian villages, Basehra is nominally governed by a 13-man elected village council. Because of their numerical strength, the lower and middle castes control the council, which is headed by Bishwanath Prasad, a gray-bearded Kushwaha. In practice, however, the council has little power here, apparently because the upper castes simply will not accept the rule of the lower castes. The real authority, therefore, seems to lie with an informal seven-man council made up of three Thakurs

(Alam Singh, the village's oldest man; Brij Bhan Singh, Dhan Bahadur's brother, and Bhagwati Singh), two Kaisthyas, one Ahir and one Kushwaha.

The Thakurs and other landholders employ the lower-caste landless laborers, chiefly the Kols, to till their fields—usually for about two and a half pounds of grain a day.

Some of the Kol families have relationships with Thakur families going back three, four or more generations. Budhu, a 60-year-old man blind in one eye, is the leader of Basehra's Kols. "We've always worked for Alam Singh and his family," says Budhu. "My grandfather worked for them, my father worked for them, my son is working for them now, and I guess his children will, too."

The relationship is a deep and many-faceted one, extending far beyond mere agricultural labor. Budhu's family, including the women, perform all sorts of tasks for Alam Singh—cleaning the yard and house, making the cow-dung cakes used for fuel, building the thorn hedges used to keep the cows out of the fields.

Those Kol families, like Budhu's, which have long-term relationships with Thakurs are relatively well off. Such Thakurs feel a sense of responsibility for "our Kols," as they describe them. Even when there is no real work to be done, they try to find something the Kols can do around the house to earn a little grain. When that is impossible, they may advance them a little grain to be deducted from their wages in a good year.

Other Kols and landless laborers are not so fortunate; there has been little work—or grain—to sustain them this past year. Some have tried to eke out grain on the *batai* system, under which they work a bit of land and split the crop with the owner, but this has produced virtually nothing this year.

Bhulai, a skinny young man in a red loincloth who is a Chamar, the lowest caste in the village, lives with his uncle, his two brothers, their wives and children—a family of 11. In a good year the family is not too badly off because there are three young men to work in the fields. They own about an acre and a quarter of rocky land, and for the past few years Bhulai has cultivated another three acres belonging to a Thakur widow.

This year Bhulai got no crop at all from his own land. "I got about 40 pounds of wheat from the widow's land, but by the time I paid her half and returned what I'd borrowed in seed I had almost nothing left. Nothing, I tell you. And my brothers didn't get any real work this year, either. It's been bad."

When food gets very scarce, the women of Bhulai's family and of other low-caste families wander to one of the Thakur houses. They sit down before the Thakur's wife, rub her ankles and legs, and look up at her with doleful eyes. Sometimes she will reach behind her into one of the huge earthenware jugs and drop a fistful of grain into their hands.

This kind of relationship breeds mutual bitterness. Some of the Thakurs are outspoken in their contempt for the Kols and Chamars. "Kols are to human beings what parrots are to birds," says Thakur Ram Avadh, a stocky farmer with a smear of yellow paste on a forehead heavily scarred by smallpox. "You can feed a parrot for years, but the moment it is released from the cage it flies away. The Kols are just like that. For years they work for you. Yet the moment they find a man who will pay them a little extra they run away. They don't have the slightest regard for human relationships."

Dhan Bahadur agrees. "After dusk you can hear their shrill voices for miles quarreling among themselves," he says. "They are very selfish and undependable."

Normally, the lower castes, brought up in a tradition of humble servitude, are reluctant to express their real feelings about the Thakurs. However, declarations about the equality of all Indians which come from Lucknow and from far away New Delhi are beginning to penetrate even here, and occasionally the lower castes let fly with a revealing gibe.

The other day, Tribhuvan Singh, younger brother of Bhagwati Singh, was lounging under a *peepul* tree before his brother's big stone house—the only well-built house in the village—when Rukmina, a leather worker's wife, came by. In a sardonic drawl, Tribhuvan Singh asked, "What do you want now? Do you want the food thrust down your throat? Can't you work in the fields?"

Stung to anger, Rukmina shot back, "How can you say that when you turn us out when we come begging for work?" Then, shifting to another tack, she asked, "How can we work when we can't even lift our feet for lack of food?"

Tribhuvan Singh stalked away. To smooth over the tense moment, a listener, looking up at the cloudy sky, asked Rukmina and a crowd of curious Kols who had gathered whether they thought it would rain.

"Rain?" asked a young Kol named Goli. "How can it rain in this village of sin where one man eats and another man doesn't?"

Goli was exaggerating somewhat, but there is a wide difference between what a Thakur or a Brahman eats and what a Chamar or a Kol eats in these days of acute scarcity.

The Thakurs and other upper castes usually breakfast around 7 on a dish of roasted mixed grains—wheat, barley and gram— that looks a little like Rice Crispies. Some eat it with milk, and others with *mahua,* a small apricot-colored fruit. For their second and third meals—at noon and 6 P.M.—they eat rice, a few *chappatis* (thin cakes of unleavened bread), lentils and perhaps some *cholai saag,* a wild leafy vegetable which the villagers pick when they graze their cattle in the fields.

Even the upper castes, of course, are eating less this year than they do in a normal year. "Once we ate four to six of these *chappatis* a meal," says an upper-caste woman as she pounds the cakes flat on a large rock. "Now we've cut down to one or two. And mind you, they're made of sorghum now, not the wheat we're used to."

Some years ago, the upper castes would also have supplemented their meals with liberal servings of milk, ghee (clarified butter), curds and perhaps even some milk candies. However, few dairy products are available now, because more than 120 of the village's cattle have died during the past year for lack of fodder, and the roughly 500 that remain—scrawny and lethargic—are giving little milk.

Most of the lower castes work from 6 A.M. to 9 before eating a breakfast of either roasted sorghum or, when they have no money to buy sorghum, a patty of crushed and roasted *mahua.* At noon, the lucky ones have a little of the same; the unlucky ones have nothing. In the evening, they eat their "big" meal— probably a few sorghum cakes and a little *cholai saag.* When they have no sorghum, some of the families try to make do by gathering a wild millet, called *sowan,* which grows around the village. "It takes hours of sifting," says Rukmina, "but if you're lucky you may be able to get enough of the little grains to make a *chappati* or two."

More and more of the families are living on the *mahua* fruit, but even this takes some money. The *mahua* trees are valuable assets in the village and those who own them rent them out to the less fortunate at 25 rupees a season. Some of the lower castes cannot raise that much and they must go without even *mahua*. "I swear by the Ganges that I have lived without any food for two or three consecutive days," Bhulai says.

One other food is available to the lower castes, but though it helps fill the aching void in the stomach it takes its toll later. This is *khesari dal,* a drought-resistant lentil which can grow even when wheat and sorghum wither for lack of rain.

Excessive and prolonged consumption of the lentil causes "lathyrism," a paralysis of the legs. For this reason, state authorities have banned it. "No *khesari dal* is grown or eaten in Basehra," the district health officer says flatly.

The villagers tell a different story. "Oh, yes," says one Kol, "the officials say we shouldn't grow it. That's all very well for them. They have wheat and rice to eat. But we have to eat what we can get. Sure, we eat *khesari dal.*"

The ravages of the grain can be seen everywhere in the poorer parts of the village. Few Kol families in Basehra do not have at least one cripple. They hobble painfully along the dusty lanes, supporting themselves on wooden staves or, in acute cases, sit propped against a mud wall gazing out at the world with dulled and apathetic eyes.

Bhaggu, Sumer and Mudair—three Kol brothers—are all cripples. "Once we used to earn our living sitting on a platform in the Thakurs' fields throwing stones at birds that tried to peck the crop," says Bhaggu. "Now there is no crop and even the crows have gone elsewhere."

So they earn some money breaking rocks in the grim expanse of brush and stunted trees which the state calls a "forest." The Forest Department pays the villagers 10 rupees for breaking up 100 cubic feet of rock, which is then used to make roads.

A healthy villager can earn about three rupees a day breaking rock, but Bhaggu, Sumer and Mudair—teamed with two other cripples from a neighboring village—made only 20 rupees all together for a recent week's work. Two of them dug out the stones while the other three, their crutches laid beside their bent legs, cracked the stones with small hammers.

About 60 men and women from Basehra have been working at breaking rocks in the "forest" this summer. The work is irregular. Sometimes the supervisors come with their trucks and sometimes they do not.

But for many landless villagers it is the only work available since the relief project closed. This project—construction of a water storage pool—began in March and provided work for hundreds of men and women at 12 cents a day, but it was halted with the first rains in June.

One of its benefits remains—the "fair price" shop which is supposed to sell grain at prescribed prices. The shop had been in a village two miles away but was moved to Basehra when the relief project began here. A low-roofed mud house with a grain-splattered verandah, the shop usually gets about 40 ninety-kilogram bags of Indian sorghum and about 20 bags of American wheat flour a week (recently, there has been no wheat flour "because the mill broke down," but that matters little since most villagers now consider wheat a delicacy to be served only when guests call).

The "fair price" shop would go a long way toward meeting the village's needs if the grains were equitably distributed at fair prices. However, they have not been. The shop is under government instructions to sell sorghum at 7 cents a kilogram and wheat flour at 8 cents. However, some of the lower-caste villagers complain they are frequently charged much more. There are also supposed to be limits on how much a man can buy, but the shop seems to be selling the more affluent villagers as much as they want.

This is typical of the government's attention to Basehra. Local officials follow time-honored practices for countering famine in the area. A 1911 gazetteer for Allahabad district recounts how British officials provided relief work, stone crushing in the forest and tax rebates during the all too recurrent famines in Meja Tahsil.

Independence has meant little to Basehra. Ironically, the village is in what is known as "the constituency of prime ministers."

Jawaharlal Nehru represented it for five years and then it became the seat of Lal Bahadur Shastri. Prime Minister Indira Gandhi, Nehru's daughter, is from the same area and may eventually decide to contest the seat. Basehra votes for Mrs. Gandhi's Congress party in national elections and for the opposition S.S.P. in local elections, but politics has little impact here. Basehra deals only with local officials who now, as in British days, do their "duty"—and little more.

In the town of Meja, four miles down the tar road from Basehra, Ram Nath Sharma, the *tahsildar,* or chief revenue officer, for the 679 villages in the Meja subdivision, sits on a raised platform at the end of a darkened room. A boy, squatting on the floor, pulls lethargically on a rope attached to a wood and green-cloth fan hanging from the ceiling. On the verandah outside, half a dozen clerks perch on their own platforms filling dusty ledgers with their long quill pens.

The *tahsildar,* a precise, conscientious man with horn-rimmed glasses, consults one of the ledgers and says the *tahsil,* or district, has rebated 1,039 out of the 1,257 rupees it would ordinarily have collected in land revenues from Basehra this year. The rebates are made on the basis of estimates of crop damage submitted by inspectors. The *tahsildar* has not collected even the small revenue due "because I don't think the villagers could pay anything now," but he will make collections after the November crop.

Up the road, seven miles on the other side of Basehra, is Koraon, headquarters of the "block development officer" who is responsible for all development activities in the block's 193 villages. The walls of his office are covered with pictures of Gandhi and Nehru and posters illustrating the pest-control and family-planning programs.

B. N. Misra, the block development officer, recounts patiently what his staff has done for Basehra in this year of scarcity. Loans of 1,000 and 1,200 rupees were made to two villagers to dig irrigation wells, and five other villagers got loans to build or repair drinking-water wells. Other villages have dug more wells than Basehra has, the officer says, but Basehra's soil is very rocky. "In most parts of the village you hit bed rock a few feet down and you have to blast. That's very expensive."

Basehra has benefited from the Kapuri Service Society, a co-operative set up with the aid of the block office to provide seeds, farm implements, pesticides and fertilizers on credit. Seventy-one of Basehra's farmers are members of the society, which also serves four other villages. A farmer can get a loan from the society up to eight times the share capital he has in the society. The loan must be paid back at the end of the crop with 8½ per cent interest. If the loan is not paid back, no new loan can be obtained. Block officials say this regulation has been relaxed to allow Basehra's farmers, who could not possibly pay back last year's loans, to borrow for the coming crop. However, the farmers say they have been refused new loans.

Therefore, many villagers fall back on more traditional ways of raising money. They borrow from moneylenders in Sirsa, a nearby market place. Interest rates vary by caste. A Thakur—who is presumed to have good credit—can get a loan at 3 per cent a month, or 36 per cent a year, but a Chamar must pay about 6¼ per cent a month, or about 75 per cent a year. This year, villagers hard up for cash also sold jewelry, cows and even land.

Officialdom's most intimate contact with Basehra is the *gram sewak* or "village level worker." Ghan Shyam Singh, the *gram sewak* for Basehra and three surrounding hamlets, is a young man with thinning hair, a ragged mustache and teeth stained red from betel nuts. He makes his rounds on a battered bicycle, taking notes in a little green plastic diary.

The *gram sewak* is supposed to act as a link between the village and the Government—relaying instructions and advice from the block and passing back the complaints and problems of the villagers. Yet, on this year's most celebrated complaint, the villagers chose not to work through him but to take direct action themselves. This was the "case of the great canal break."

The canal water which runs through but not onto Basehra's land has been galling the village's farmers this year. As one says, "It is a horrible thing to see all that water there and your fields scorching in the sun."

In earlier years, the villagers cared less. Since the canal was opened in 1958, the three-mile stretch through Basehra had never irrigated more than 21 of the village's 1,000 acres of cultivated land. In years when the rains were good, no canal water was used. Since farmers must pay 11 rupees per acre per crop for the water, they saw no reason to pay when they had rain. This year every farmer with land below the canal used the water, and 127 acres were watered. But most of the villagers, whose land is above the canal, got nothing.

The failure of either the villagers or the block officials to find some way of getting the water out of the canal and onto the fields puzzles the visitor. At one place, where the canal passes through Dhan Bahadur's land, a pipe can be seen hovering just three inches above the water. "Why don't you lower the pipe?" Dhan Bahadur is asked. "The block won't let us," he replies. "Of course we'll let him," says the block. "It costs too much money," says Dhan Bahadur. "It doesn't cost anything at all," says the block. "It's too much work; we haven't got that much energy these days," says Dhan Bahadur.

It's the same story when the visitor asks why diesel pumps or bullock-driven "Persian wheels" aren't used to raise the water as they are in other areas. "We've asked for them but the Government don't give them to us," say the villagers. "We don't give them out. The villagers have to get them themselves," says the Irrigation Department. "A Persian wheel costs too much, and what's more, it wouldn't work here," say the villagers. "Of course it would work and it could be built very cheaply," says the Irrigation Department. Why don't you go out and show the villagers how to do it, the department is asked? "That's not our job; it's the block development office's job," says the Irrigation Department. "We're too busy," says the block development office.

So it was no surprise when seven men crept out one night last October with shovels and staves and broke through the dikes of the canal in nine places. The water, under heavy pressure from up the canal, seeped across the land. The culprits were apprehended but never charged because, as the *tahsildar* said, "We wanted to take a lenient view. The villagers were in distress and we didn't want to drag them into a court of law."

Despite the food shortage, Basehra has had little other crime of consequence this year. The village may be spared some violence because the *tahsil's* most renowned criminal is from Basehra and does not strike his own village. He is Mangal Singh, a gaunt, long-nosed bandit, who with his 10-man band has been terrorizing the *tahsil* for the last four or five years. Two months ago he pulled off a particularly daring job in neighboring Manda, stealing money and jewelry from some wealthy Brahman women.

Once Basehra was known for its virile men, particularly wrestlers like Banke Singh, the huge, walrus-mustached Thakur who could pin any man for miles around. Today its pleasures are more sedentary. The villagers like to lounge on string cots under the leafy *pakar* tree by the twin temples and gossip. (Only the upper castes sit on the cots, of course. The Kols and the Chamars squat deferentially on the ground at the edge of the shady circle.) Sometimes the villagers play the old Indian card game of *kot-pis*. Some of the Thakurs who can afford it smoke marijuana and most of the villagers drink *daru,* the strong almond-colored wine made from *mahua,* when they can get it.

Most of all, the villagers get solace and pleasure out of telling and acting out tales from the Ramayana and the Mahabharata, two of the great Hindu epics. Some years ago, Basehra boasted a prodigious story teller, Raghubir Prasad Srivastava, and on balmy evenings 50 or 60 persons gathered in front of his house to listen for hours to the adventures of Ram and Krishna.

Raghubir is dead now, and nobody in the village can tell the tales as he did, but the villagers take joy in the October Dashahara festival, during which they assume roles in the Ramayana tales. Several men known for the roles they play each year use those names year-round.

Basehra takes its religion seriously. The village boasts four tiny white-domed temples—three devoted to the worship of Shiva, the god of destruction, and one to Hanuman, the monkey god. All of the temples are served by one Brahman priest.

At this time of year farmers perform the traditional *havan* ceremony to implore the gods for rain. Early one recent evening 12 farmers and their families gathered around a small fire to begin their all-night *havan* vigil and prayers. Led by the Brahman priest with a trident smeared in red and white powder on his forehead, they chanted, "hail Ram, hail Shiva," as they poured clarified butter and roasted gram onto the fire. Clouds of incense rose from brass pots as the priest blew four blasts on his conch horn and the other villagers turned their eyes upward into the star-speckled sky.

The next morning the stars gave way to sun again, but nobody was particularly disturbed. "We will produce what God gives us," said Bishwanath Prasad. This refrain is heard over and over again in Basehra, usually accompanied by a shrug of the shoulders. Religious fatalism prevails all over India, but those who know Basehra well believe it is particularly strong there.

"Basehra is a poor village because it just doesn't care," says Kamta Prasad Singh, chairman of the development block's elected council. A vigorous, articulate man who does care, Singh says Basehra's villagers are "royal," a word used in this part of the country to describe a man with a "don't give a damn" attitude. "We have other villages around here which might be just as poor as Basehra, but they try to develop. Basehra doesn't try. The block dug compost pits all over the village, but the people never put compost in them. They just fill up with mud."

A few villagers have managed to shake off Basehra's pervasive lethargy. The most energetic and progressive family in the village are the descendants of the rajah's patwari, or record keeper, at Basehra. Members of the traditionally "intellectual" Srivastava caste, some of them have now moved to Allahabad. At 30, Sudhir Chand Srivastava is a lecturer in botany at Allahabad University. Kedar Nath Srivastava is a parcel clerk at Allahabad's railway station. They speak with affection but sadness about their ancestral home.

"Certainly ours is a backward village," says Kedar Nath as he sits in the station's new canteen. "Only 20 per cent of the villagers are literate. Family planning has not reached the village yet. Most of the farmers don't use chemical fertilizers. But it really isn't their fault. A child doesn't know how to walk at birth. Adults must help him. Basehra needs help."

Two other Srivastavas from the village are studying in Allahabad today—one at the Law College and one at the Agricultural College—the only villagers now at the university level. Both agree that Basehra needs help, but neither wants to go back. "I'll have a Master of Science degree in agriculture soon," says Suraj Prasad Srivastava. "What would I do in Basehra?"

Part 2

BARRIERS (MOSTLY MAN-MADE) TO ECONOMIC DEVELOPMENT

ALL COUNTRIES, developed and underdeveloped, must cope with obstacles to the realization of their economic and social objectives. The fact that some countries are materially richer than others suggests that at some time in the past the barriers to their own development were less important, or the methods for overcoming them more successful. All countries have grown economically at one time or another; variations in the rates of growth account for current differences. Where obstacles were overcome on a sustained basis, not only did growth occur but development took place as well.

The articles in this section explore the range of barriers to development, from the population explosion to the debilitating impact of a nation's currency gone wild. The most important thing to bear in mind when considering the issues discussed below is not so much the obstacles themselves but the setting in which they occur and the way in which that setting contributes to their becoming obstacles. The military may check needed reforms and economic progress in one situation; in another it can become a positive force, contributing significantly to economic development. Under still other conditions, it may be neutral.

All discussions of economic development inevitably turn to population growth. Professor Davis' analysis of current population growth singles out three major issues which can no longer be ignored. Standards of living probably have no chance to be raised until the growth rate of population is slowed; it is possible to slow the population explosion, as Japan has demonstrated; and the developed nations, especially the United States, must adopt new attitudes toward providing birth control assistance.

In Roman Catholic Latin America, where birthrates are the highest in the world, birth control is still political dynamite. Without official backing, the prospects for birth control assistance look rather dim. But entrenched attitudes about the values of large families are not monopolized by Roman Catholicism, as Joseph Lelyveld shows in his article on India. Having many sons has been one way of providing old-age insurance in poor countries. When life expectancy was short, a large number of sons was required to insure survivors. With death rates now dramatically reduced, the old attitudes have become significant obstacles to progress.

Inability to cope with the obstacles to development is closely connected with the strengths and weaknesses of a nation's political system. Weak, corrupt, or brutal political regimes do nothing to meet the underdeveloped nation's problems. In many instances, as in the case of Duvalier's regime in Haiti, the government itself becomes the major barrier to economic development. More often, inertia and bureaucratic corruption simply stifle national initiative.

Getting economic development under way is difficult. But there are plenty of possibilities for failure even after it gets started. Cases of arrested development are perhaps the most tragic of all; in these instances, it is clearly man's institutions which have gone awry. Once that occurs, it can be almost impossible to reverse the process, as illustrated by Chile's monstrous inflation.

Analysis of the
Population Explosion

by Kingsley Davis

THE INCREASE of mankind has been so rapid, so overwhelming and utterly unprecedented in recent years that it is commonly referred to by scientists as a population explosion. We now number 2,750,000,000, about twice as many as seventy years ago; and there is every sign that that number will double within another forty years. Moreover, the rate of increase is growing faster all the time. The world's population rose by 6 per cent per decade between 1850 and 1950, and by 7 per cent between 1900 and 1930; by 10 per cent between 1930 and 1950, and by 17 per cent, on a decade basis, in the seven years since then. At present the number added to our globe each year is 47,000,000 (greater than the population of France) and before long it may be 75,000,000 annually.

This explosive human multiplication, unanticipated and unexampled in history, clearly cannot continue indefinitely. It would give us nearly 6,000,000,000 by the end of this century and nearly 13,000,000,000 by the year 2050. How this growth is eventually stopped, and when, will play a tremendous role in human destiny.

Although a climax in population growth is approaching, noth-

From the *New York Times Magazine,* September 22, 1957, copyright © 1957 by The New York Times Company.

ing indicates that the peak has yet been reached. The total may climb faster in the next twenty years than it did in the last twenty. Even if the rate of increase begins to decline, centuries may pass before it falls to simple replacement level; and new billions will have been added to the human horde in the meantime. Unless a catastrophe intervenes we and our children will share the earth with a lot more people than we do today.

A strange fact is that in general it is the poorer and less-developed regions, the regions least able to support additional millions, that are exhibiting the biggest demographic inflation. Briefly, according to the United Nations, the explosion is greatest in Latin America; next in Oceania, Africa, and most of Asia; less in the United States and Canada; and least in Europe, especially Western and Central Europe. The Latin Americans, for example, are multiplying more than four times faster than the people of Northwestern Europe; the people of East Asia more than three times faster.

In the past the greatest numerical increase occurred in the more successful nations—those that were expanding economically and raising their level of living. Now, however, it is primarily the peasant-agrarian countries, where poverty is most intense, that are ahead in the population marathon. Ceylon, Taiwan and Malaya; Paraguay, Costa Rica, Colombia and Mexico; Turkey and Syria—these are among the countries that have attained or are approaching a rate of increase that will double their numbers every twenty-three years. Our neighbor, Mexico, which now has 31,500,000 inhabitants, will have about 63,000,000 in 1980. The only industrial countries that have better than half of this rate are the new ones—such as Canada, the United States, New Zealand and the Soviet Union. The older industrial countries are far behind, despite their postwar baby boom.

The recent acceleration in world population growth is not due, as is often assumed, to rising birthrates. In advanced nations birthrates did rise after the depression, but for the most part they have slipped back to comparatively low levels.

The main factor is the revolutionary reduction in death rates in the underdeveloped countries, where most of the world's people live. And this spectacular drop has been gathering speed since 1935. Most notable is the case of Ceylon, where the death rate fell 34 per cent in a single year and 70 per cent in ten years. Other cases are similar: Since the nineteen-forties the average death rate in Puerto Rico dropped by 82 per cent in a single decade; in Cyprus by 64 per cent; in Trinidad by 45 per cent; in Mexico by 43 per cent; and in Jamaica by 30 per cent. As the United Nations shows in its latest Demographic Yearbook, the countries with the highest mortality have generally shown the most remarkable declines. This new achievement in death control is revolutionary not only because its speed has never before been matched but also because it is occurring at a more primitive economic stage than did the fastest death control in the now advanced nations.

The miraculous conquest of death in the less developed areas springs mainly from the application of new scientific and medical discoveries to the control of infectious diseases. These discoveries—new knowledge of diseases, new means of treatment (from insecticides to antibiotics), new modes of public health organization—do not originate in the underdeveloped regions. They come chiefly from the advanced countries, which furnish much of the money and personnel for their application.

In Ceylon, for example, it was the DDT destruction of malaria mosquitos that smashed the death rate—not only from malaria itself but from other connected causes as well. This technique has achieved startling success in many other countries, such as Cyprus, Sardinia, India, Greece, Taiwan, Iran and the Philippines. Not only more efficient than older malaria measures, it is also cheaper. In India a whole household can receive a year's protection from malaria at less cost to the Government than an American spends on one haircut. Health experts believe that malaria can be eradicated from whole regions before the mosquitoes develop DDT immunity, thus making even the negligible expense of spraying unnecessary.

In Yugoslavia a WHO and UNICEF campaign utilizing penicillin wiped out endemic syphillis among half a million people. Related diseases such as yaws and bejel have been successfully attacked under international auspices in Haiti, Indonesia, Iraq, the Philippines and Thailand. The cost of eliminating these widespread diseases is expected to fall to as little as 10 cents per person examined and to one dollar per person treated. Such mass health programs, with bulk purchase of supplies and use of governmental authority, can wipe out at a low individual cost one after another of the infectious diseases that formerly afflicted millions.

Further reductions in death rates can confidently be expected from the same international effort. The United States, for instance, is currently planning a world-wide war on malaria, to be managed by international agencies at a cost of more than half a billion dollars, a fifth of this sum to come from us. And whether the non-industrial countries develop economically or not, their death rates will be further reduced by additional discoveries, funds and technical personnel from the advanced nations.

If birthrates were dropping as fast as death rates, no acceleration of world population growth would be occurring. But birthrates in most countries have not declined. The recent baby boom has given the industrial nations—particularly the new ones—a greater increase than the experts anticipated. In the agrarian countries birthrates have remained high, largely because the amazing reduction of mortality has been accomplished with minimum disturbance to local customs and often without any rise in the level of living.

The old attitudes that encouraged prolific childbearing—necessary when death took most of the children before adulthood—thus persist even when high fertility no longer makes sense. The same industrial nations that have helped the poorer nations to get rid of diseases have done little to help them get rid of excessive reproduction. Actually, a sharp decline in mortality tends to raise the birthrate, because women are healthier, have fewer miscarriages and are less frequently widowed. For these reasons the birthrate in underdeveloped areas is currently about twice as high as it is in the advanced countries.

How will the acceleration of the earth's population growth and the spectacular increase among backward peoples affect future economic development?

Too often this question is misunderstood as simply the problem of getting enough food to feed the world's people. To do this requires economic expansion, and certainly such expansion is actually taking place; otherwise the huge population increase could not have occurred. But a rise in production that just matches the increase in human beings is not economic development. What brings prosperity is an increase in production per unit of human labor.

The product per unit is not enhanced by merely multiplying workers, but rather by adding things to human labor—fuels, hydroelectric power, machinery, rational organization. The task of economic development is therefore not to keep up with population growth but to get ahead of it. An increase in national income just sufficient to support ever more people at a near-subsistence level offers no solution to the problem of poverty; instead, it makes that problem bigger.

Poor people are more numerous today than ever before, because population is skyrocketing in the poorer countries. If two-thirds of the earth's population was impoverished a century ago and only one-third today, there would still be more poor people now than there were then. With many countries multiplying at a rate near 3 per cent per year, their economies must somehow move ahead at 4 or 5 per cent per year if poverty is to be reduced. This is no easy task when the ratio of people to resources is already excessive and the poverty so great that capital can hardly be accumulated for long-run industrial development.

In countries like India, Ceylon, Egypt, Pakistan and Haiti, to mention only a few, per capita income has risen little if at all, despite a rise in national income. An economist, writing recently about Ceylon, had this to say. "The issue is plain: Any check to population growth will make economic progress more likely or speed it up. Continued or accelerated population growth will make progress slow down or stop. In one meeting of Government officials I attended, the problem of development was put as that of keeping the standard of living from falling—not of raising it."

A further consequence of tumbling death rates and surplus reproduction is the creation of the youngest populations ever known. The reason is that the greatest gains in saving lives are made among infants and children under 10 years of age. A swift drop in mortality therefore has the same effect as a sharp rise in fertility. It increases the proportion of children in relation to older age groups. In Algeria, for instance, 52 per cent of the

Moslems are under 20 years of age, whereas in the United States only 37 per cent of the populace is under 20, and in France, 31 per cent.

Peasant-agrarian countries consequently have an excessive number of dependents for each person in his productive years. One of the ways of meeting this situation is to put children to work at an early age, a practice hardly conducive to education or to economic development. But in fact a great problem of these countries is to find jobs for the ever larger waves of youths that enter the working ages each year. If the young cannot find employment they naturally seek remedies for their plight. They are ready to follow any revolutionary leader who promises a quick and preferably violent way out.

A leader who rests his political career on the whims of these swollen cadres of youth is usually incapable of making solid economic improvements. He is driven to embrace the safest and most inflammatory of all issues—nationalism. He can persecute and expropriate the foreigners, the Jews, or the Christians. He can threaten war on neighboring states. He can play the communists against the free world to get emergency funds for staving off calamity or for buying weapons. He is the unstable political offspring produced by the monstrous marriage between rapid population growth and national destitution.

Fortunately, not all impoverished or overpopulated countries are in irresponsible hands. In some there is a genuine attempt to make economic progress. In such cases, a government may ignore the population trend, but this policy entails a gigantic risk; for it assumes, first, that economic improvement will be possible despite the population avalanche and, second, that the economic gains will ultimately bring a drop in fertility and stop the runaway population growth.

The second assumption is probably correct; for if a country achieves a high level of living and becomes heavily urbanized, its better-educated people will plan their families, and its birthrate will fall to something like a reasonable level. But the assumption that skyrocketing population growth will not obstruct economic development is so dubious that several governments have decided against the gamble of ignoring the population trend.

They are striving to bring fertility control to their people in order to insure and hasten economic growth.

One industrial country that has officially decided to lower its birthrate is Japan. With a population that rose from 55,000,000 in 1920 to 91,000,000 today, with an area no bigger than Montana and with 617 persons per square mile, the Japanese do not think the number of people on their crowded islands has nothing to do with their economic future.

In 1948 the birthrate was 34 per 1,000, the death rate 12 per 1,000 and the resulting population growth sufficient to double the population in thirty-two years. In that year the Japanese Diet passed a law, backed by the five major political parties, legalizing abortions and sterilizations and setting up marriage-advice centers throughout the country. Subsequent liberalization and expansion of this law was accompanied by a semi-official nationwide propaganda campaign for family planning, by the formation of a Population Problem Council under the Japanese Cabinet and by the formation of private family-planning associations and publications. Increased emphasis was placed on contraception, with more than 800 Government-subsidized health centers and with some 30,000 birth control guidance officers.

The consequence has been an amazing drop in the Japanese birthrate. The 1955 figure was 19.4 per 1,000, and the birthrate now is substantially below that of the United States. The rate of population growth has already been cut in half.

Among less industrial countries, India has the boldest population policy. Nehru and a majority of his party have long held that avoidance of excessive population growth is essential to social and economic welfare for the Indian masses. The first Five-Year Plan, initiated in 1951, allotted 6,500,000 rupees for a program of research and education in family planning under the Ministry of Health. Under the second Five-Year Plan, 2,000 rural health centers and 300 urban centers are scheduled to be opened, with family planning an essential service of each center.

Several Indian states and cities have independently taken an interest in the subject; influential citizens are leading a strong birth control movement. Surveys have shown that Indian peasants as well as urbanites, pressed by poverty and by big families, yet aspiring to a better life, are not averse to the idea of birth control. One cannot expect the program to affect India's birthrate immediately, but Indian leaders are looking to the future.

The most recent and surprising convert to family planning is Communist China. Until 1953 the Chinese followed the standard Communist line that overpopulation is a vicious figment of the bourgeois mind. However, the census completed in 1954 gave mainland China a population of 583,000,000, some 15,000,000 more than the Chinese themselves had estimated and over 100,000,000 more than others had been estimating. Believing this huge population to be growing faster than the world average, the Chinese officials speedily did an ideological somersault, maintaining that "overpopulation" is still a myth but that the Communist program would fare better if population growth slowed down. Family planning was justified as conducive to maternal and child welfare.

The Government, which had begun to spread the idea of birth control as early as 1953, stepped up its work in 1954 and 1955. Contraceptive supplies went on sale at Government-managed stores; a propaganda campaign was started. On March 5, 1957, the Communist party newspaper, People's Daily, carried an editorial saying that contraceptives should be widely and cheaply disseminated. Of late, a family-planning propaganda campaign has been intensively pursued throughout the country.

When the Population Commission of the United Nations had its eighth meeting in New York in 1955, the Soviet delegation firmly opposed the very idea of a national birth control policy. At the 1957 meeting, this position was changed. The Soviet delegate (the same man who was there in 1955) maintained that for *his* country no such policy should be adopted, but he said that other countries should be free to adopt whatever population policy they wished. This was an important shift in the Soviet line. What else could the Soviet delegate do with the example of Communist China and neutral India before him?

Officially, the United States and most other Western countries are more afraid of family limitation than the so-called backward nations. Such official silence, prompted by strong religious opposition to birth control, would be impossible if it were not for the fact that these nations are relatively prosperous and that their citizens limit the size of their families anyway. In some under-developed countries, such as Colombia and Peru and the Congo, the full effects of unrestricted propagation have not yet had time to manifest themselves. But in countries with extreme population pressure, responsible leaders cannot afford to adopt an ostrich attitude toward the population problem.

The American policy of improving the lot of the world's poorer peoples is seriously impeded by our official inability to aid them in their population control. A runaway inflation of people in the underdeveloped nations is not in our national interest.

"It's God's Will. Why Interfere?"

by Joseph Lelyveld

NADIAD, INDIA

ATTA JINA, called Attabhai Jinabhai as a mark of respect, let down the rope bed that had been upended against the whitewashed mud walls of his house and motioned the foreigner to a seat. Then he eased himself down onto the doorsill and passed out *bidis,* mini-cigarettes hardly larger than matchsticks, to the villagers crowding onto the stoop. For the foreigner there was a more luxurious smoke, a strong oval-shaped cigarette wrapped in brown paper that suddenly appeared from the folds of his dhoti. Finally, after tea had been summoned, he signified that conversation could begin.

He could guess which way it would turn, for a family-planning worker—a type that has become almost ubiquitous in the villages of this part of Gujarat, mainly as a salesman of sterilization operations—was hovering at the foreigner's elbow. Didn't the villagers, Attabhai was asked, still want large families?

"Nah, nah, nah, nah, nah," he sputtered, then clicked his teeth as many times as if to furnish each syllable with an exclamation point. "That has all changed. A few years ago we used to beat

From the *New York Times Magazine,* January 14, 1968, copyright © 1968 by The New York Times Company.

people who came to talk about small families. Now we know we must listen."

But didn't a man with a large family feel proud? "Nah, nah, nah," he started again, shaking his head; only this time he stopped himself short, smiled, shrugged and amended his answer to: "Maybe."

"I have two views," he explained. "No one in the entire village of Manghroli is against small families. But children are God's gift. The size of your family, that is up to God."

Did a man have to have sons? "Of course," he replied with a solemn shake of his head and the indulgent smile of someone repeating a self-evident truth to a simpleton. "A man needs his generation. A man needs sons."

Attabhai himself, at the age of 60, had only one surviving son, a 14-year-old boy; he also had five acres. If God wanted to bless a man with a holding that size, how many sons would he have? "Ah," he sighed, "even one son can be too many." But if they were good sons? "Ah," he smiled dreamily, "with good sons, he could make his five acres grow to 25. With good sons, there could never be too many."

Those who persuade themselves that this part of Gujarat and maybe even India as a whole stand on the verge of a breakthrough in the business of population control listen to villagers like Attabhai and take comfort from his first view. Others who are sure that it is a wild dream hear only the second. But the confusing truth is that both Attabhai's views can be heard in any village around here, very often from the same man. Both say something about what is happening to the stepped-up drive to contain India's swelling human numbers.

The idea of family planning seems to be gaining remarkably, but the actual practice of it spreads more slowly, possibly because it has come to mean different things to different groups of villagers. Some of those who have grasped the idea of the small family still haven't been persuaded to insure it through contraception. Others see advantages in contraception but not a small family. Still others see the advantages of both—but not for them.

Ranchode Chagen, a Harijan or former Untouchable, in the village of Manghroli is emphatic: three children—the officially sanctioned number—are enough. He himself, however, has five, a son from his first wife and three daughters and a son from his second. Not only that, he is still determined to have another boy so there will be someone responsible for looking after his wife should anything happen to him and her one son. He deeply regrets that his circumstances don't permit him to limit his family yet. But he will certainly quit after his next child, unless, of course, it is a girl. No one can say he isn't planning his family.

Manghroli is fairly typical of villages here in Kaira district, which in family planning and agriculture is probably the most progressive rural district in Gujarat, one of India's most progressive states. Its literacy rate is higher than the national average. But so is its rate of infant mortality. And so, though family-planning workers have been active in the district now for eight years, is its birthrate.

Today Kaira is among the small number of India's 335 districts that already have a virtually complete task force on hand for the promotion of birth control. Each of its 973 villages has a family-planning worker assigned to it. That is true of not even one-third of India's 560,000 villages. Thus Kaira district should be way out in front. It doesn't follow that its successes could be easily emulated in more backward districts which the program is just beginning to reach. But its failures will almost certainly have to be run through again countless times before the ambitious population strategy pays off in a lower birthrate.

The district's population—now 2.4 million—has doubled in the last 30 years; it will double again before the end of the century if it continues to grow at the present rate. Similarly, the population of India, now estimated at 518 million, will go shooting across the one-billion mark in 1991 if the growth rate remains unchecked. At the very least that would doom hopes for development.

But numbers can soothe as well as frighten. Having resolved on what one United Nations report termed a frontal "attack on fertility," Indian planners talk glibly about preventing 75 million births between now and 1975 in order to reduce the birthrate from 41 to 25 for every 1,000 of the population. If accomplished, that would be one of the most fantastic feats of social engineering on record, virtually without precedent. For everywhere else population control has been effective it has come mainly as a by-product of modernization and social change. The Indian aim is to reverse the process—to make population control an agent of social change.

The targets may invite skepticism. But with a population grow-ing by one million a month, debates about sociological theories become luxuries. Indian officials are busy, instead, trying to imple-ment a master plan that calls for training an army of 125,000 family-planning workers, only one-third of whom have been re-cruited so far. They are impelled by the realization that left to itself, the growth rate might well climb, not drop. To reverse the trend there will have to be a sharp cut in the birthrate, for mortality rates now are shrinking so fast, thanks to effective pub-lic health measures, that the life expectancy of the average Indian goes up one year every year.

As if that were not enough, the population burst of the past 20 years—more than half the Indian population is under 20, with 100 million under 8—has already guaranteed vast increases in the numbers of reproducing couples. The future isn't rosy even if they learn all there is to learn about contraception.

The standing-room-only projections of the demographers are very impressive, but they have nothing to do with the calculations of the villagers who must make the crucial choices. In Manghroli, for instance, probably all of the 526 "target couples," as they are known to the field workers who canvass them, have a rough idea of what family planning is and how it is done. At one time or another most of them must have peered curiously into the glass cases at the health center at Alindra, three miles away, with their cut-away models of male and female organs, loops, con-doms, diaphragms, jellies and pills.*

But probably only one in six or, at best, one in five of these couples has actually tried any of the methods. Most of those have gone in for sterilization. The effect on the village's birthrate, calculated to be 45 for each 1,000 but probably higher, has been

---

* Actually, only the first two of these devices are in any use here. The pill is just now being tried out in India, in the face of warnings from experts that it can never succeed on a mass scale in an underdeveloped society because of the tremendous difficulty of maintaining regular supply and of making illiterate village women understand it must be taken regularly.

imperceptible so far. There is, in fact, no place in India as yet where a decisive and continuing decline in the birthrate has been proved beyond reasonable doubt.

Indeed, no one in India has really figured out who is likely to go in for family planning, when, or why. To a remarkable degree, the program is fueled by a kind of desperate faith. Seen from departmental headquarters in New Delhi or the state capital of Ahmedabad, the problem of reducing the birthrate is mainly one of logistics, of tooling up to implement the gigantic master plan—training so many thousands of people, getting them into what is called "the field" with the necessary numbers of jeeps, films, pamphlets and condoms; then setting targets for them to meet and when they miss, rushing in more workers, jeeps, films, pamphlets and condoms in a big push to meet the revised targets.

The unrelenting pressure has a strange effect on the family-planning workers who actually venture into villages. Timetables were drawn up to be followed week in, week out like a military drill. But the targets come on inexorably and the timetables are put aside. The mood finally becomes evangelistic. "Camps" are organized for the performance of sterilization operations. Special family-planning days, weeks or months are "celebrated." Those who have been saved—i.e., sterilized—are called on to give witness while the tireless field workers carry the gospel of the small family to the unredeemed.

It is hard to say what emerges from all the commotion and propaganda, from the puppet and film shows, touring dramatic companies, and lectures. But somehow there are results and a sense of momentum. Of the 10,000 sterilizations performed in Kaira district in the first 10 months of last year, nearly half took place in one frenetic family-planning "fortnight" in September. In those two weeks more Kaira men were sterilized than in the previous 7½ years.

The advantage of sterilization is that it is normally final. Its disadvantage follows from that: people don't try it till they are certain they won't want any more children. Obviously there can't be much effect on the birthrate if they wait till they have had five or six. But in an area in which infant mortality is seven times what it is in the West, it is prudent for parents to make sure their children are growing up healthy before calling their family complete; in the meantime, there may be another addition. In Kaira district 42 per cent of all the people who submit to sterilization have had five or more children. It is considered remarkable that 27 per cent have had three or fewer.

Male sterilization, accomplished by an operation known as a vasectomy, is an astonishingly short and simple business. The patient is given a local anesthetic. Then a small incision is made in the scrotum and a duct called the *vas deferens* that carries semen from the testes is cut and tied off. The patient is almost invariably back on his feet inside of 10 minutes. Just as invariably, if you ask him how he feels he will wag his head sidewards in a characteristically Indian way that means everything is all right.

Everyone agrees that a man who has had a vasectomy is never (well, hardly ever) teased about it in his village; it may even enhance his sex appeal, it is said. But joking on the subject is far from unknown. In Manghroli a man who had submitted to the operation was interrupted, as he was explaining why, by a friend curious to know what the field workers wanted. Here it was the sterilized man who had the laugh. "They want to cut out your future generations," he said.

The zeal of some of the field workers cannot adequately be explained by the pressure of, in the case of the medical officers who get cash incentives, by their material rewards. These people believe in family planning the way others believe in revolution or peace. It is their cause.

There is, for example, Dr. Babubhai S. Patel, the medical officer at the Mahudha health center, who is to vasectomies in Kaira district what Jack Nicklaus is to the professional golf circuit. The analogy may sound farfetched, but not after you have seen the two silver plaques and six loving cups Dr. Patel has garnered for his prowess in population control. The most recent award was for coming in first in vasectomies in the September fortnight with a score of 681.

"During those days we were moving like anything," he recalls. He must have set a record for a single day on Sept. 18, when he performed 71 vasectomies. Though it was sometimes close to midnight when he finished operating he would then jeep into the villages to help the field workers corral candidates for the next day. At 7 rupees an operation, he was also a big money winner; like some of the other medical officers in the district, what he earned from vasectomies in the year was more than his basic salary.

As soon as the fortnight was over his health broke down. So did the program. There were one-fifth as many vasectomies in the next two months as there were in those two weeks. By December the spirit of the workers was rising again for the annual targets were slipping away.

"There's no question about it—we've got to perform 10,000 operations this month," P. S. Amin, the district family-planning officer, solemnly vowed when the month was already one-third gone. Mr. Amin, an M.A. in sociology who stores and emits data about the program like an overstrained computer, had a weary, almost obsessed look that his dark glasses couldn't quite conceal.

His family, he explained, lives in Ahmedabad only 30 miles away. He hadn't seen them for a week, nor did he expect to see them, he said, for three weeks more now that December had been proclaimed a family-planning month. In those three weeks he would try to take his station wagon with the triangular red symbol of the family-planning program on the sides to at least one village every night.

"You must worry about them," a visitor said.

"Oh, I do," Mr. Amin replied, referring not to his family but the vasectomies. "I'm not at all sure that we can do 10,000."

The higher castes were the first to show an interest in family planning in Kaira district, then the lower castes, then gradually the mass in the middle. Each group, for reasons that make sense if someone bothers to listen to them, tended to have its own distinctive likes and dislikes in birth-control methods.

The first people to take to family planning here were the Patels, a caste of landowners and traders who live in the big brick houses with the tiled roofs in the center of the village. Early in the program they were sold on female sterilization, which was more popular in Gujarat, alone of all Indian states, than male sterilization till last year. The operation, involving the cutting of the fallopian tubes, is known as a tubectomy. In India the woman is usually required to spend a week in bed convalescing afterward.

Other Indians sometimes type Gujaratis as calculating people. The answer the Patels give when they are asked why they settled on the tubectomy, the most difficult of the available birth-control measures, tends to bear this out. Women in their caste, they explain, cannot remarry if they are widows, but a man whose wife has died is free to seek a bride. If he has been sterilized his search may prove difficult: it is a question of market value.

When they are setting their targets, the planners sometimes forget how very easy it is for things to go wrong in a family-planning drive. An ambitious surgeon trying to pioneer a new technique almost finished off the tubectomy program in Manghroli and other villages near here. He thought he had found a safe way of making tubectomies reversible, so that women could change their minds about being sterile. But, since in his zeal for science he had neglected to make them sterile in the first place, a number of his patients soon found themselves pregnant again. For a while thereafter tubectomies were hard to sell.

But that was nothing to what happened to the intrauterine device known as the loop. When it was introduced, foreign experts concluded that it was almost ideal for Indian conditions, being cheap, safe and long-lasting. The big drive for the loop in Kaira district started in June, 1965. Several thousand women came forward to receive it every month. Then abruptly, after only a few months, hardly anyone was interested.

Rumors did it (some of them, it is alleged, traceable to an American drug company in Bombay with an interest in marketing the pill). From Kaira district the rumors spread all over India.

The more lurid of them—that the loop causes cancer, or gets into the bloodstream and lodges in the brain, that it gives the man an electric shock during love-making, or causes man and woman to stick together—have probably all been dispelled by now. But the story that the loop causes excessive menstrual bleeding is still widely believed, even by many of the family-planning workers who are supposed to be promoting it. The experts contend that that actually happens in only 4 per cent of the cases. Now in some places the loop is steadily winning acceptance again. But most Kaira women still won't hear of it.

Thus the switch of emphasis from the loop to the vasectomy in family-planning programs throughout the country was especially timely here. (The switch at one point threatened to become overemphatic, with a Health Minister, Dr. Sripati Chandrasekhar, enthusing over off-the-cuff proposals to award transistor radios to those who agree to undergo sterilization, or even make the operations compulsory. Now officials say wryly that the exuberant Minister was merely "thinking aloud" and they try not to look too smug or satisfied about the recent appointment of a new Health Minister to whom Dr. Chandrasekhar, whose responsibilities have been limited to family planning, must answer.)

In Kaira district the first "acceptors," as the field workers call them, were found at the bottom of the social scale among a so-called backward caste known as the Vaghris. Upper-caste Hindus here still show very little interest in the vasectomy. When the suggestion is made, their reaction is anything but casual. Either they laugh just a bit too hard, shake their heads and wave their hands, or their facial muscles tighten and they withdraw from the conversation, fast.

The Vaghris, who are mostly landless and illiterate, have their own good reasons for preferring it. Divorce in the caste, one Vaghri in Manghroli explained, is easy and common. So is re-marriage—for the woman as well as the man. A woman who returns to her family leaves her children behind; in her next marriage she may be expected to bear children again. She cannot contemplate sterilization. Since whatever happens, the man is left with the children, he is the one who really has to worry about limiting the family's size.

Upper-caste field workers often remark on how eager the lower castes are for their advice about family planning. "If we tell them, they do," one said. But significantly, it was a field worker named Laksman Vaghri who made the case for sterilization among his own people, becoming Gujarat's champion vasectomy salesman.

Mr. Vaghri relies heavily on personal contacts and always refrains from even mentioning sterilization or his connection with the family-planning program until he can feel he has the confidence of the villagers. Then he comes on strong, starting off with an analogy between seeds and children and what happens to them when they are planted too close together, following up with the baleful tale of his own Uncle Mothibhai who died of drink and tuberculosis leaving seven young children in the care of a deranged wife, finally going into grateful raptures over his own good fortune in having been born as an only child. His method is to keep the context local, his claims easily verifiable.

Even before it can occur to the Vaghris to worry about whether vasectomies lead to impotence, he has cited the example of someone they are likely to know who had the operation without, as he puts it, "falling from the human level." When they worry that Khodiyar, their goddess, might disapprove of small families, he assures them, as one Vaghri to another, that she is a mother goddess and wants her children to be happy. A mother knows what unhappiness big families bring, he says.

Foreign observers, especially those belonging to the subgenus *Americanus masculinus,* tend to wonder at the readiness of the Indian male to submit to sterilization, however simple and safe the operation. Usually the foreigner ends by telling himself that the Indian must enjoy greater psychological security. There have not been many careful studies of Indian attitudes to sex, but what there is—notably, a book called "The Twice-Born" by a British social scientist, G. M. Carstairs—suggests that an Indian villager is unlikely to be free of neurotic anxiety.

Mr. Vaghri hasn't read Freud or Carstairs, but he knows his people. Not without a measure of cunning, he promotes the vasectomy as the solution to one of the psychological dilemmas Carstairs describes. This derives from a traditional belief, still widely held, that it is debilitating for a man to part with his semen, the source of all his strength. For what is lost is not easily restored: it takes 40 days and 40 drops of blood, according to tradition, to produce one drop of semen. The masculine ideal is *Bhramacharva,* the ascetic self-control practiced by holy men. Celibacy is less a sacrifice than a health cure.

The most revered Gujarati of modern times, Mahatma Gandhi, recounted his struggle to attain this state in his autobiography. "It took me long," he wrote, "to get free from the shackles of lust and I had to pass through many ordeals before I could overcome it."

As Laksman Vaghri sees it, the vasectomy provides instant *Bhramacharva,* without fuss or bother. With charts he shows the villagers how the semen is blocked by the cutting of the duct. The miracle is that normal sexual relations are still possible. The vasectomy can offer much more than a small family.

"A man who keeps his semen always looks bright. It gives him strength," Mr. Vaghri says, repeating the ancient Hindu belief. During the September fortnight this argument helped him persuade 412 men—most of them, finally, outside of his own caste—to submit to the vasectomy.

Family planning in India has been promoted either as a patriotic duty or a public-health measure. Mr. Vaghri's success suggests there is an equally strong appeal in the possibilities it affords for marital happiness. This theme is also taken up in one of the two touring "dramas" being shown to villagers in the district as part of the family-planning campaign. The play tells the tragic story of a young man with an insatiable lust for his wife. His father—fulfilling one of the functions of the Hindu parent—tries to teach him self-control. But the only way, finally, that he can curb his son is to lock him in a box. The young man breaks out; catastrophe threatens. Then at the critical moment the hero of the play—the family-planning worker—enters with free condoms to distribute. Lust is blessed.

It is hard to say how much that kind of appeal has had to do with the success of the vasectomy program. But it is a fact that more than 800,000 vasectomies were performed in India in the six months between May and October, a total nearly equal to that achieved in the previous 12 months.

In Manghroli the other villagers like to joke about the Vaghris. With measured cruelty, they say that the family planners are welcome to them because they're all thieves; the fewer the better. Anyway, they say, everyone knows that the Vaghris are enthusiastic about vasectomies only because of the cash incentives the Government offers—15 rupees ($2) for the man himself, 3 rupees for any other villager who is said to have persuaded him.

Mr. Vaghri, who gets nothing more than his own small salary, denies that the money is the bait. So do the Vaghris. "Of course," a Vaghri in Manghroli added with a grin, "if the Government is giving away money, you can't expect us to refuse."

Though the villagers in the middle castes don't like to admit it, it seems that the example of the Vaghris has helped to start some of them mulling over the possibilities of family planning. These people are arrayed in a dozen different subcastes, all claiming connection to the Kshatriyas, the warrior caste. Some of them are probably concealing lowlier origins behind their flaring, martial mustaches. But that just makes them all the more insistent on showing off the martial virtues, among which they reckon a large family. "Get 100 children" is still a common greeting to a bride at their weddings.

Mostly small landholders not above tilling their own soil, they make up the majority of the population of most Kaira villages. Politically alert members of higher castes suspect they want large numbers for the power they bring. Undeniably the Kshatriya subcastes have been the least interested of all the groups in the villages in family planning. Field workers type most of them as "rigid castes."

Usually, it seems, it is the women among them who get interested first. One afternoon at the Akhdol health center there were two men and three women waiting to be sterilized. All but one, a Thakur (Brahman) woman, claimed to be Kshatriyas. Somewhat lugubriously, the men said they were there because of pressure from their wives. The women said they were there because they had failed to persuade their husbands to submit to the operation.

One of them, Dahai Ben, was calmly nursing an infant child as she watched the doctor go through the routine of boiling water on a kerosene burner. She had six children, which she thought were more than enough. In fact, she had wanted to have the operation a year ago, before the infant in her arms had been conceived, but couldn't get her mother-in-law's approval. Now she had come without it.

"My husband knows I am here," she said, with a nervous titter, "but if he told his mother she would come and carry me away."

The readiness to defy a mother-in-law is the kind of change that suddenly makes the family-planning program look promising. But it will probably be some time before there are many Kshatriya women like Rukhi Ben, the Brahman woman who was being operated on that afternoon. She was only 26 and had only two children, but she was through with childbearing.

"It's the problem of keeping house," she said, almost seeming to step from the pages of McCall's. "With too many children, it's impossible."

Rukhi Ben's youngest child was 4. She no longer felt she had to worry about losing him. Childhood diseases are no longer the killers they once were. The other women don't yet share Rukhi Ben's sense of security, perhaps because so many infants die. No doubt, as infant mortality declines further, they will become more confident. But, of course, the immediate effect of such declines will be to boost the population.

The family planners now realize how different and fickle people's preferences in methods of contraception can be. This realization has led to what they call the "cafeteria" approach, making available any recognized device or method. There is still the hope that some laboratory somewhere will come up with something ideal for India, a miraculous serum, herb or pill that would be immediately and universally acceptable.

But without that, the Government is stuck with the task of manipulating or, to choose a nicer-sounding word, managing people, making them want what it thinks they want, or simply what it wants them to want. In the United States, students take courses in "group dynamics" and "extension education" to learn the technique. India is still innocent of it. But if the family-planning program is to move steadily ahead, it will no longer be enough—it never was—for the legions of field workers to lecture people on what is best for them. The people have to be goaded into standing up and asking for it. That means moving the unmoved movers, the village leaders.

In Gujarat and most other parts of the country these are the leaders of the village's castes and subcastes. In other words, the program will depend on getting what many Indians would consider the society's most conservative elements to take the initiative.

A group of caste leaders was gathered for this purpose one recent afternoon at Bamangam, a village in the district where the program had been lagging. Dr. Paul R. Ensign, a public-health specialist brought here from Salt Lake City by the Ford Foundation three years ago, drove down from Ahmadabad to coach a young, inexperienced extension educator named D. J. Talati, who would have to deal with the elders.

"What are you going to say?" Dr. Ensign asked, speaking ever so slowly in order to be understood. The eager young man hesitated, then remembering something from a circular on how to be an extension educator, replied earnestly, "Why and How."

"Why and How what?"

"Why family planning and how family planning." For just an instant, Dr. Ensign looked tired and discouraged. The young man missed the look.

Recovering, Dr. Ensign had a determined smile fixed on his face as he slowly and patiently explained that the idea was to provoke the village leaders with questions so that they ended up providing the why and how themselves. When the doctor had finished speaking, he searched the young man's face for some sign that he had gotten across. He didn't seem to find it.

The meeting took place in the schoolhouse. The villagers sat on the floor in ranks by castes, with the Brahmans up front, the Kshatriyas in the middle according to their various subcastes, and the Harijans, or former Untouchables, way to the rear, with a stretch of floor serving as a kind of no man's land between them and the higher castes. The village leaders didn't look hostile but they didn't look interested either. They had been asked to be there. So they were.

A flushed and self-conscious Mr. Talati, rolling a pen between his palms and nervously tapping his pointy shoes under the table, started off with a soaring 20-minute address. It left the villagers inert. "Come on," Dr. Ensign advised in an impatient stage whisper. "Wake them up. Throw some questions at them."

Mr. Talati obliged, but couldn't wait for the answers. When a discussion got going in spite of him, he seemed relieved to find he was being ignored. Fortunately, Indian villagers aren't half as solemn about family planning as the program's promoters. Soon there was a variety of ribald suggestions.

"Why don't you try keeping men and women apart? That would do it," a toothless old man from one of the subcastes in the middle called out with a cackle.

A Brahman said he had been thinking of sending his wife for sterilization. Why not himself, he was asked. "Nothing doing," he replied. "If the operation went wrong and my wife became pregnant again, everyone would say she had been fooling around with other men."

While he was speaking, the Harijans rose as a group and indicated how impressed they had been by the proceedings by exiting through the rear door with hardly a word. No one seemed to notice.

A man in a turban in the middle said he could be counted out because he only had one son. Dr. Ensign broke in to say he himself had only one son, and that because there had been only one he had been able to make sure the boy received the best of educations.

"Yes, but you're from a rich country," the villager replied. "If your son dies you'll get a pension from your Government. If my son dies, who will look after me?"

Now the toothless old man was on his feet. "It's God's will," he was insisting. "Why do you want to interfere?"

"They don't mind interfering with God's will when it's a case of sterility," Dr. Ensign remarked in an aside.

Mulshankarbhai Patel, a Brahman father of six who was chairing the meeting, answered the old man. "We used to have droughts. Then the Government built a dam so that there would always be enough water. You didn't say that was interfering with God."

In the end the village leaders promised to locate five candidates for sterilization. Dr. Ensign told Mr. Talati he would come back and work with him some more. He did and a couple of weeks later the young man led a meeting at which 43 sterilizations were pledged.

Implicit in the kind of approach the young man was learning was the faith that there is an appropriate technique this side of compulsion or terror for persuading people to make new assumptions about the things that matter most to them.

Most of the family-planning workers in Kaira district already have this faith. They say they will have the birthrate down to 25 in only a few years.

Dr. Ensign has the faith, too, but he knows the technique won't be mastered so easily. He thinks it will be about eight years before the rate gets down that low. "I guess I'm a pessimist," he says apologetically.

But since the evidence isn't in, it is still reasonable to call the doctor an optimist and imagine that progress will come even more slowly, without any sudden breakthroughs. The other afternoon some of the members of the Manghroli *panchayat,* or council, were asked if they could think of any reasons why the universal acceptance of family planning about which they had been boasting hadn't yet been reflected in the number of births.

The question had to be repeated before one of the village elders answered with an even prouder boast. "We have strong mothers and fathers," he said.

Beautiful, Cruel, Explosive—Haiti

by Tad Szulc

PORT-AU-PRINCE, HAITI

THE HAND OF God crumpled it like a piece of parchment and tossed its improbable mountain-creased shape onto the western edge of the Caribbean island of Hispaniola. History for centuries played glorious but unspeakably bloody and cruel games with it, then let it lie forgotten for nearly 160 years. It became the first Negro republic in the world and Latin America's first sovereign state.

This land, so singular as to belong to a dimension all its own, is Haiti. Unrelated as it long seemed to the tides of modern politics and economic change around it, it has abruptly become the center of the latest Caribbean crisis and a matter of high-priority interest to the United States, concerned that what has been happening here may lead to a complete breakdown of law and order and, conceivably, a Communist take-over.

It is Haiti's incongruous but explosive brew of bizarre dictatorship, of voodoo mysteries, of an atavistic social and nationalistic revolution and of the menace of communism—all swirling in a surrealistic setting—that has brought this tortured country back to the mainstream of history.

From the *New York Times Magazine,* June 9, 1963, copyright © 1963 by The New York Times Company.

Haiti is a nation in search of its lost history and greatness, and it is going about it both consciously and instinctively.

The conscious quest has been reflected in the methodical policies of President François Duvalier, the strange and sorcererlike little dictator in the black suit and homburg with the submachine gun at hand. He has hammered on the theme of Haiti's Negro origins and identity, trying to fit it into the mold of the new African nationalism rather than into the context of Latin America, to which it happens to belong geographically but in no other way.

Superficially, Haiti's language is French—it is only spoken by the élite—but basically it is Creole, an amalgam of French patois with Breton, Basque, English, Spanish and African words. So overwhelming is the domination of the Creole and that which it implies in terms of acculturation that a popular Haitian proverb proclaims that "to be able to speak French is not proof of cleverness."

Haiti's religion is officially Roman Catholic, but virtually the whole population practices the rites of voodoo, which is a true folk religion rather than the sinister black magic that tourists believe it to be. Mixed with Roman Catholicism, it is, according to Dr. Jean Price-Mars, Haiti's leading cultural authority, "a syncretism of beliefs, a combination of Dahomeyan, Congolese, Sudanese and other animisms," brought here by the slaves that the French imported to populate their colony.

Because of its simplicity and symbolism, it is the religion best suited to the primitive and superstitious population, which is more than 90 per cent illiterate and lives almost entirely isolated from outside influences. In fact about 95 per cent of Haiti's population, which is somewhere between four and six million inhabitants (there has been no census since 1950, and even then a great many peasants feared to answer the census takers' questions), lives in the forbidding countryside, wholly unaware of the outside world.

The country's economy is the most backward in the Western Hemisphere, despite its vast colonial affluence of two centuries ago. Vague statistical guesses place the annual per capita income at $70, but this is a meaningless figure because at least three-fourths of the Haitians live all of the time or part of the time outside the money economy. They eke out a living planting coffee, sisal and yucca, existing on an impossible average daily intake of 1,500 calories and succumbing to disease and death at a rate unequalled in the Americas. Yet, and such is the perversity of nature, Haiti is a country in the midst of a tremendous population explosion, with its excess humanity spilling over into Cuba, the Dominican Republic and elsewhere.

Thus what can be called the Haitian national culture emerges from the sum of these linguistic, historic, religious, social and economic factors. Under the Duvalier regime it has stood out as something along the lines of a Negro national socialism in which the whites and the once-ruling mulattoes are the racial pariahs. Politically, it is a monstrosity. Socially, it is a heart-breaking tragedy because it holds no promise of a brighter future.

Strangely, however, Haiti also is a land of art and beauty. The beauty lies in the flowers that cover this improbable, heat-suffocated and slum-ridden capital and in the breath-taking views of its mountains and seashore. The art explodes in the treasures of almost intoxicating primitive paintings that, in their brilliant colors and subject matter, portray better than an anthropologist's treatise the complex Haitian soul. Take a look at the painting of a sheep crucified on a cross atop a cloud-shrouded hill and you will understand what Dr. Price-Mars means about animism and voodoo and why every other Haitian proverb speaks of animals.

With all this, however, to speak of Haiti in the terms of a static primitivism is to tell only one part of the story. Like the rest of the underdeveloped world, it has begun to stir, and these stirrings seem initially to have taken the form of a search for the country's forgotten history, even before it attempts to relate itself to the present and future.

The quest for a new Haitian identity has been embodied, almost pathetically, in the efforts to bring back to life Haiti's incredible past when its liberated slave leaders, Toussaint L'Ouverture and Jean Jacques Dessalines, broke Napoleon's thrust into the Americas, forced him back into Europe after decimating Leclerc's armies on the island and established, in 1804, the sovereign nation of Haiti.

Those were the blood-drenched days of Haitian glory, the days when John Adams treated L'Ouverture as an equal and sent him ships and supplies to smash Napoleon's offensives (and thus saw the Emperor back away from America and sell Louisiana to the United States); when Wordsworth wrote sonnets to the "first of the Blacks"; when Haiti was so wealthy that it made the buccaneers' fortunes and led the French to invent the expression "as rich as a Creole"; and when, early in the 19th century, the Haitians subjugated their Dominican neighbors for 22 years.

But today nothing is left of this past and this glory, for time has eroded both the Haitian mountains and the Haitian man. The country has virtually no immediate hopes of betterment, only a new ferment so powerful that it could again explode in the awesome blood baths that have dotted its history.

Dr. Duvalier, with his Negro dictatorship, seized upon Haiti's history as the instrument for perpetuating himself in power and for constructing the weird "Duvalier revolution," utilizing the Haitians' tradition of violence, their sensitive pride, and deep mysticism, and desperate need for even a semblance of social justice.

Thus it may have seemed grotesque, but it was really in harmony with Haitian history when Dr. Duvalier brought out youths dressed in flaming red coats and tricornes—reincarnations of Jean Jacques Dessalines—to stir up the crowds of peasants in Port-au-Prince in May during the celebrations of the "Month of National Gratitude" in his honor.

It was in tune with this history that the central patriotic celebration of the "Month of Gratitude" was the "Day of the Flag," the anniversary of Dessalines' act of defiance against Haiti's French masters, when the white section of the tricolor was torn out to make the Haitian flag—a rectangle of blue and red. Similarly, President Duvalier established diplomatic relations with Dahomey, Liberia and Ethiopia, sent emissaries to the African conference at Addis Ababa and dotted Port-au-Prince with posters speaking of the African heritage.

It is also in keeping with Haiti's terrible history that the regime's speakers have harangued the crowds with Dessalines' old Creole cry of *"Brule tête, brule kay"* (burn heads, burn houses) with which the slave leaders led the Negro mobs to the immense massacres of tens of thousands of whites and mulattoes in 1791 and 1803.

The heritage of violence is perhaps the only constant in Haiti's history, and Dr. Duvalier and his associates have used it in all its primitive forms along with modern methods of police terror to maintain their dictatorship intact.

Appealing to the memory of Dessalines, a Duvalier leader like Dr. Jacques Fourcand, who improbably holds the post of President of the Haitian Red Cross, warned of a "Himalaya of corpses," should the regime ever be attacked. The Duvalier militias and the gangs of the regime's toughs (officially known as the Movement of National Renovation but called by the people the Tonton Macoutes, meaning in Creole, "Uncle Grab Bag," in an allusion to a folkloric bogyman) consider murder and torture as routine acts of state security.

In this terrorized country, tales of refined executions, wholesale assassinations and brutalities are commonplace. The regime's enemies are said to have been literally crucified, shot in the Presidential Palace, machine-gunned in prisons and their homes, or tortured by the Tontons. When Dr. Duvalier smashed a military conspiracy late in April perhaps 100, perhaps 200 persons were executed at the Fort Dimanche prison here. A Tonton squad machine-gunned the elderly parents of an Army officer who was hiding in a foreign embassy, burned his house to the ground and kidnapped his 18-month-old son.

Humiliation has been another weapon of the regime's oppression. With cruel delight, President Duvalier forced Haiti's outstanding citizens, usually his opponents, to make public speeches praising him as part of the extraordinary personality cult of the dictatorship.

The Mayor of Port-au-Prince, who had shown reluctance to speak out for the President, was put in prison, then released a few weeks later in time for the May celebrations to make his speech. A well-known businessman was tortured, beaten and made to drink his own urine to break his will. Then he was paraded to one of the daily ceremonies of "popular rejoicing" to praise the President.

The brutalizing features of the "Duvalier revolution" help to explain why Haiti's few technicians and teachers have found jobs in the Congo and why much of the country's tiny élite is in exile or in asylum at the Latin-American embassies here. Those who remain at home go through the motions of participating in the Duvalier cult while trembling for their lives.

But if terror is such an all-present fact of Haitian life, its counterpoint is the gaiety, sensitivity and love of pageantry of the Haitian people. An anthropologist may reconcile the violence with the nation's mysticism and its readiness to sing and dance by citing the highly primitive state of Haitian society. In Dr. Duvalier's hands this peculiar combination of traits has proved a tool for self-aggrandizement.

Politics invaded the folklore to create the ostensibly benevolent figure of "Papa Doc," another name for Dr. Duvalier, and mambos, merengues and sambalike African chants have been sung with lyrics praising the President. One of them, not atypically, tells of *"Petit Bon Dieu,"* the "Good Little God," who provides all the good things and, therefore, gave the people the gift of Duvalier.

Massed in front of the white-domed Presidential Palace, peasants from the countryside have swayed and sung about the Duvalier glories. The "rah-rah" bands, ensembles of drums and long, bamboo flutes, have paraded the city's dusty streets to the tune of Duvalier songs.

During the official celebrations, they have patiently allowed themselves to be herded to the Champs de Mars before the Palace or elsewhere by the rifle and submachine-gun-wielding militias. They have cheered for Dr. Duvalier when he has come out on the steps of the building or appeared in a window. They have listened attentively to his harangues, breaking into song and dance as he stiffly jerked his arms up and down in a sorcerer's gestures.

To conclude from this automatic obedience that the masses of Haitians support Dr. Duvalier is to apply to this country the political standards of other countries—Cuba, for example—which in contrast to Haiti are superdeveloped and sophisticated. The most that can be said of the Haitian demonstrations (and in Haitian terms this is extremely important) is that even the pathetic pageantry of the Duvalier regime provides for the masses their only sense of excitement and release from the misery of their daily lives.

A physician and ethnologist with a deep psychological understanding of his nation, Dr. Duvalier—himself a figure of strange mysticism who is said to have a *houngan* (voodoo priest) in his immediate entourage—has known how to exploit these characteristics of the Haitians for the purposes of his dictatorship. As the modern ingredient in this political witches' brew, he added the cry of the social revolution, a notion that even in its most elementary outlines could not fail to evoke a response from the abysmally poor Haitians.

To be sure, the "Duvalier revolution" adds up to vast deception and, in the words of a bewildered European diplomat, to a *danse macabre* in which the terror blends weirdly with the voodoo rhythms and the "rah-rah" bands.

All that can be found in Haiti to justify the Duvalier talk of a social revolution are two partly completed, virtually uninhabited housing projects, not surprisingly named Duvalierville and Suzanne Duvalier (after his wife). In the former, the most imposing structure is the cock-fight arena, a Duvalier version of the Roman circus. A highly advertised "Road to the South" has been inaugurated three or four times, but it still does not lead anywhere. A mysterious project known as *"Le Over-pass"* apparently was abandoned before anyone discovered what it was. The only serious development project in Haiti, the Artibonite Valley irrigation scheme, ground to a halt when the United States, horrified by the corruption of the Duvalier regime and its dictatorial practices, stopped all aid to the country.

The "Duvalier revolution" seems, then, to be motion in a vacuum. When a loyal officer of the Presidential guard, Dr. Duvalier's Praetorian Corps, was asked to explain this "Revolution of National Renovation," he fumbled for an answer, finally saying that "it is good for the people."

But, without any question, Dr. Duvalier has set in motion with his demagoguery and his appeals to Haiti's African past a new set of explosive forces. The concern among Western diplomats here is that, in the long run, the Communists may be the beneficiaries of the "Duvalier revolution," now that the people have been stirred but have had no rational alternative offered to them.

Haiti's hopelessness begins, of course, with the mountains. A favorite proverb has it that "beyond the mountains there are mountains again," which describes accurately the corrugated-metal topography of the country. Erosion has done away with much of the cultivated land of the French days. If the Artibonite Valley project is ever revived, it may bring some life to Haiti, but at the rate the population is growing, it will make only a dent in the national problem.

Land reform, the battle cry of modern revolutionaries, has no meaning here. Haiti has no huge estates to speak of; most peasant families own their bit of land, which is largely unproductive land. If investments are ever attracted here, industry may absorb some of the vast labor force, but the consumers' market is so narrow at present that large industrial development is not feasible.

Stop-gap and palliative solutions are, of course, necessary, and if a rational government ever achieves power, perhaps a beginning can be made toward leading Haiti into the 20th century.

Meantime, everything in the country cries out for change, peaceful or otherwise. Even a cursory tour of Port-au-Prince, so immensely better off than the rest of the country, suggests that Haiti has become an untenable proposition. The spectacular mansions of the tiny élite of merchants and plantation owners rise in the cool hills of Pétionville, the suburb of dusty Port-au-Prince, side by side with the hovels of the masses of the poor. In the unpaved downtown streets, naked children beg for coins among the cars of the regime's officials.

Along Harry Truman Boulevard, bordering the sea, pigs and goats search for scraps of food on the great expanse of untended lawns. The modernistic Government buildings that are the city's pride—a leftover from an international fair—seem to have been dropped along the bay by an absent-minded architect. The peasant women riding side-saddle on their *bourriques* and the naked children carrying tins of water on their heads are much more of a Port-au-Prince reality than the expensive effort to make this a modern capital.

This basic reality of the Haitian hopelessness and destitution could not be erased during the May celebrations even by the insistent Duvalier efforts at pro-regime pageantry. Instead, the unending appearances of the Dictator in his black limousine behind the ceremonial cortege led by an Army band and made up of motorcycles with screaming sirens, troop-filled trucks and his ubiquitous (and only) armored car provided just another jarring note, just another illusion of the "Duvalier revolution," and just another eerie attempt at restoring Haiti to a place in the world and in history.

Survival Issues for the New Africa

by George H. T. Kimble

FEW IF ANY political events of recent times have kindled the imagination of free men so strongly, or been so widely acclaimed and celebrated, as the "rebirth" of Africa. Nor is it difficult to see why. For here is a new thing: a brood of nations—twenty since 1957 alone—sired by colonialism out of tribaldom. But birth is a time of concern as well as celebration, of stock-taking no less than back-slapping, and it has a habit of posing as many questions as it answers. The child may be lively, but will it live? If it lives, will it be strong, and what will be its destiny?

While it is as easy to be wrong about the future of nations as it is about the future of children, there is nothing obscure about either's requirements for growth. They both need the will to live, schooling in the business of living and gumption in the practice of it; and they both need a sound "constitution" and the sustenance to keep it sound. How do the new African nations stand in these respects?

The will to live is clearly present. No one can visit any of the newly independent countries without being made aware of their exuberant vitality and their determination to conserve and nourish it. What is more, they have the leaders to articulate the will. The

From the *New York Times Magazine,* November 26, 1961, copyright © 1961 by The New York Times Company.

Nkrumahs, Tourés and Houphouet-Boignys of Africa are among the most eloquent and persuasive of men.

And the new nations are certainly getting the schooling. Facilities for formal education remain far from adequate in most places, but first-class schools of experience are mushrooming everywhere. There is no teacher like responsibility, and in the past few years the new nations have discovered that they have plenty of responsibilities they were ill-prepared for: among them the running of banks, corporations and armed forces; the raising of revenues and the balancing of budgets; and the winning of other nations' confidence in their ability to do these things. While they undoubtedly still have much to learn they have already mastered enough to confound some of their earlier critics.

Of gumption, too, there are growing signs, though not perhaps as many as we should like to see. One might well question, for example, whether, in countries where most of the people are still unshod, unwell and poorly housed, there is room for the kinds of pleasures and palaces with which some of the leaders are surrounding themselves. It may also be questioned whether there is room for interference in the internal affairs of one's neighbors and obsessive concern with the wrongs of others when there are so many wrongs to be righted at home. More questionable still is the suppression of the very freedoms—of speech, assembly, movement and self-determination itself—by which the present leaders came to power, and the tendency to consider political opposition (as Ghana, Guinea and the Sudan have done) as a kind of malaria to be stamped out at all costs.

What of the soundness of their "constitution"? What sort of stock do they spring from, and how well adapted is it to the austere environment of nationhood? Here it is much more difficult to generalize, for no two nations have quite the same inheritance. Even if they are alike in nature, they differ greatly in the nurture they received while coming to birth.

Ghana, for instance, was rather better supplied with "welfare and development" funds during its period of gestation than Guinea; and Guinea fared better than Gabon. And all three had more opportunity to gather political and administrative strength than the (ex-Belgian) Congo. However, this much is true of almost all of them: they are not homogeneous nations in the sense in which Denmark and France are. Thus, the inhabitants of Ghana—to name only one country—have no common tongue and share no common creed, morality or history. Although they have had their men of destiny and their martyrs (whose blood is the seed of nations no less than of churches), they have hitherto lacked the means of memorializing them.

Rather are these new nations collections of tribal states or groups. Ghana has approximately 100 such groups, each with its paramount or head chief. The Congo has many more. Even so small a country as Sierra Leone has over a score.

It is true that the new elite in these countries are coming increasingly to think of themselves as Ghanaians, Congolese and Sierra Leonians, but the common people still think of themselves as Ashanti, Baluba, Mende and so on. For these, the tribe remains what it has always been, the ground and reference of daily life, the bourn to which all travelers return, the home, sweet home of every prodigal son.

Further, most tribes have their own language or dialect, and their own ideas about the kind of world they want to live in, who shall run it, and for whose benefit. Many of them continue to regard themselves as "peoples" in the United Nations' sense of the word, with the implied right "freely to determine their political, economic, social and cultural status." Dictatorship may curb the expression of these loyalties, but it shows no sign of destroying them, or even of fusing them into a commonwealth.

It is equally difficult to generalize about their sustenance— that most necessary of all growth requirements—for no two of the new nations are alike in size, situation, physical character or resources.

Some of them are larger than others. The Congo is nearly three times the size of Texas; Togo, on the other hand, is only about the size of West Virginia. Some, like Chad, Niger and Upper Volta, are landlocked and far from the sea. Malagasy and Somalia have more coastline than they need.

Some, such as Gabon and Cameroun, have all the looks of a Hollywood set of the tropics—complete with sunny fountains, palm trees and surf-beaten strands where every woman pleases and only man is vile. Others are neither very "tropical" or very "African." There are permanent snows in the Congo, and there are parts of Mali, Mauritania and Morocco where rain has never been known to fall.

Some, like the Ivory Coast, Ghana and Cameroun, are rich in woods that provide fuel for home and industry, shade for crops, and timber for plywood, veneers and an ever-growing range of synthetic products. Some, like the (former Anglo-Egyptian) Sudan, are rich in waters that can be used for transport, power and irrigation. The Nile already provides the Sudan with irrigation water for well over two million acres, and could provide as much again. Others, like Somalia and Chad, have neither woods nor waters in large amounts.

There are similarly striking contrasts in the mineral realm. The Congo is the world's largest source of gem and industrial diamonds, and Nigeria of columbite (an essential ingredient of many high temperature alloys). After 400 years, Ghana is still one of the world's largest producers of gold, and gold figures prominently on the export lists of five other countries.

Mauritania, Sierra Leone, Guinea and Gabon are believed to have enough high-grade iron ore to take care of the expected needs of the entire free world for years to come. The same is true of the Congo for cobalt, of Gabon for manganese, of Guinea and Ghana for bauxite. At the other extreme come Niger, Somalia, Mali, the Sudan, Togo and Upper Volta, where minerals make no money worth talking about and feed few hopes.

But, here again, some things are true of most of the new countries. *First,* they are either hot or humid—or both—the greater part of the time, and they are not the most healthy of places any of the time. Sustained effort, manual or mental, is irksome, and it is easy not to be inclined to do today what should have been done yesterday. What is done tends to be done slowly and inefficiently by Western standards.

Second, they are poorly off for manpower. Only three of those that have become independent in the past six years have populations of more than ten million. These are Nigeria, the (former Belgian) Congo and the Sudan. Sixteen have populations of less than five million; eleven have less than three million; three, Mauritania, Gabon and the Congo Republic (formerly the French Middle Congo), have less than one million.

To aggravate the manpower problem the rate of population

increase in some of the poorest countries appears to be exceedingly small. In Somalia (which has less than two million people), the rate is reported as being less than 1 per cent per year. In Gabon the population (reported to be less than 500,000) is barely holding its own.

Even if their incomes were high, these countries would find it very hard to support the paraphernalia of self-government including, as it does, military installations, embassies and consulates, to say nothing of hospitals, schools, prisons and other necessary services. With the annual incomes in these countries averaging less than $100 per head and government revenues less than $20 per head, the task of paying one's way becomes formidable indeed. Somalia's annual domestic revenues of—at the most—$10,000,000 will scarcely provide a second-rate school system, let alone an army or an air force.

Third, their economies rest on rather slim—often slippery—foundations. In Somalia, the economy rests on bananas (hitherto subsidized by the Italians), for these provide about two-thirds of the country's export income. In Sierra Leone it rests on iron ore, palm products and diamonds, all of them subject to the play of forces beyond the control of their producers.

Even in Ghana, which fares far better than most of the new countries in this respect five commodities account for all but 5 per cent of the export revenues. Of these, cocoa (another commodity that is not nearly as indispensable to the world as it is to Ghana) contributes more than one-half.

Efforts to broaden the base of these economies have so far met with little success, either because the environment proved too much for man or man's machines proved too much for the environment, or simply because the capital and running costs proved too high. While every country is yearly increasing the range of its offerings, almost every country continues to rely heavily on the earning power of its traditional staples. Indeed, for every territory that became less dependent on its traditional staples during the past decade, another territory became more dependent on them.

Considered from these standpoints, few of the new countries have all the requirements of national growth. Of those that have come into existence since the late nineteen-fifties, only the (ex-

Belgian) Congo, Ghana, Nigeria and the Sudan appear to be well enough endowed with resources, human and physical, potential and actual, to support the burdens and exercise the responsibilities of autonomy. And, at the moment, not all of these have the "constitution" needed to make the most of their endowments.

What of the rest—the Togos, Chads and Somalias of Africa? Given time, they can undoubtedly acquire the skills, sophistication and experience needed for the satisfactory conduct of their domestic and foreign affairs, for none of them is friendless. To Somalia alone in the past year or two have come suitors from a dozen countries, laden with gifts and good words, seeking to sell its leaders the keys to their kingdom.

But what of the earthly requirements of national growth—the things that cannot be conjured out of a suitor's bag, or as yet synthesized out of thin air?

There are at least three possibilities. *One,* the needy nations can try to get along with what they've got. That is, they can go on being poor and puny—pygmies in a world of giants—much as the Liberians were before the Firestone-Tubman era. But in these days who wants to live like pygmies? To judge by their growing interest in the outside world, not even all of the pygmies.

Two, they can pool their poverty. This, some of them are beginning to do, with the help of customs unions, common markets and federations of one kind and another. But usually, it is only the poor who help the poor, and to share poverty is not, alas, to halve it or even, it may be argued, to make it more tolerable. At any rate, it is difficult to see what material benefits are likely to accrue to Somalia as the result of fusing the former Italian and British Somalilands. Both are nine-tenths desert; both are deficient in the things that make nations grow, and such resources as they do have are almost identical.

It might be a different matter if the wealthy were willing to pool their resources with the poor, but philanthropy is still a minority movement among nations. Anyway, no nation, in or out of Africa, is eager to be cast in the role of a poor relative.

Three, they can sell themselves, and even the poorest among them have some things to sell. To begin with, they can sell their economic potential, limited though it may prove to be. There is not a country in Africa that has yet been fully prospected for underground water supplies, oil and other minerals. After more than five years of systematic prospecting by foreign companies, the Somalis still hope to hear that their land flows with oil, if not with milk and honey. (Meantime, the companies concerned are annually putting several million dollars into domestic circulation.)

They can also sell their neutrality and for this, as we are seeing, there are already a number of bidders, both in the council chambers of the U.N. and elsewhere. Some, it is to be feared, may even be tempted to sell their integrity and become pimps of the great powers looking for lovers. Whether they do or not, it is hard to put aside the feeling that the recent loans made by the U.S.S.R. and other powers to Ghana, Guinea, Somalia and Sudan are intended to do a mighty love-making work in those lands.

Be this as it may, the territorial changes now taking place in Africa mark only the beginning—not the end—of the continent's reshaping, for they create more problems than they solve. How the new countries will deal with these problems none can say, for there are no precedents. But some of the omens are unpropitious.

Governments that have few scruples about snuffing out internal opposition can hardly be expected to have many about dealing with external opposition to their plans for federation, fusion or any other form of alliance. If the giants cannot woo the pygmies with song and dance, maybe they will resort to war drums. And they already have the drums. The military buildup in countries like Guinea, Ghana and the Sudan is quite impressive. Since these countries have no reason to fear their former masters or America, or even the U.S.S.R.—from which, and its satellites, most of the arms are coming—it would almost look as if the only people against whom they can use these arms are their neighbors.

One thing, at all events, is fairly certain. Twenty years from now the political map of Africa will be very different from what it is today. It may not be more rational in design, but it will be simpler in appearance. The pygmies will have gone.

Chile's Nightmare— Case Study of Inflation

by Tad Szulc

SANTIAGO, CHILE

THE PRETTY YOUNG housewife's long silver earrings shook in a gesture of defiant indignation. "Do we save money?" she asked, then laughed derisively. *"Mi Dios,* we don't even dream of it any more. I don't know how we manage to keep body and soul together."

She sat talking to a visitor in the clean but sparsely furnished living room of an apartment on the third floor of a gray concrete housing-project building in Santiago's cheerless middle-class district of Llano Subercaseaux. It was a Saturday afternoon and the feeble sun of the Chilean winter shone outside on the drab, dusty street with its ugly apartment buildings and dilapidated one-story houses, their paint peeling off, doors and windows sagging.

Her soft-spoken husband, a 26-year-old clerk and messenger, nodded gravely as she related in her high-pitched Spanish voice, punctuated with little laughs, her version of the universal and age-old story of how a family budget can be stretched to the breaking point while, almost miraculously, the family survives and keeps its pride and self-respect.

But there was a special touch of drama in the Santiago version

From the *New York Times Magazine,* October 13, 1957, copyright © 1957 by The New York Times Company.

of this ancient tale, the same touch of drama that, monotonously yet poignantly, underlies the stories of all wage-earners, from the northern nitrate fields of Antofagasta to the southernmost city of Punta Arenas, in this long and narrow land of nearly seven million inhabitants on South America's West Coast.

This touch is Chile's staggering inflation, which has made a mockery of the whole notion of salaries and prices and their normal relationships, and has forced over half of the population to engage in a continuous juggling act with their incomes to keep ahead of the next rise in prices and retain a semblance of solvency. It had turned the national economy into something approaching chaotic nonsense at the peak of the crisis in 1955 and, though Chile has escaped complete stagnation or breakdown because of its inherent dynamism and its natural resources, such as copper, its rate of development lags painfully behind most of the other Latin-American countries.

There have been bigger and worse inflations than Chile's in recent decades and the Chilean peso, never quoted at a lower rate than about 800 to one United States dollar, did not reach the abysmal depths of depreciation of the German mark of the Nineteen Twenties, the Chinese dollar as the Communists conquered the mainland, or even the boliviano in neighboring Bolivia. But these other inflations accompanied or followed major political upheavals and were of relatively short duration.

In Chile, inflation has been a household fact of life for well over seventy-five years, a tremendous problem for twenty years, and an acute and exhausting nightmare for the last two or three years.

The Government has tried hard to control the inflationary spiral and the success of this program, launched on Jan. 1, 1956, with the advice of a United States group of private consultants, can be measured by the fact that the rate at which inflation had been progressing is now arrested. Whereas the cost of living in 1955 rose 88 per cent, the increase last year was 37 per cent. This year's figure should be roughly the same.

Plans have been drawn up for a major economic development scheme designed to strike at the very roots of Chile's inflation— low industrial productivity and insufficient agricultural output— and the United States, through official aid and private investments, is helping along in the endeavor. But plummeting copper prices —and copper is the nation's main source of revenue—are complicating these plans. Meanwhile, the Chilean wage-earner is still waging the battle of the monthly budget.

Statistical figures of the Chilean inflation are so astronomic that they tend to become meaningless unless they are translated into the shocking realities of daily life. The cost-of-living index, in terms of the peso, has soared from 237.1 points in 1946 to 763.4 points in 1952, and to over 3,000 points by January of this year. This means that in the last five years the price of rice has gone up from 22 to 78 pesos a kilogram; sugar (an important energy food here) from 8 to 85 pesos; salt from 3 to 50 pesos; meat from 50 to 500 pesos; a man's cheap suit from 3,000 to 21,000 pesos, and a pack of cigarettes from 4.60 pesos to 100.

In terms of United States dollars today's prices are not excessive—by American standards. But look at the Chilean salaries: an unskilled worker averages 15,000 pesos monthly, which equals about $24 at the current rate of exchange. This means that he has to work longer than a month just to buy a suit, and half a month for a decent pair of shoes. A white-collar employe averages 50,000 pesos. And the real income of the Chilean wage earner, his purchasing power, has risen only 40 per cent since 1940.

The basic cause of Chilean inflation—if such a generalization is possible—is that for decades the nation has been living far beyond its means. In the strictly financial field, beginning with the Popular Front governments of the late Thirties, Chile embarked on a grandiose program of social legislation whose payments threw the treasury into continuous deficits, forced the printing of more money and thus depreciated the currency. Military budgets out of all proportion to the nation's real defense needs aggravated the trouble. Both these problems still exist.

Simultaneously with the weakening of the currency for immediate fiscal reasons, inflation worsened in the postwar years because neither agriculture nor industry could provide the goods that an expanding economy and a growing population required. With most of the land in the hands of a relatively few families, no serious effort was made to increase productivity and modernize agriculture, with the result that Chile has to depend on costly imports for many key foods. In industry, antiquated methods plus the reluctance of local capital to invest quickly depreciating money in the expansion of plants, when returns were greater in import or real-estate transactions, resulted in scarce and expensive goods. Finally, the Government, instead of encouraging private enterprise in industry, embarked itself on uneconomical programs in the fields of steel, petroleum and electric power.

In these circumstances, what sort of standard of living can a worker maintain, particularly since he is likely to be married and have three or four children? (The average size of the Chilean family is 5.6 persons but those with seven or eight children are not uncommon.)

The answer comes easily, at least here in Santiago. At the end of a twenty-minute drive from the center of the city, where well-stocked luxury stores cater to the wealthy but tiny Chilean upper class and to the many to whom inflation is a bonanza, are the *Callampas,* the wretched homes of Santiago's very poor.

Callampas means mushrooms. Horrible, unsanitary and degrading shacks slapped together from old boards, packing cases and strips of corrugated iron, they have spread like ugly fungi. *Callampas* children go barefoot and clad in rags—and winter here is chilly and rainy—because their parents cannot afford shoes and clothes. They are unhealthy and anemic because at 50 pesos a liter milk is unattainable and, at 16 pesos apiece, an apple is unthinkable, despite the fact that Chile is a big fruit producer. In the old days, before inflation hit them with such a wallop, the *Callampas* people and other Chileans with small incomes could afford occasionally a *cazuela,* the national dish, which is chicken or meat cooked into a soup with potatoes and vegetables. Today, brown beans are the daily fare.

The difference between the Chilean *Callampas* dwellers and their counterparts in most other places is that they had once lived better; that, measured by the Latin-American yardstick, they have a high degree of education and belong to a society with traditionally one of the highest living standards in this part of the world.

What inflation has done then to the Chilean worker and his family—and they account for 45 per cent of the population—is to force him into social and economic regression, and this runs dramatically counter to the Latin-American trend.

The middle class, like the workers, is also taking a powerful beating in the backwash of inflation and the current anti-inflationary measures. If its troubles are less visible, they are just as real for, along with the working class, they form the legion of Chile's wage-earners.

Chile's middle class consists of privately employed white-collar workers and the thousands of government functionaries on the federal, provincial and municipal rolls. This social group is important here because of its role as a key consumer of domestic and imported goods—the essential ones as well as those designed to meet its fairly sophisticated tastes. Its emergence as a national force in recent decades did much to bridge the old chasm between Chile's very poor and very rich and, as such, was a positive social and economic development.

But inflation saw to it that the healthy evolvement of the middle class was slowed down, if not altogether arrested. And yet this group is showing a remarkable resilience.

Take the story of Juan Muñoz Gonzalez, a 31-year-old Santiago bank clerk. The son of a street-car driver, he is a high-school graduate and now earns a basic monthly salary of 50,000 pesos. He is married and has four children, which means that he receives from the Government another 2,500 pesos under the family-allowance scheme. Out of the total of 52,500 pesos, 10 per cent is taken away in taxes and multifarious social security contributions. The rent—they live in four small rooms in a crowded neighborhood—is 18,000 pesos. Food costs them 36,000 pesos —the Muñozes eat modestly and Señora de Muñoz stands in line for hours every day to buy milk and meat—so, with only taxes, rent and food, their expenses have exceeded their income.

The rest, of course, is deficit spending. The family's clothing bill runs to over 200,000 pesos annually—nothing frivolous, just the essentials for the six of them to be reasonably dressed. All clothes are bought on the installment plan, which means a 20 per cent markup. Merchants who have been carrying huge inventories as a hedge against inflation, insist that these markups are necessary or else, they say, their profit margin will be wiped out by anticipated currency depreciation during the lapse between purchase and final payment.

Items like refrigerators and other appliances are also sold on time and have to be paid for in full within six to eight months. The stores claim they cannot risk carrying customers for a longer period. It is this vastly inflated but clearly unavoidable credit system that keeps most of Chile's tradesmen and businessmen solvent and prosperous, despite—or, rather, because of—inflation.

(Commercial bank credit, on the other hand, has been severely curtailed as part of the twenty-month-old anti-inflation program. While it has been a helpful measure on the whole, it has had the immediate adverse effect of making money tight for new construction and for the industrial expansion that is so badly needed in Chile; building has fallen off about 40 per cent.)

The inflation-blessed new class of the Chilean wealthy—the big importers and exporters who enjoyed political favor in foreign-trade transactions before the peso was freed last year, the speculators, the middlemen and all those who knew how to parlay the chaotic situation into personal fortunes—is represented by the luxurious private homes that have sprung up in Santiago's residential districts almost as fast as the shacks in the *Callampas*. Avenida Pedro de Valdivia has become the special enclave of this fortunate group.

But aside from the two extremes of the *Callampas* and the homes of the newly rich, the impression the visitor gets is one of solid, if somewhat seedy, lower-middle-class prosperity, reminiscent of the prewar English cities. The stores are full of customers most of the time; people who do not at all look badly off stroll briskly during the day along the Bandera and Agustinas and the other busy streets of the business district; at night, there are crowds at the coffee-shops, cinemas and theatres.

One has to reserve a movie seat well ahead of time, and on Sundays there are long lines at the entrances to the stadiums as the *aficionados* troop to watch soccer, the Chilean national sport.

But how is this possible? Juan Muñoz, the bank clerk, has the explanation.

"Every Saturday night the wife and I go to the movies," he says. "Every other Sunday, if there is a good game on, we go to see football. It costs us 500 pesos each time, but we've got to live, no?"

And this remark, as much as anything else one hears in Chile, tells the story of this nation's adjustment, if it can be called that, to the extraordinary pressures of inflation. The Chileans have, of necessity, learned how to live with it and they simply take it in their stride. They find relief from their troubles in their football games, their movies, their lotteries, their conviviality, in their liking for the military pageantry (parades and change-of-guard ceremonies are almost a commonplace here) and, basically, in their human hope that things will some day get better. In the meantime, they improvise with their budgets, borrow a little from relatives and friends, try to placate creditors with partial payments, hold off as long as possible on the rent, and so forth.

How long can Chile go on like this before coming to the boiling point of social unrest? There is no ready-made answer to this question, but most people, experts and the victims of inflation alike, agree that if the Government had not embarked on its anti-inflation program late in 1955—the year the cost of living shot up 88 per cent—something terrible might have happened.

The Santiago and Valparaiso riots in April of this year, when nearly thirty persons were killed and hundreds injured, were a fair sample of what may lie ahead if popular discontent is adroitly exploited by interested political groups, be they Communists or even certain factions within the Government.

Wages are being strictly controlled, though the same doesn't apply to prices. Until January, 1956, workers were legally entitled to an automatic annual raise equivalent to 100 per cent of the increase in the cost of living during the previous year. It was a vicious circle and this system has been abolished. This year, for instance, the across-the-board wage increase was just over 30 per cent, while the over-all cost-of-living rise in 1956 had been cut down to 37 per cent from the previous year's 88.

The experts of the Klein-Saks Mission, a United States firm of business consultants retained by the Chilean Government since September, 1955, at $25,000 a month plus expenses, to draft the anti-inflation program, feel that the nation may now be over the hump.

The people are not so sure, though. Prices are still going up, though at a slower rate, and Chileans are complaining bitterly. The Klein-Saks specialists argue that price controls would be unenforceable and that the way to slow down inflation and let prices become stabilized is to create a healthy economic climate in Chile.

This, they say, can be accomplished if the budget is balanced and Chile becomes convinced that it must try to live within its means. In other words, the cost and the scope of Chile's cradle-to-grave social legislation—it now accounts for 28 per cent of the annual budget—must be drastically curtailed because the nation just does not produce enough to pay for it. The same reasoning applies to the military expenditures, which eat up nearly 30 per cent of the budget.

Widespread monopolistic practices must be abandoned and the free play of competition must be allowed to raise productivity and lower the prices. Tax evasion by the wealthy must be stamped out—the wage-earners resent the idea that they are expected to bear alone the burden of saving Chile from inflation—and Chilean capitalists must learn that it is essential to invest in their own economy for nonspeculative purposes. Chile has been assisted importantly by the United States, by the International Bank for Reconstruction and Development and by steady investment of private American capital, but, in the final analysis, Chile can be saved only by Chileans.

To carry out in full this program, the Government of President Carlos Ibañez del Campo will need a good deal of political courage to face the vested interests in Congress, in the political parties and even among its own friends. So far, the President's political weakness and other influences have made him slow to act on many ticklish aspects of the anti-inflation campaign and, to judge from remarks made by many Chileans, the nation does not seem to have much faith in the regime.

It would be unfair to say that all the current problems are man-made or Chile-made. This year the country was hit by a ruinous drought and agriculture has suffered heavily. The prices of copper and nitrates on the world market have slumped beyond all expectation and these two commodities are the mainstays of the Chilean economy.

Even though the prospects for improvement seem brighter now than they did a year ago, critical times still lie ahead for Chile. A lot of determination, good luck and sacrifice will be needed before the *Callampas* dweller can think of leaving the shanty-town, before the wife of the bank clerk can make ends meet without going into debt, and before the whole Chilean economy settles on a rational basis.

"We've Never Had It So Bad"

by Khushwant Singh

NEW DELHI

IT WAS FIVE in the morning and bitterly cold. The morning star shone brightly and there was a suspicion of gray on the eastern horizon. I locked my car and made for the dimly lit tea stall. A couple of peasants wrapped in quilts were warming their hands by the hearth. The *chaiwallah*—tea vender—sat on his haunches with his eyes fixed on the saucepan.

"*Jai Ram ji ki* [Victory to God Rama]," I greeted them.

"*Jai Ram ji ki,*" replied the peasants, shuffling apart to make room for me. The *chaiwallah* grunted: "*Chai?*" I nodded and sat down. I stretched my hands toward the glowing embers. "How are things?" I asked. In the countryside, the word "things" means only the state of the crops.

"Don't ask!" replied one of the peasants, who had a thick walrus mustache. "We've never had it so bad. There was hardly any rain in the summer. Half of the *rabi* [winter] crop has been lost. Here in Jharsa things are really terrible."

The other peasant took up the theme. "We have good land. What we need is rain. A few drops will make an acre of desert

From the *New York Times Magazine,* January 23, 1966, copyright © 1966 by The New York Times Company.

worth 100,000 rupees. Without those drops it is not worth a *naya paisa* [one-hundredth of a rupee]."

The *chaiwallah* poured a cup of milk and several teaspoonfuls of sugar into the pan of boiling tea and sat back on his haunches to let the brew come to the boil again.

"What is the Government doing about it?" I asked.

The peasant with the mustache considered the question a while and replied: "If resolutions could produce rain, we would have had a good monsoon. And if officials' speeches could raise crops we would surely have a bumper harvest."

The *chaiwallah* handed us our cups. The peasants poured their tea into the saucers, blew over it and began to sip noisily. "What are *you* going to do about it?" I asked.

No one answered; the question stayed in midair between the hurricane lantern hanging from a beam in the ceiling and the steaming saucepan.

Two Goojur milkmen alighted from their bicycles, put them against a tree and joined us. *"Jai Ram ji ki,"* greeted one, pulling off his gloves. "Brothers, it is cold riding a cycle at this hour of the morning." The *chaiwallah* poured more water, tea, sugar and milk into the saucepan. "Sardarji [polite title for a Sikh] here wants to know how things are in the villages," he said, nodding toward me.

The second Goojur, who had joined the semicircle around the fire, laughed and said, "If you really want to know our plight, put away your car and cycle 20 miles with us from Teeghra to Delhi at 4 A.M. with six large canisters full of milk dangling between your legs and your behind. The cold eats into the bones. As for the bottom . . ."—he explained what the cycle seat did to his posterior with full-blooded, rustic bawdiness. Everyone burst out laughing. "Except for that," he said, giving his rump a hearty smack, "Ishwara [God] has been good to us. Ishwara gives to everyone," he concluded, pointing to the ceiling.

The Goojurs drank their tea and rode off on their cycles. The rattle of their milk cans faded away in the dark. Once more it was the *chaiwallah,* the peasants and I in the yellow circle of light of the lantern and the amber glow of the fire.

"The Goojurs didn't sound so despondent," I remarked.

"You know what Goojurs are! Cattle thieves!" replied the mustached peasant. "They loaf about all day while their buffaloes graze in other people's lands. All they do is milk their cattle and sell it in the city. If the yield is not enough, they'll stop by the nearest pond and add as much dirty water as they think will go unnoticed. Do you know of anyone who gets pure milk in Delhi? But these Goojurs will also learn their lesson when there is no fodder and the ponds are dry. Their cattle will die of hunger and thirst. Then the only people who will gain are the *harijans* [untouchables] who skin carcasses and make shoes of their hides."

He spat on the ground and brushed his mustache with the back of his hand. "Where are you bound for?" he asked.

"Shamaspur."

"Ah, Shamaspur! That's the Government's showpiece! It is an Ahir village. They have some *harijans* too, but in Shamaspur there is no caste or creed. Don't believe what all these Ahirs tell you. We have a saying: 'All castes are God's creatures, but three are ruthless and without shame: the whore, the moneylender and the Ahir.' They are a shameless lot."

The sky had turned gray; the morning star lost its luster. Long lines of crows flew overhead. From a remote distance came muffled thuds of sporting guns. A minute later, a flight of teal and mallard whistled past overhead. "There's hardly any water in the marshes, but these incestuous *shikaris* won't leave the birds alone," remarked one of the peasants. "In their next birth they will be born as ducks and the ducks in human form will shoot them. So it is written in the sacred texts."

I left the tea stall of Jharsa and made my way to Shamaspur, a mile away.

Why did I choose Shamaspur? Simply for the reason the peasant at the Jharsa tea stall had mentioned: It was "the Government's showpiece." The administration had tried out most of its rural development schemes in this village and declared them to be good. Foreign visitors were brought to Shamaspur to be shown how India's democratic revolution had succeeded. And now Shamaspur was hit by drought. Was it facing the challenge any better than others similarly afflicted?

I drove into Shamaspur just as the sun was coming over the rim of the range of hills which semicircled it. Partridges were calling in the pampas grass; peafowl, which are numerous in the region, were in the fields.

Shamaspur is unlike any other Indian village. Instead of the usual huddle of mud huts, it consists of blocks of little houses, many with kitchen gardens of their own. Instead of the usual village well with women drawing water and filling pitchers, a 60-foot water tower and taps are in the lanes. What struck me most was that at that hour of the morning there were no peasants defecating in the fields. In Shamaspur, every home has its own private latrine.

I pulled up outside the house of the *sarpanch* (president of the village council, the *panchayat*). Prithipal Singh was revving up his Russian-made tractor. He came down from his perch and shook hands. He was in his early 30's, a little bald in front, but athletically built and handsome. He noticed my notebook and pen and switched off the Diesel, grumbling: "The self-starter won't work; I'll have to have it pushed again." He indicated in no uncertain manner what the intrusion meant. "I am already late with my plowing; everyone else in the village finished more than a week ago."

I apologized. I was forgiven with a friendly hand on the shoulder and taken indoors. It was a cold room with a charpoy bed, three cane chairs and a table with a radio. The walls were of a cold blue color, bare except for three old calendars: one bearing a picture of Gandhi, another of Nehru and the third of a tractor. Before I had finished inspecting the room, Prithipal Singh's wife came in with a tray of tea and steaming hot *halva*.

I got my statistics first. Population, about 500, half Ahirs—a pastoral tribe claiming descent from the Hindu god, Krishna— and the other half *harijans*. Most of the 400 acres of land are owned by Ahirs, who live in the slightly better homes in the western half of the village.

Shamaspur has electricity, all but three of its 100-odd homes lighted by power from the Bhakra Dam (built by an American engineering firm) over lines stretching 200 miles across the Punjab. Eight families have radio sets. Shamaspur has its own primary school, with 71 children (51 boys and 20 girls) studying Hindi, arithmetic and geography. They tell me that there is not one child in the village who does not attend school.

Shamaspur has 24 drilled wells irrigating 60 per cent of its land. The remaining 40 per cent has been hit by drought. The winter crop of gram (a kind of bean), barley and mustard (its leaf forms the staple diet of the northern Indian peasant) sown on land dependent on rain has already withered. If the drought continues, the same proportion of the *kharif* (summer) crop of millet, pulse, corn and fodder will be similarly lost.

Prithipal Singh is known in bureaucrat jargon as a "progressive farmer." He is a college graduate. Two of his younger brothers have master's degrees and are teaching in colleges. The youngest joined the army when the Chinese invaded India in October, 1962. His one sister is in her last year at high school. The family jointly owns 45 acres, all of it farmed by Prithipal Singh. He is the only one in the hamlet who owns a tractor.

I asked him about the effects of the drought in Shamaspur. "No doubt," he said, "land which is entirely dependent on rain will produce nothing, but there are canals and tanks and wells. I am cultivating only 32 acres of my land, which I can irrigate with my wells—I would have had to leave some of it fallow in any case. I have had more time to plow; I've put in more fertilizer, I have sown a new variety of Mexican wheat, Sonoro 64, which I am told will yield three times more than the indigenous strain. I expect to reap as much as I did last year—if not more. Come and see for yourself," he said and leaped up from his charpoy.

I followed him out of his little bungalow. We passed by his yard, where a buffalo and a calf were tethered. "Those are the only animals I have. The cow gives me enough milk, butter and ghee [clarified cooking butter] for the family. When I bought the tractor I sold the oxen I had for plowing. Diesel oil costs less than the fodder, and the tractor does the job more thoroughly and in a tenth of the time. I use it for threshing as well. What took the bullocks two days of treading I now do in two hours."

Behind the yard, women were winnowing sorghum. "They are hired labor," explained Prithipal Singh. "Yesterday there was no breeze; I would have had to pay them without getting any work out of them. So I fixed a table fan. The entire village turned up to see the winnowing." He was pleased with himself.

We passed stacks of dung cakes. Even Prithipal Singh had not been able to prevent this valuable manure from being used as fuel for cooking. "We have no coal or wood," he explained, "and we cannot afford electric stoves. It will be a great day when we can feed our soil with dung instead of chemical fertilizers."

We went around the fields. I saw a field of young Sonoro 64, next to another that was growing what seemed to be a more lush Indian variety of wheat. "Appearances are deceptive," said Prithipal Singh. "Indian wheat grows bigger but has less grain and more chaff. The Mexican is smaller but infinitely richer. Ten years ago, I could never get more than 20 maunds of wheat from an acre; today, I get at least 35." (One maund equals about 90 pounds.)

We then came back into the *harijan* quarter and Prithipal Singh introduced me to two of them. Badla, who owns four acres of land, is the best-off among the *harijans*. Niadar, who has been a member of the *panchayat,* owns only two acres. Neither can make a living out of his land, more than half of which is out of the range of the cooperative well. With their antiquated plows and limited supply of fertilizer, the best they get out of an acre is 28 maunds. They had tried growing vegetables and citrus fruit, but never got enough to feed themselves. Niadar has resumed the ancestral craft of making shoes. His sons have taken on jobs as unskilled workers in an ammunition factory five miles away. Badla's son has joined the army.

Both the *harijans* were despondent. "This year our harvest will be less than half of last year's. But for the money our sons bring in, we would be starving. It is the same for all the other *harijans."*

They did not have any complaints of discrimination by the higher caste Ahirs. "We drink out of the same taps. Our children go to the same school and play together. Our womenfolk gossip together in the *mahila mandal* [women's club] at the community center. We are much better off than the *harijans* in Jharsa or any of the other villages in the neighborhood."

Shamaspur has a community center of three large rooms. The walls display charts on rural themes—growing more food, caring for livestock, preventing disease, providing healthy diets, having smaller families, etc. It has a community radio set (which has been out of order for several months), and a harmonium and drum used for community singing.

Across the road is the old *panchayat ghar* (village council house), a ramshackle hut made of mud and thatch. It is preserved as a relic to give an idea of what Shamaspur buildings were like some years ago. Beside it, bricks are stacked to prove the intention to knock it down and build anew. Today it is the haunt of the flying fox and the owl. An old banyan tree spreads its arms over its dilapidated roof sloping down to the village pond. No one uses the pond any more. Sandpipers run along its muddy banks. A pair of adjutant storks stride up and down as if on patrol. On the other side of the pond is the village primary school.

We returned to Prithipal Singh's home. The *harijans* left and I continued my cross-examination. How many trees have you planted? "Quite a few—but not as many as we should have." How many compost pits have you dug? "None; the compost-pit idea hasn't really caught on."

What about family planning? "Very little of that," concedes Prithipal Singh. "For many years there was only talk of limiting families. They talked of the rhythm method to people who did not know the calendar. Then they gave us rosaries of colored beads; at night, people couldn't tell the red for 'don't' from the green for 'go ahead.' Then they sent doctors to operate. We've had only six cases of voluntary sterilization—five women and one man. No, family planning has not made much headway."

Prithipal Singh's wife came in with another tray of tea and the subject was discreetly dropped. When she left the room, Prithipal Singh resumed his discourse. "People here are not as opposed to the idea as they used to be. At one time they refused to have B.C.G. [Bacillus Calemette Guerin, an anti-tuberculosis vaccine] injections because somebody spread the rumor that the letters stood for 'Birth Control Government.' Now women with large families are quite eager to be sterilized. It's the men who refuse to be operated upon. They believe it makes them impotent."

I asked him about the pill and the intrauterine loop. Prithipal Singh had heard of neither; he has five children. His wife came in to collect the tea things and he changed the subject to wheat coming from America. "It's a shame that an agricultural country like ours should have to import food. We should be selling wheat to America instead of begging for it."

Prithipal Singh was full of hope for the future. I left him to resume his plowing and went on to meet other Shamaspurians. I learned that in two important areas of rural development, the *panchayats* and cooperatives, the picture was not as rosy as Prithipal Singh had painted it.

Government schemes to bring about radical change in the countryside are based on the assumption that in due course the villagers will, through their elected *panchayats,* assume responsibility for all aspects of development—agriculture, education, health, social welfare. The *panchayat* is an old institution which the Government has sought to revive and adapt to present-day requirements. It is a statutory body whose rules require it to have at least one woman and one representative of the untouchable castes, and to meet at least once a month. Each is provided with a proportion of the land revenue and house tax, and some have additional income through ownership of pasture lands or wells. Its functions, once largely restricted to settling internecine disputes, have been enlarged to cover policing, maintenance of schools, sanitation, co-ordination of plans for agricultural improvement, etc.

Panchayat Raj ("People's Rule"), however, has not generated democratic enthusiasm to the degree that was expected. Much of the blame can be laid at the door of the administration, which has been tardy in parting with the right to collect money and in handing over judicial powers. Elections have increased factionalism in the already faction-ridden villages.

The *panchayat* of Shamaspur consists of representatives of three hamlets, Shamaspur, Teeghra and Ghasauli. A 55-year-old *harijan* woman, Champi Devi, a mother of five children, is both the *harijan* and the female representative. The *panchayat* gets 400 rupees a year ($80) from its share of land revenue and 800 rupees a year ($160) through lease of common land. It has not yet been able to levy a house tax. With this modest income of $240 a year it tries to run a primary school with two teachers and keep its road in good repair. It is now engaged in sinking a well to irrigate the common land. Since the well will cost three times more than the annual revenue it will be quite some time before the Shamaspur well begins to spout water, unless the Government gives an additional grant.

Despite the enlightened leadership of Prithipal Singh and the high proportion of educated farmers, the Shamaspur *panchayat* is only a little better than the *panchayats* of other villages. Prithipal Singh faithfully calls meetings by rotation in the three hamlets, but sometimes there is no agenda (just an opportunity for the elders to get together) and at other times there is no quorum. At all times, the meager income inhibits ambitious schemes. The Shamaspur *panchayat,* like many of its counterparts all over India, has little money and less to do.

Cooperatives have been another of the administration's trouble spots. For many years, Socialist-oriented planners believed that the only way to overcome the problems of small holdings and to introduce modern techniques was cooperative (if not collective) farms on the Russian and Chinese patterns. Collectives were abandoned as impracticable but determined efforts were made to set up cooperatives for many purposes—credit, seed and fertilizer, wells, tractors, marketing. In some spheres, like banking and services, the cooperatives worked reasonably well. In others, notably farming, the experiment has been a dismal failure.

Shamaspur's experience illustrates the limited impact of the cooperative method. In 1953 the villagers were persuaded to knock down their mud huts and rebuild their homes with brick. To do so, they set up a cooperative society to manufacture bricks. The venture was a success; Shamaspur got its bricks at cost. This experience encouraged the *harijans* to set up a Harijan Better Farming Cooperative Society, pool their savings and sink a well. They erased the boundaries of their holdings, farmed the land as one block and apportioned the harvest on the basis of prior ownership.

For a couple of years, things went well. Then bickerings began. Good workers complained about sluggards and drones, and then became indifferent. Production fell. Boundary lines went up again and each began to plow his own holding. Today, all that remains of the Harijan Better Farming Cooperative Society is the well. There is no way of dividing a well.

I left Shamaspur in the afternoon to drive back to Jharsa. The sun was bright and warm. The partridges were silent but skylarks filled the heavens with song. The green of the young wheat, mustard and sugar cane gave way to brown earth with rows of withered crops. Then came a stretch of dry, hard ground with nothing except clusters of pampas and camel thorn.

When I pulled up again at the *chaiwallah's* stall in Jharsa, the clouds of dust my car had raised overtook me and spread all around. I emerged from the car with my muffler drawn across my face. Dust today is the presiding deity, omnipresent and all-covering. It hangs in the air, and falls on the faces of the people like a powder. The leaves of the jujube trees hang limp under its weight.

Hoshiar Singh, headmaster of the Government Middle School, and the Government-appointed Village-Level Worker join me at the *chaiwallah's* and we proceed on a tour of inspection. We wade through a foot of soft powder. We make way for a herd of buffaloes. A troop of girls follow the herd and race one another to claim the steaming offal. At every open space in the lane there are stacks of dried dung cakes; the walls of houses are pock-marked with dung left to bake in the sun.

The streets get narrower and narrower. The gray stream of slime which runs in the middle gets correspondingly broader till we have to walk sideways like crabs with our backs to the walls of the houses. We have to tread warily because the children squat on their haunches to defecate; dogs and pigs scamper along without any notion of the right of way. Swarms of flies rise from heaps of rotting garbage. The stench from the gutter forces me to place my handkerchief over my nose.

"We have been planning to pave the streets and cover the drains," explains the Village-Level Worker.

"When? The sixth five-year plan?" I demand. He ignores my sarcasm. "These things take time," he replies blandly.

I turn to the headmaster and ask him about the school. He

has 1,100 boys and girls, taken in two shifts. Education is not compulsory but there are hardly any children in Jharsa who do not go to school. "Education has certainly caught on," says the headmaster proudly. "Everyone is keen to send their children to school. The only ones who don't come are the retarded.

"Twenty years ago you could have counted the number of people who could read and write on your finger tips. In another 20 there won't be one who will be unable to do so. From total ignorance to 100 per cent literacy—that is no small revolution!"

We enter the school premises. On either side of the entrance stretch rows of classrooms. I can hear the drone of children chanting multiplication tables. In front is a large courtyard a few feet below the level of the school building. At either end of the courtyard are beds of carrots, radishes and marigolds ("planted by the students," explains the headmaster). Troops of boys and girls march up and down, exaggeratedly swinging their arms. A man in a green beret yells commands in English. He orders them to halt, turn right and "standatees." He steps in front and salutes smartly.

I walk down the line like a V.I.P. inspecting a guard of honor. I stop by the prettiest girl. She is a strapping lass of 15, olive-skinned, doe-eyed, with hazel-brown hair.

"And what is your name?" I ask her.

She springs to attention: "Shashi Bala."

"What caste are you?"

"*Harijan.*"

I am surprised that an untouchable could be so light-skinned: usually they are darker, often faintly Negroid. I ask her more questions. Her father is a peon in an office in Guargaon. There are four children in the family, all at school. Most *harijans* of Jharsa are *chamars,* skinners of dead buffaloes and leather workers making fancy slippers for the Cottage Industries Emporium in New Delhi. None of them own any land. They are the poorest community in Jharsa. But all their children go to school.

"Is there any discrimination against you *harijans?*" I ask Shashi Bala.

She does not answer. I encourage her. "Do you feel discriminated against in this school?"

A look of fear comes over her pretty face and she glances nervously on either side and at the headmaster. But she does not open her mouth.

"Why don't you answer?" admonishes the headmaster. "Do you suffer from any injustice here?"

"No." And she again casts nervous glances at her companions. I give her an avuncular pat on her dimpled cheek and move on.

I go into the classrooms. They are crammed with children sitting in serried rows on the bare brick floor. They stand up, cry *"Jai Hind"* in unison and sit down. There is not a stick of furniture in any room—no blackboards, no charts, no benches— not even a table and chair for the teacher. Most children have wooden slates to write on, a few have books. They are all there —Jats, Brahmins, *mahajans* (moneylenders) and *harijans*. The headmaster explains that in school the children eat and drink (UNICEF milk) together—something their parents will not do to this day. "The caste business is finished and done for. Not 5 per cent of what it used to be," he assures me.

I am not sure he is right. The official report of the Commissioner of Scheduled Castes (so called because the names of untouchable castes are listed in the schedule of the act outlawing untouchability) states that we are still a long way from eradicating untouchability. I tell the headmaster of a statement made in the United States by a *harijan* Member of Parliament that the American Negro is infinitely better off than the Indian untouchable.

"These things take time," says the Village-Level Worker.

We go out of the school through evil-smelling lanes till we come out of Jharsa at the other end. A cane-crushing machine is at work, operated by a pair of oxen going around in a circle. A full-bosomed lass of 18 strides behind and lashes the oxen with a two-thonged whip. Half a dozen men and women sit on one side hacking the leafy tops off the cane to prepare it for the crusher. Behind, a group of women are winnowing millet.

I exchange greetings with the menfolk and sit down on the ground beside them. I begin with the usual question about the state of crops: In the countryside this is as customary as an inquiry about the other's state of health.

"Between a third and a half of our crop has been destroyed," answers an old man, Pirbhoo, who has been peacefully smoking his hookah. "The wheat took root and then rotted. We haven't even sown gram. Last year we were able to sell wheat and cane; this year we won't have enough to fill our own bellies."

I discover that old Pirbhoo is one of the more prosperous peasants. He owns more than 40 acres of land. He has one son in college. His other children, four daughters, are not educated. "It wasn't the fashion in those days to educate girls," explains Pirbhoo.

"Why haven't you more wells?"

"Ask the Government!" he says looking at the Village-Level Worker. "We have about 200. Another 50 have had machinery installed but have been awaiting electric connection. 'Come tomorrow,' says the babu at the office. That tomorrow we've been awaiting for the last three years. How many of us can afford to sink 4,000 rupees in a well for three years? And these moneylenders go on charging us interest."

"We are short of electric power," explains the Village-Level Worker. "These things take time."

I ask Pirbhoo about the cooperative. He dismisses it as a *"kaghazi karwai"*— a paper transaction. I ask him about the *panchayat*. *"Kaghazi karwai,"* he replies. He dismisses all the Government's projects for the improvement of the peasantry with the same two words. And each time the Village-Level Worker interposes: "In due course; these things take time."

When I ask Pirbhoo about family planning, he pushes away the nozzle of his hookah and spits on the ground. "Why should we limit the size of our families? Who will stop the Chinese and the Pakistanis if the Jats and Sikhs do not provide warriors to stop them? In any case, we work hard all day; by the evening we are too tired for anything but sleep. It's not we who have large families. It is these moneylenders, who sit in their shops all day doing nothing but passing wind, and their fat-bottomed women who breed like sows—they and the city folk. You should talk to them about family planning, not us."

So much for the rhythm method, the pill and the loop. I learn from the Village-Level Worker that out of Jharsa's 10,000 people, fewer than 30 have been sterilized in the past 10 years. "Family planning hasn't caught on," he explains. "These things take time."

Old Pirbhoo turns to me and asks: "Is it true that the Americans have reached the moon?"

I came out with the reply before the Village-Level Worker. "Not yet; these things take time."

When Generals Take Over in Latin America

by Herbert L. Matthews

IN LATIN AMERICA, as elsewhere, old soldiers never die. But there, only too often, they decide that the good of their country requires them to take power—or to decide which civilians will rule in their name. During the past twelve months alone, military leaders have intervened in Brazil, Argentina, Ecuador and Peru.

The hemisphere was especially shocked by the recent coups in Argentina and Peru because, in both cases, the officers acted to nullify the results of elections whose honesty and fairness were obvious. In each country, they suppressed popular reform movements that are attracting from a quarter to a third of the electorate—*Peronismo* in Argentina and *Aprismo* in Peru.

The Argentine officers struck on March 28. Five days later, chiefs of the armed forces in Ecuador lined up with a conservative political group and presented President Carlos Julio Arosemena with an ultimatum: Ecuador must break diplomatic relations with Cuba, Poland and Czechoslovakia—or else. President Arosemena obeyed.

Peru held its Presidential and Congressional elections on June 10. The candidate of the American Popular Revolutionary Alliance (A. P. R. A.), Victor Raul Haya de la Torre, did not

From the *New York Times Magazine,* September 9, 1962, copyright © 1962 by The New York Times Company.

quite get the required one-third plurality, but he got more votes than any other candidate. The leaders of the armed forces quite literally hated Señor Haya de la Torre, fearing his reform movement, and so they took over.

In Brazil, the military elements, which have been a decisive power behind the civilian government since independence, had already intervened. They had at first tried to block the constitutional assumption of power by Vice President João Goulart after the sudden resignation of President Janio Quadros on Aug. 25 last year—and had then compromised with him on a government formula which weakened his powers. The new system has worked badly and Brazil is in another grave crisis.

The wars of independence in Latin America from 1810 to 1825 were led by military chieftains, often professional officers and usually men of high moral qualities inspired by the ideals of the American and French revolutions. They were succeeded in the next fifty years, however, by a different type of officer—the *caudillo,* who was out for personal power and wealth in a feudalistic society. He was a tough, dangerous, rapacious, mettlesome type who made a jungle out of politics and was at home in it. A praetorian-guard tradition soon developed, with the "outs" always trying to get in to make their leader president. And as one conspirator reached the top, another would seek to oust him by winning over part of the army.

Although no accurate count is possible, one authority, Prof. Edwin Lieuwen of the University of New Mexico, has estimated that there were 115 successful military revolts south of the border between 1810 and 1914. In other words, the normal way of changing the government in many Latin-American countries all through the nineteenth century, and even into this century, was the *cuartelazo* (a garrison or barracks or palace revolt).

This type of revolution caused few deaths and hardly disturbed the regular functioning of society. Life in the countryside went on uninterruptedly and the isolated peasant would, as a rule, not even know that a revolution had taken place in the capital—and he certainly would not care since it made no difference to him.

The "pure" type of militarism—*caudillismo*—began to die out, however, as the nineteenth century approached its end. Wealth from trade was bringing the businessman and banker into the ruling élites. The middle class was growing; political experience was spreading; a wave of European immigration was introducing Italian and German as well as Spanish and Portuguese blood, and the growth of better communications was helping to break down isolationism. Armies became more professional and national.

Today, the rank and file are conscripts—often illiterate, usually apolitical and almost never playing a role of their own. (The one big exception was the "Sergeants' Revolt" in Cuba, led by Fulgencio Batista in 1933.) Generally speaking, the enlisted men follow their officers blindly, so that today in Argentina, for example, one army unit is quite willing to fight another.

Almost all the Latin-American countries have compulsory military service for a year or two. But as middle and upper-class families can get their sons into officer-training schools—or even have them excused—this leaves the sons of poor peasants and workers as the Latin-American equivalent of G.I.'s. They are a mass to be maneuvered—not a living, articulate, intelligent force.

The officers come from a different class—overwhelmingly from the urban middle class. (In the nineteenth century, they came from the rural upper and middle classes.) Since World War II, all the social and political pressures of our time have been at work on them. They are no longer just representatives of landowners or bankers. Many of them had tours of duty in the United States. All are educated men. They serve as military attachés in foreign embassies; they become officials of the government, even cabinet ministers.

In a crisis, it is almost always the garrison of the capital that swings the balance. Thus General Batista, in his second coup on March 10, 1952, seized Columbia Barracks in Havana and was master of Cuba. The overthrow of President Juan Perón of Argentina in September, 1955, was an exception in that the revolt began in the provincial city of Córdoba—but it had to end in Buenos Aires. In the recent Peruvian coup, only Lima counted.

But postwar military revolts are rarely one-man shows. (Batista's coup in Cuba was an exception and so was the 1948 revolt led by General Manuel Odría in Peru. Normally, they are staged by groups of officers from whom a single leader may or may not emerge with time. General Marcos Pérez Jiménez, for example, was one of a three-man *junta* in Venezuela in 1948. General (then Colonel) Juan Perón was one of a group of officers when he skyrocketed into power in 1943. There is, as yet, no outstanding military figure in Peru or Argentina where the officers have taken over.

Revolutionary emphasis used to be exclusively on stability and the maintenance of law and order, which meant keeping the traditional ruling classes—and sometimes military dictators—in power. Nowadays, however, the officers often insist they are acting not only in the interests of law and order but in the name of democracy and constitutionalism. But whatever their views, the military are not called upon to perform the customary function of national defense or territorial conquest.

"Our generals have never seen a battlefield and their armies have never waged a war," wrote ex-President Eduardo Santos of Colombia six years ago. "Their first battle, and one in which there is no physical enemy, is the seizure of power by virtue of the sheer weight of armaments put into their hands. They then proceed to occupy, as though it were conquered enemy territory, the country which they are determined to rule by force of arms."

From the international and hemispheric points of view, the Latin-American armed forces have only one important use—and this is valued more by the United States than by the Latins. It is to defend their countries against subversion by Left-Wing, Communist and *Fidelista* activities.

The political situations in the twenty Latin-American countries are in no case simple. The wave of outwardly democratic revolutions that began with the overthrow of General Perón in 1955 was very complicated. Peronism itself, for instance, is a social reform movement that is Fascistic in form and Leftist in composition. Its mass support comes from the workers (the so-called "shirtless ones") but its political leadership is Right-Wing. The military component has now had to go underground and consists only of some lower-ranking officers.

The generals scrambling for power in Argentina run from extreme Right to Center-Right. Their common denominator is nationalism—which throughout Latin America, and in Argentina especially, has an anti-Yankee coloration. Thus, one of the developments most to be feared in the threatened tidal wave of militarism is an intensification of this kind of nationalism.

For all the confusion and complications involved in the many Latin-American military coups during the past three decades, it is possible to pin down the primary factor that sets the machinery in motion. The armed forces are defending the social and economic structures of their countries; they honestly believe they are "saving the nation."

There are about a dozen countries where the armed forces are either in control or in a position to take over any time they want to. The exceptions include four of the most politically mature nations of Latin America: Costa Rica, where the army was simply abolished, Uruguay, Chile and Mexico. Colombia is a borderline case. The Dominican Republic is just beginning a new life under a civilian government. In Bolivia and Cuba, where social revolutions are under way, the regular armies have been destroyed.

But in the countries where the armed forces are preponderant, the ruling classes are traditionally composed of landowning, business, banking, Church and Army elements. The purpose of military intervention, therefore, is to defend the status quo. Yet few, if any, students of Latin-American affairs (and practically none in the Kennedy Administration) believe that the status quo *is* defensible. This is why the recent revolts by the military are so dangerous. They do not settle a situation. They merely fan smoldering fires and set new forces in motion outside their own hitherto isolated ranks. The military act, but they are also being acted upon.

Nowadays, the generals usually do not seek permanent office for themselves. They might be Provisional Presidents—as Gen. Pedro Aramburu was in Argentina after Perón or Rear Admiral Wolfgang Larrazábal in Venezuela after Pérez Jiménez. Or they may form *juntas*—as in El Salvador after Col. José María Lemus, the elected President, was ousted in 1960, and as they have done in Peru today. Their long-range preference is to be the power behind a civilian government or, as they would say, the guardians of law, order and constitutionalism.

These contemporary officers are not always easy to label.

They are by no means all reactionary, Rightist, traditional and anti-democratic—although on balance, they do favor the present ruling classes and fear social change, whether it be *Peronista, Aprista,* Communist or *Fidelista.*

There is perhaps nothing more significant for the future, however, than the broad cleavage often found between the generals and colonels, who tend to be more conservative and traditional, and the majors, captains and lieutenants, who are younger and more likely to come from less wealthy and socially prominent families. These younger officers, when they are politically conscious and active, are eager for social change, often radical in their politics and, in Argentina, for instance, often pro-Peronist.

Nearly all the popular revolutions of the past fifty years were led by young officers. The Argentine and Peruvian coups of this year were exceptional. Even the young officers, however, are not usually democratically inclined. They approve of social reforms but believe they should be instituted by authoritarian governments. As a result, their aim is first to get power and then to back governments that will win and keep popular support by measures that favor the workers and peasants.

The strongest force operating on the Latin-American scene today is the popular demand for social justice. It stands to reason that progressive, ambitious young officers are going to put themselves at the head of such movements. The United States cannot object since the Alliance for Progress is based on the encouragement of social reforms.

The historic role of the United States until this postwar period was to accommodate itself to military dictatorships in Latin America, regarding them as natural phenomena conducive to temporary stability. Dictators were easy to deal with and the corruption of their regimes made bribery simple and useful. After the Spanish-American War of 1898, American Marines intervened in Cuba, Nicaragua, Panama, Haiti and the Dominican Republic. In every case, we built up or trained the local military forces; in every case the result was military dictatorship and appalling corruption.

These interventions ended with the Good Neighbor policy of President Franklin D. Roosevelt in the early Nineteen Thirties and were supplanted by U.S. military aid and training. But the results have not been much more fortunate than with the previous direct intervention. Our military assistance has been used by the worst type of dictators to help them stay in power and oppress their people. This was true, for instance, of Trujillo in the Dominican Republic, Batista in Cuba, Somoza in Nicaragua and Pérez Jiménez in Venezuela.

It was widely noted throughout the hemisphere that the palace gate in Lima, Peru, was smashed down on July 18 by a Sherman tank commanded by a Peruvian officer trained at the Ranger School of Fort Benning, Ga. Senator Ernest Gruening of Alaska has pointed out that "three of the four military commanders who staged the Peruvian coup had tours of duty in the United States," while four of the new military Cabinet members were recipients of the U.S. Legion of Merit.

Yet it was over Peru that the first determined effort by a United States President was made to condemn the overthrow of democratically elected governments by the armed forces. On July 19, the day after the coup, Mr. Kennedy denounced the officers and suspended diplomatic relations and economic and military aid. He could not make it stick because the Peruvian people accepted the dictatorship, the American business community applauded the coup (our investments in Peru total about $800,000,000), and the military *junta* promised to hold elections next year. We have had other Presidents—notably Woodrow Wilson and Harry S. Truman—who expressed disapproval of military coups, but none who acted with the vigor and clarity that President Kennedy displayed.

His reaction showed that the United States would like to use the potential leadership provided by its power and wealth to discourage the political role of the military in Latin America. But, the meager and uncertain results of our policy toward Peru demonstrate how difficult it is going to be to break down traditions and customs that go back 150 years.

The problem is to bring about control of the armed forces by civilians in those countries where military leaders hold decisive power. With a small ruling élite, however, of which the military forms a part, the civil authorities, the courts, the Congresses and other institutions simply cannot control or contain them.

Unhappily for us, a democratic form of government is not the only way to curb military leaders. In the Soviet Union, for instance, it is effectively done by the Communist party system and, in Latin America, by the "Marxist-Leninist" system of the Cuban regime. Since we are determined to do whatever we can to prevent any more Cuban-type regimes, we are restricted to a policy of reluctantly accepting military take-overs and domination—as in Argentina and Peru—while we do what we can to encourage the growth of democracy as we practice it.

A baffling feature of such a role by the United States is that Latin-American societies, with a few exceptions, are not adapted to an Anglo-Saxon or Western European type of democracy—and what is more, they do not especially want it. We have to accept the fact that there are different kinds and degrees of democracy. In the end, there was nothing President Kennedy could do about Peru except express condemnation and the hope that the military leaders would fulfill their promises to maintain civil liberties and hold an honest election next year. It is only realistic to add that they will only do these things if civil liberties do not threaten their power and if the election can be made to bring a result they find acceptable.

Meanwhile, with our Mutual Defense Assistance Pacts, the Inter-American Defense Board, the tours of duty spent annually by hundreds of Latin-American Army, Navy and Air Force officers and the American military missions in Latin America, we can only keep hoping that our democratic ideals will rub off by contact. One result so far is that the top officers in the different countries are getting to know each other personally—which is one reason why militarism can go in a wave of sympathy from one country to another. But our democratic principles are not, unfortunately, spreading in a similar way.

"None of the goals of the [United States] program have been achieved," Senator Gruening said in a speech in the Senate on Aug. 2, "not hemispheric defense, not standardization, not modernization, not a reduction in forces, not even that much-to-be-desired by-product, indoctrination of the military in their role in a modern democracy."

A widespread sense of frustration and disillusionment has led many Congressmen to wonder whether we should keep up our military aid and mutual defense programs with Latin America.

Yet to abandon them would be no solution. Machine-guns would be enough to support a coup if the other side was unarmed. In any case, military establishments in Latin America absorb 30 to 40 per cent of the national budgets. Felipe Herrera, a Chilean and President of the Inter-American Development Bank, recently pointed out that "our countries maintain approximately 650,000 men under arms and our [annual] military expenses amount to the equivalent of $1,400,000,000." In contrast, the U.S. contribution to the Alliance for Progress is only $1,000,000,000 a year.

In the short run, it has to be recognized that the United States can do little to discourage militarism in Latin-America. The Latins themselves must find the remedies and I believe they will if the Alliance for Progress, with its emphasis on social reforms, economic development and democratic institutions, succeeds. Latin America is not going to settle down in our generation. When there is ferment, the generals and admirals will feel it is their duty "to save the nation" and "to set things right." Some day the people of Latin America, in democratic fashion, are going to set their generals and admirals right—but that day is far off.

Myths About Africa— and the Reality

by Chester Bowles

IN ADDIS ABABA, Ethiopia, 32 African nations recently concluded a Chiefs of State Conference to develop the maximum basis for political and economic cooperation. Only the Republic of South Africa was absent. This is but one mark of the changes that have swept Africa from a position of unheeded obscurity to a place of primary world interest—and sometimes confusion.

Eight years ago, when I first visited Africa south of the Sahara, 29 of these nations existed only as colonies or as trusteeship territories. There was no Bureau of African Affairs in the State Department, and only two centers of African studies in the United States. In all of Africa there were only four American embassies.

In the weeks that my wife and I spent traveling down the African west coast to the Congo, across to the Rhodesias and west to Uganda, Kenya and Ethiopia, we came to see Africa as an awakening giant, stretching its limbs and opening its eyes to the first faint prospect of freedom.

Yet with notable exceptions, largely in British West Africa, European civil servants appeared as serenely confident of the permanence of things as their grandfathers had been in the days of Queen Victoria. How, some would ask, could we expect the

From the *New York Times Magazine,* June 16, 1963, copyright © 1963 by The New York Times Company.

European settlers of East Africa to compromise their pleasant and profitable existence under pressure from "uneducated natives"?

Outside of British West Africa only a handful of forward-looking European leaders were conscious of the trend toward change and were ready to move with the times, and even for them the pace was too swift. Before the war, they had been doing things *to* the Africans. Now, belatedly, they were striving honestly to do things *for* them. With a few exceptions they had not yet learned to do things *with* them.

On each of the half-dozen trips which I have taken to Africa since then, I have seen the pace of change rapidly accelerating and our own efforts expanding in response. The four American embassies of 1955 have now become 31, headed by an extremely competent group of ambassadors, most of them vigorous younger men. Our United States Information Service libraries have increased to 51; Americans serving in Africa in our embassies, consulates, U.S.I.S. posts and Agency for International Development missions now total almost 3,000, in addition to 1,500 members of the Peace Corps.

In the meantime, here in the United States the flow of books, documentaries, articles and lectures on African history, politics, geography and culture has reached flood-tide. The African Bureau of the State Department, non-existent eight years ago, has grown into a remarkably dedicated and effective organization, manned in large part by younger Foreign Service Officers.

Our present policies by and large appear admirably well keyed to the realities of the new Africa, and our new administrative apparatus is competent to carry them out. What is urgently needed now is deeper Congressional and public understanding of the economic and political forces that are shaping Africa's future, and a clearer recognition of the degree to which developments in Africa affect our own security interests.

In this framework let us examine some of the current popular stereotypes in regard to Africa which stand in the way of such understanding:

Racial antagonism—black hating white—is still a dominant factor.
Contrary to this general impression, Africa's new leaders—

with few exceptions—are neither anti-white nor anti-European. In spite of the long and often humiliating colonial experience, few hold grudges against either the former colonial powers or their own European minorities.

For instance, the African leaders of modern Kenya insist that while their first concern is to secure independence, this should be accomplished in such a way that the European minority will be given a sense of personal security and participation in building the new nation. In what was once known as French West Africa we find the same friendliness toward the former colonial rulers —the same willingness to live and let live, to forget past wrongs.

The Republic of Guinea offers a dramatic example of this resilience. In 1958, when President Sékou Touré decided to leave the French Union, the exasperated French reduced their investments in Guinea and recalled many of their doctors, technicians and teachers. Then, when the United States was slow to respond to Touré's desire for American assistance for fear of antagonizing our French allies, Guinea turned to the Soviet Union for economic aid. The Kremlin responded favorably, and some American policy-makers promptly wrote off this new African nation as a probable Communist satellite.

Yet, in the face of the most difficult pressures and adjustments, Guinea's young leaders have maintained a refreshingly sound perspective, which includes a genuine desire to re-establish friendly relations with the French, for whom they continue to express respect and even affection. In this cold-war period of violence and bitterness such tolerance is heartening.

Nor are these isolated cases. With the exception of Algeria, transition from African colonialism to African freedom has been achieved with surprisingly little violence. Indeed, in the recent interval of difficult adjustment—during which 25 African nations south of the Sahara emerged from colonial rule—fewer than 8,000 people have been killed, and this includes the Mau Mau revolt in Kenya and the Congolese civil war. When we compare this relatively orderly transition with the mass killings that accompanied comparable revolutionary changes in China, Russia or even the Indian sub-continent, it seems miraculous.

It should be added that the Africans responsible for this mature style of transition are themselves notable for their youth, enthusiasm and humility. In country after country, these new leaders have appeared to come out of nowhere; most of them are under 45 and many are in their thirties.

African leaders are unrealistic visionaries in their views on economic and social developments.

On the contrary, the objective visitor will be impressed with the sophistication with which most African planners are approaching this challenge. In 1955, to be sure, the few African nationalist leaders with whom I was permitted to talk were dreaming of independence in terms of nuclear reactors, global airlines and steel mills. These visions of economic grandeur, however, have long since been replaced by a remarkably down-to-earth understanding of achievable goals and priorities.

When a foreign visitor asks African leaders to list their requirements for national development, he will find their replies not only realistic but also surprisingly uniform.

Their first concern is for expanded and improved education, including technical education; the new African faith in education is passionate.

Second, they are likely to emphasize rural development, with particular stress on more productive agriculture through extension work, experimental farms, low-interest credit cooperatives and commercial fertilizers.

Third is the need for improved communications—roads, railroads, telephone and telegraph installations.

And, fourth, they may stress the need for small industries that can manufacture the inexpensive consumer goods that in non-Communist countries must be relied upon to provide the incentives for increased production in both rural and urban areas.

Many African leaders point out that a major share of such industries should be located in the small provincial towns so that the headlong rush into the large cities can be slowed down and a more rewarding life created near their homes, where the people feel more secure.

All of Africa is the same—a single great mass of land and problems.

Against this, sensitive American visitors to the new Africa will be impressed with the diversity of this great continent and the pride that each new nation is taking in its own future.

Africans want to be masters of their own destinies—and for this reason most African leaders demonstrate an acute awareness of the threat to their independence posed by international communism. Because they know by experience how uncomfortable it is to be ruled by others, however generous and well-intentioned, a fierce sense of independence is everywhere evident. This is often expressed in an almost belligerent determination to build their own future within the framework of their own culture and, above all, not to appear to be influenced by outsiders—particularly by white foreigners.

While this new sense of national identity may strike us as a distorted and often exasperating reflection of the spirit of freedom, the world Communist movement—still dreaming great dreams of dominant ties with the new African states—will find it a formidable political obstacle to its ambitions.

Yet the new Africa is surprisingly free of provincialism. Side by side with a fierce dedication to independent growth is a sober realization of the need for cooperation among neighbors in viable geographic units. Although hopes for a full-blown, all-African political federation at this stage are unrealistic, there is a steadily growing movement toward forms of multinational cooperation in both East and West Africa, as the conference in Addis Ababa demonstrated.

Most African leaders are realists who believe that small African nations of a few million people each, many of them with crazy-quilt borders that are a legacy of clashing 19th-century European colonial ambitions, have much to gain by merging development plans and governmental services with those of their neighbors. Far-sighted Africans even see these economic ties as a first important step toward increasing political integration.

Africa's problems are so vast that major economic progress is impossible in the foreseeable future.

The very opposite is the case. Africa's economic potential is limitless. By 1975, when its short supply of educated and technically skilled manpower will be substantially eased, the rate of per capita income growth in most of Africa may be faster than in either Latin America or Asia.

Although the obstacles created by inadequate education and inexperience in public administration are formidable, they are likely to be overcome more rapidly than many observers think. And, once this is accomplished, Africa's vast economic promise will become dramatically evident.

For one thing, only two or three African countries are plagued with the deeply rooted resistance to political reforms on the part of an entrenched élite that one often finds in other underdeveloped continents. And although some observers regard the tribal system in most parts of Africa as a similar barrier, they may be surprised to see the relative ease with which many of these tribal arrangements, including the common ownership of land, evolve into constructive systems of cooperative ownership and management.

Another important African advantage over the long haul is the extraordinarily favorable ratio, in most African nations, of people to natural resources. The Congo and the Sudan, in particular, illustrate the possibilities. Each of these new countries is about two-thirds the size of India and may be expected to possess a similar percentage of India's natural resources. Yet the population of India is 440 million, while the population of the Sudan and the Congo is approximately 13 million each.

The economic implications are self-evident. Once sufficient numbers of trained and educated Congolese and Sudanese are available to help organize and develop their vast natural resources, the per capita incomes in both countries may be expected to grow far more rapidly than in India, in spite of the demonstrated vitality and capacity of Indian democracy.

This development is likely to be spearheaded by the rapid introduction into Africa of labor-saving machinery, with the consequent growth of a well-paid core of industrial workers and a developing middle class. While the more heavily populated Asian countries may be resisting modern machinery because its first impact is to throw people out of work, the new African nations are likely to face an increasing labor shortage and a consequent rapid increase in wages and purchasing power as machinery is introduced to fill the gap.

Although on balance Africa's present development and long-term future prospects appear remarkably promising, we should not overlook the dangers. A sober view must take into account certain built-in political traps which in several areas could turn the present generally favorable situation into disaster. One of the most important and pressing of them has been the Congo.

Before the Congo achieved independence in 1960, the province of Katanga, through its vast copper exports, supplied the Central Government with nearly half of its foreign exchange and half its annual tax income. Not only its transportation system, but much of the rest of the Congolese economy was financed by this single natural resource.

If Katanga had ultimately seceded, we would almost surely have witnessed a bloody civil war in the heart of Africa and the political disintegration of a potentially wealthy country nearly one-third the size of the United States. This would have invited Communist intervention in the very heart of Africa.

Faced with this situation, the United States would have been forced to choose between turning its back on a dangerous political debacle or acting unilaterally and at substantial cost to pick up the pieces. Fortunately we made the right choice—to support a request from the Congo Government for U.N. aid—and today the United Nations is striving to help this once profitable colony transform itself into a viable, unified nation. History will view this as a fateful decision. American failure to support the U.N. effort would have produced an impact far beyond the Congo itself.

How, then, should the United States deal with the new Africa?

The first requirement is continuing, courageous support for the right of all peoples to determine their own forms of government. Respect for this fundamental right is an intrinsic part of our American faith which we can never afford to compromise.

In 1825, Prince Metternich, the spokesman for reaction in post-Napoleonic Europe, in referring to American support for the Greek war of liberation from the Turks, said: "Wherever a subject people seek revolutionary change, there you will find the Americans applauding those who succeed and bemoaning those who fail." In today's revolutionary world, similar support for self-determination must be an integral part of our political strength.

Second, while wholeheartedly supporting the right of all peoples to govern themselves, we should recognize the difficult adjustment facing our friends in Europe. Once the strength of the African independence movement became clear, the British, the French and the Belgians (with some admitted lapses) have conducted themselves generally with understanding, flexibility and skill. Let us then forgo patronizing lectures in dealing with our European associates. Our joint interests will best be served by an earnest effort to understand their problems and to work with them toward realistic solutions.

Third, in the last few years, the Bureau of African Affairs in the State Department has developed great sensitivity and competence under the leadership of Assistant Secretary G. Mennen Williams. Let us continue to strengthen this key organization.

Fourth, the Peace Corps appears to be ideally suited to the needs of Africa. In Ethiopia, Tanganyika, Nigeria, Cameroon and Liberia, I have met serious young Americans who are a profound credit to this country and a promise of increased world understanding among the younger generation. The Peace Corps is the most outstanding new contribution to foreign policy in the last decade. In Africa, as elsewhere, it should be expanded rapidly.

Fifth, we should join with other capital-exporting nations to make sure that those African countries that are able to absorb economic assistance are supported, and, equally important, that they are given the *right kind* of help. In line with the priorities set by responsible African leaders, education should be given major emphasis, followed by integrated development of the rural areas, agricultural extension, public administration, health services and road construction.

Insofar as possible, we should encourage local initiative in these undertakings, particularly in the construction of schools, clinics and roads. A simple, bamboo-mud school or a connecting road built by parents and other villagers in the tradition of our own rural development will contribute far more to the orderly political growth of a village than a better constructed road or a "show place" school built with no local involvement.

Some American observers suggest that the ex-colonial countries —Britain, France and Belgium—should be urged to take the lead in furnishing economic assistance to Africa. In effect this has already occurred. In 1962 the contribution of the former colonial powers amounted to $1.1 billion while the U.S. assistance was a little more than one-third that amount. However, we must be careful not to allow others to put a ceiling on our own efforts. The emerging African nations will continue to need substantial American help not only to speed their development but to underscore their new independence from European domination.

Sixth, we should not compromise our own interests or principles in an effort to win African applause on short-term issues where we honestly believe that they are wrong and we are right. A strained effort to curry favor by agreeing with African leaders, regardless of the circumstances, will not create the solid ground necessary for an enduring partnership. In the U.N., for example, we find ourselves on most issues voting with the African nations because we share with them a desire for a freer, more prosperous, more peaceful world. But when issues arise about which we fail to see eye to eye, we have not hesitated to say so.

However, let us curb our impatience when particular situations fail to develop as we think they should. The new African nations, having at long last thrown off British, French and Belgian rule, have no desire to be either Russianized or Americanized. They want to be Africanized, and in a hurry.

Although they share our hopes and fears on most aspects of world affairs, they are anxiously and often belligerently determined to maintain their own identities. When they sense that their independent judgment is being compromised they will go out of their way to assert it regardless of what we say or think—and even regardless of their own immediate interests.

In this regard, we should also keep our perspective when African leaders make speeches or offer U.N. resolutions which we consider to reflect undue impatience and emotionalism. We should remember that early in our history—and even from time to time today—we have done likewise. Furthermore, many African capitals do not yet have large and experienced civil-service systems, aided by extensive research and public-information organizations. This sometimes results in speeches or resolutions based on inadequate or outdated information. With the passage of time, however, this situation will correct itself.

Finally, let us remember that in the postwar years, when we Americans were learning by hard, painful experience about the nature of communism and the deviousness of Communist diplomacy, most of the present crop of African leaders were living under colonial governments as obscure civil servants, budding young lawyers or university students, absorbed with their own affairs. As in our own case, experience is the only reliable teacher, and experience takes time.

Part 3

WHAT IS BEING DONE, AND HOW WELL IS IT SUCCEEDING?

THE CATALOG OF obstacles to economic development is interminable. Underdeveloped countries, it would seem, must do everything at once. But they cannot; underdevelopment means you are poor and can do only a few things at a time. There are few hard and fast rules under these circumstances, which is why there seem to be about as many strategies for development as there are countries trying to develop. In this selection of articles, the discussion of policies and programs ranges from Guatemala's adult literacy campaign to Mexico's single-party political machine, which slides easily between left ideology and right-of-center policies.

Almost every underdeveloped country in the world today has a government agency ostensibly concerned with national economic planning. The formulation of broad national plans has occupied numerous university-trained intellectuals, who often cannot find other employment in their home countries because of limited industrial development. It has also employed a bevy of international experts provided under various technical assistance schemes. The preparation of plans often takes place under the encouragement of aid-providing nations and such international aid organizations as the World Bank. The United States, which ideologically rejects national economic planning at home, actively encourages it in the less-developed countries which receive American aid.

The formulation of a national development plan is easy compared with its execution. This is why very complicated plans tend to fall apart. Where an efficient machinery exists for executing projects, formal and complicated long-range plans are probably not necessary. Involved planning may work to replace action.

These articles examine the political machinery and strategies being tried in a number of countries. Hal Lehrman shows how a politically powerful development board attempts to channel a country's resources into carefully screened projects. Despite its seeming rationality and favorable political position, the board faces severe handicaps, and there remains the all-important question of whether the current strategy is improving the lives of those who need help most. The vast majority of the world's impoverished are rural people. The village is where the results of different strategies must ultimately come to rest. What is happening in the village is literally what is happening in the nation. Barbara Ward's article examines this crucial role of the village and explores the relationship between agricultural and industrial development.

Perhaps the most important single ingredient in any development strategy is a central purpose, a common goal which serves to unite people for a national, cooperative effort. David Lilienthal thinks Nigeria may have found such a central purpose in the development of the Niger River. For most poor countries the outlook remains decidedly bleak, and it is difficult to maintain great enthusiasm for long on an empty stomach. The strategies employed up to now leave too many questions unanswered.

Iraq Tries
"Operation Bootstrap"

by Hal Lehrman

NOT LONG AGO the tomb of an obscure Moslem holy man, over-looked in the road-planners' charts, turned up across the path of wreckers and steamrollers cutting a modern boulevard through Baghdad. The awesome taboos of sainted ground paralyzed further advance; it appeared the thoroughfare might have to make a detour. Then one morning the city awoke to find the sepulchre gone and the area around it transformed into a delightful park to grace the new street. Before so clear and benevolent a miracle, not even the most pious could cry desecration.

Baghdad's Mayor of the moment was the responsible magician. Covered by darkness, after secret preparations, a small army of workmen with machines and all essentials including trees and grassy turf had moved in under his intrepid command and accomplished the feat in a single, incredible, new-style Arabian night.

Such phenomenal energy rarely stirs in sun-cooked Iraq (or anywhere else, for that matter). Yet Iraq itself today is making a prodigious national effort no less remarkable in the Arab world.

Seventy per cent of the state's revenues from oil have been flowing unswervingly into the account of a Development Board

From the *New York Times Magazine,* February 24, 1957, copyright © 1957 by The New York Times Company.

established in 1950 to build up the country. The board has begun digging dirt for a score of massive projects and has actually completed a few already. It has installed Western experts in key positions, has given some of them a full vote in policy-making and has never gone counter to their major recommendations.

This is precisely the sort of "bootstrap" self-help the United Nations and the United States have long been urging if the Arab world is ever to lift itself up out of medieval backwardness and mass destitution. President Eisenhower's special cache of $200 million for Middle East aid would be intended to assist just such programs—with the long-range aim of soothing Arab nationalist fevers by reducing the virus of poverty.

Yet nowhere else among the Middle East's independent Arab states can comparable progress, or even an inclination toward improvement, be detected. Like Iraq, Saudi Arabia has been enjoying a mammoth oil income—more than a quarter of a billion dollars yearly. But King Saud spends more on one extra palace than on his Government's entire budget for education. After his numerous brothers and sons have drawn their annual allowances, and a legion of tribal sheikhs their stipends as a fee for non-rebellion, little is left over for public works and welfare. In Egypt, Gamal Abdel Nasser's start on economic reform has limped to a halt. In hypernationalist Syria, even free economic aid has been rejected as "colonialism."

By contrast, Iraq's seven-man Development Board executive committee, working with the Prime Minister and the Ministers of Development and Finance, has an average annual budget of $250 million to disburse. Its five native members—an ex-Premier and four senior statesmen, all former Cabinet members—authorize nothing without the concurrence of their two full-ranking foreign colleagues, an American and a British engineer. Its irrigation and drainage section is headed by a Dutchman and an American, the bridges and highways section by an Englishman, industry and mining by a Frenchman.

In the bazaars 500 fils ($1.50) is the standard "price" for a smuggled copy of any confidential board document; and every foreign firm is assailed by agents offering to purchase the ear of a high official for a fee.

Immersed in this classic baksheesh climate, the board nevertheless screens contracts and projects rigorously on merit. Perhaps the one dubious item is an air-conditioned palace for 21-year-old King Faisal, to cost $7 million. But even this can be justified as part of a public-building program that includes a new Parliament building, a royal guardhouse, a museum, a library, a jail and a tourist hotel to cost $6 million.

The board's program of major public works will literally change the face of the country. Already a set of dams at Samarra on the Tigris and at Ramadi on the Euphrates has lengthened to a cycle of five years instead of one the prospect of regular and ruinous inundation for the Mesopotamian Plain. Two more dams, one of them 450 feet high, are now being erected on Tigris tributaries.

A gasoline refinery has been completed at Daura with board funds, an asphalt refinery is going up at Qaiyara, a cement plant near Sulaimaniya and a cotton textile plant at Mosul. Contracts have been awarded on another cement plant, a sugar factory and two thermoelectric power plants totaling 85,000 kilowatts. A six-year road program has laid down 400 miles of first-class highway so far and is scheduled to complete 1,000 miles by late 1957. Of twelve new main bridges projected for Iraq's great rivers, three are already in use at Kirkuk, Kufa and Hindiya, and two will be opened at Baghdad before the year's end.

The bridges symbolically point to another Iraqi eccentricity—by Arab standards. When five iron bridges span the Tigris at Baghdad, according to ancient prophecy, "an invader will come down from the North." On modern maps this means the Soviet Russians. The two new bridges will give Baghdad a total of five for the first time in history—and another two are already being planned.

Not that the Iraqis are indifferent to menace from Moscow. On the contrary, Iraq is the only Arab state sufficiently aware of it to have entered a Western-led regional defense system, the so-called Baghdad Pact, with Britain, Turkey, Pakistan and Iran. Iraq's defense forces get weapons and training from Britain and substantial armaments, by separate treaty, from the United States. Early this month Crown Prince Abdul Illah, uncle of the King, turned up in Washington to negotiate still more arms aid.

Iraq faces squarely Westward, despite abuse from her neutralist "allies" in the Arab League. Outwardly, she takes the same angry stance as they against Israel—and even against Britain in the Suez crisis. After the Franco-British attack on the canal two meetings of the Baghdad Pact states were ostentatiously held without inviting the British. But that estrangement, churned up mainly for public Arab consumption, seems safely past. The Hashemite dynasty which reigns in Baghdad feels much less threatened by Western "imperialism" than by nearer dangers.

The dynasty that rules in Saudi Arabia has long been a hated rival; and the carefully contrived Washington meeting of Saud and Abdul Illah obviously cannot be expected to erase the old enmity. Ambitious Egypt and quarrelsome Syria, both under increasing influence from Moscow, have been driving for Iraq's isolation in the Arab world. King Saud, Nasser and the Syrians are deep in intrigue inside Jordan, which sits at Iraq's door and has a Hashemite kinsman of Iraq's King Faisal on the throne. The Soviet Union, within easy march of Iraq's oil fields, looms larger still.

Against all these perils, and in mutually profitable oil exploitation through the British-controlled Iraq Petroleum Company and other outlets, Britain remains Iraq's closest ally—and the United States her strongest friend. When the Soviets were making alarming military gestures in the Middle East last autumn, it was Washington which warned Moscow that any move hostile to Iraq or her Baghdad Pact neighbors "would be viewed by the United States with the utmost gravity."

Iraq has much to defend. Other territories in the Middle East possess oil or water or an excess of potentially fertile land over inhabitants. But Iraq alone has all three combined.

Once, populous Sumerian and Babylonian civilizations flourished in antique Mesopotamia. On the great plains between the Twin Rivers there are desert stretches paved with remnants of classic pottery that turn up at every step. One can still see the vestigial mounds of ancient cities, some of them five miles long. As late as the ninth century A. D., Baghdad under Harun al-Rashid was the Eastern capital of Islamic culture and power. But afterward came Mongol destruction of the irrigation system, the Turkish conquest, unrestrained floods, erosion, deforestation and other hazards. By World War I the region was the "Siberia" of the Ottoman Empire, administered by Turkish officials temporarily banished there.

Today Iraq has a population of only 5,000,000. Egypt, with less than a third as much tillable soil, has 22,000,000 people. "Almighty God," cried Development Minister Dhia' Ja'afar in Parliament the other day "has given us a wealth very seldom bestowed on countries with such a small population!" But Iraq will need large-scale immigration if the challenge of projects already in work is to be met.

From a guaranteed annual minimum of $70 million negotiated in a 50-50 split with four oil companies in 1952, Iraq's share swelled to better than $205 million in 1955. This represented 65 per cent of total Government income. Between 1951 and 1955, Development Board allocations amounted to $470 million. For 1955–60, estimates of expenditures were calculated initially at $850 million. But within a year, with the mounting flood of oil royalties and taxes, these were revised upward to $1,400 million.

An Iraq Petroleum Corporation pipeline from Kirkuk normally carries 75 per cent of Iraq's export oil to the Mediterranean. Last November the three pumping stations on Syrian territory were blown up by the Syrian Army. The action, ostensibly a defensive military measure provoked by the Anglo-French invasion of Egypt, has been costing Iraq around $700,000 daily. The magnitude of Iraq's resources is attested by the fact that, despite this blow, the development program has continued until now without pause. Plans not yet put into work are being slowed pending negotiations with Syria for pipeline repair. But all projects already under way are going forward uninterruptedly, thanks to $385 million of board reserves banked in Baghdad and London. Iraq's credit, the soundest in the Arab Middle East, is expected to obtain financing for her abroad easily if these funds give out before full income is restored.

In other oil-rich Arab countries—Saudi Arabia, for instance—the land is either parched desert or stony steppe. Iraq, however, has so much fresh water that damage from periodic river overflow in some years has cost $80 million. Hitherto, floods that ravaged the land each spring ran futilely off, leaving a water shortage in the dry season each fall. Storage and irrigation works now in progress are expected in five years to redeem 400,000 wasted acres and bring supplementary water to a half-million other acres. The board aims ultimately at supplying extra water to 7 million of the 8 million acres which represent Iraq's total irrigated area today—and at reclaiming 6 million acres more.

Such stupendous expansion could multiply native farm output at least five times. But skills are notoriously lacking in Iraq. Despite the general advance already noted, it is far from certain that the basic long-range development program will be able to move steadily forward.

In Baghdad, modern homes sometimes get completed before someone remembers that a kitchen should have a sink and that a fireplace performs better if equipped with a chimney. A $5,000,000 railway station started under an earlier development program was finished in 1954 near the Baghdad airport—but nowhere near the railroad.

At the start, the board itself also committed monumental boners. In one case, close study finally revealed that a large patch of reclaimed soil could never drain properly and hence would yield malaria instead of crops—but the study which proved this was undertaken only after expensive canals were dug and hundreds of settlers brought in.

Under discreet foreign guidance, the passion to spend huge sums quickly has faded. If anything, the board errs now on the side of slow motion. Years of study are being put into each project. The countryside swarms with survey teams exploring potential resources.

But excessive precautions are not the main obstacle. A prime roadblock is the Ministry of Development, the board's liaison with the Government. Whenever a Cabinet falls, the board's work halts while a new Minister of Development learns his job. In four years, eight Governments have fallen.

Iraq's shortage of technical personnel is an even graver problem. There is a surplus of lawyers, but a shortage of plumbers (the Government Law College was grinding out 700 graduates yearly until a recent decree cut new classes to 100). Too few vocational and advanced technical schools exist. The board's total staff is only 1,500—including a battalion of coffee-bearers

—as against 10,000 in the United States Bureau of Reclamation, which has a program of roughly the same magnitude.

Equally serious is the bottleneck produced by Iraq's backward civil service. Between 1933 and 1956, the cost of living rose 500 per cent, but salaries of middle and upper Government employes inched up only 50 per cent. Better pay in private enterprise lured away most of the more competent personnel. Promotions for merit and discharges for incompetence being virtually unknown, the civil service suffers from a built-in apathy. Iraq has had no facilities for special training in government and, until recently, no awareness of the need for them. With a super-billion-dollar development program to manage, the state machinery might fairly be described as a one-cylinder motor in a Rolls-Royce body.

Last summer, Parliament voted a scaled pay hike up to 75 per cent for Government workers. The major immediate result was only that cigarettes and other "white-collar" items quietly doubled in price. There is some prospect of bolder reforms, however. Prodded by the United States International Cooperation Administration—which supports a 110-man Point IV mission in Iraq—top native leaders are even contemplating the possible utility of establishing a school of public administration.

The largest question-mark in the Development Board's future is its social goal. Is the program truly designed to help the whole Iraqi people, or merely to make the rich grow richer? Despite the lavish funds available, projects executed or planned for the direct short-range benefit of ordinary Iraqis were of paltry scope in the program's first half-decade.

In 1954, the Development Board invited a British economist, Lord Salter, to make a critical survey. He recommended that the board find ways to hasten the impact of its good deeds. He pointed especially at the appalling need for housing. Three-fourths of the nation still live in miserable huts, largely without fresh water or sewerage. Even in Baghdad, almost within sight and smell of Government offices, over 200,000 occupy squalid *sarifa* of mud walls and reed roofs.

A "crash program" has now been launched to erect in five cities during the next two years around 5,000 one-family houses with modern insulation and sanitation. The houses, ranging in cost up to $2,800, will be sold or rented on easy terms. Other Government departments are being assisted with housing programs for employes.

By 1960, the board intends to have spent around $70 million on perhaps 25,000 new dwellings. Even this scratching of the surface is impeded by the dearth of specialized labor. In addition, $45 million has been allotted for schools, clinics and hospitals and $242 million for roads and bridges, with priority for roads that afford farmers better access to markets.

Sober foreign observers are hopeful these noble works may yet be accomplished, along with other Grand Plans of the board. But all agree that first there must occur a dazzling enlightenment of Iraq's economic and political rulers.

The sweeping progress of which the board dreams implies a revolution in Iraq's social patterns. It would wash away the pillars of mass poverty, illiteracy and semi-feudal subjugation. It would diminish the caste which now rides high on the backs of the Iraqi people. Such drastic change could be made only with the voluntary consent of the riders—or by their violent overthrow.

Over 60 per cent of the population subsists on agriculture, but nearly 70 per cent of the land consists of large holdings which employ the bulk of the farm labor. At least four out of every five peasants in Iraq get no cash return for their toil. Their landlords pay them in kind, sometimes as little as a two-seventh share of the crop. Perpetually debt-ridden, forbidden by law to quit their places as long as they are in arrears, trapped by low productivity and high interest rates, most peasants live in virtual serfdom.

Their lords and masters constitute a corps of medieval-minded sheikhs, with some absentee urban potentates. The sheikhs are hereditary rulers. Their power rests on ingrained fealty from below and on their personal armies of tribal riflemen. In Parliament the sheikhs form the hard center of Premier Nuri as-Said's support. A measure of their rooted strength is the fact that Iraq, despite its predominantly agricultural economy, levies no land tax or inheritance tax.

The landed caste has been persuaded thus far to go along with the Development Board. Flood control, irrigation and other improvements obviously raise the worth of the private properties affected. Until now, the state has largely classified such improvements as in the "common interest," absolving the owners from having to compensate the public coffers for benefits received.

On the other hand, the rural oligarchy has no zeal for civil service reform, which might build up cadres of lively officials with reformist notions about entrenched privileges. Nor are the sheikhs likely to relish the growing unrest among their landless followers as the area of reclaimed acreage available for distribution expands. (To date only 15,000 peasants have been affected by various agrarian reform schemes.)

Will the Government give this land to those who need it, and help them survive by easy credit—or instead will the land go eventually, by default, to those who already have too much? Can the wealthy be allowed continually to grow fatter from the development program's contributions to the value of their properties, or must not some apparatus for adequate repayment on these benefits be devised? How long, finally, can sound economic and social management tolerate a fiscal regime which gives immunity from taxes to the one group best able to pay?

The best that can be said is that recommendations on all these matters have been prayerfully drawn up by foreign consultants and that the Iraqi Government has begun gravely to read them instead of filing them in back drawers. It is too early to predict whether the feudal class can recognize in time that its best interest demands a relative reduction of its own top-heavy wealth in exchange for the tranquilizing effects of reduced mass resentment.

Petronillo Learns
to Write His Name

by Alan Howard

GUATEMALA CITY

DURING THE RAINY season the best way to get into Zapotitlán is by mule. Now and then a jeep comes through, though most of the people who travel in and out of the town walk. The bus from Guatemala City goes as far as a town called Adelanto, which is set in a pocket of high, angular hills; then you make your way up the wide slope that walls the town on the east, over a bare plain, and down the rutted and twisting road into Zapotitlán. With luck, the trip from the capital takes about eight hours.

The town looks like most of the other towns in this part of the country. The low houses and narrow stone streets seem to flow toward a square of rocky dark earth, dusty at noon and filled with muddy rivulets after a rain. The square's barren space is broken by a few tall palms planted randomly along one side, and, opposite them, a couple of wooden basketball backboards facing each other.

On the near hillsides you can see an occasional white house among the dun adobes. Many of the homes have only one room;

From the *New York Times Magazine,* February 7, 1965, copyright © 1965 by The New York Times Company.

it is kitchen, bedroom and barn. One house in the town has a latrine. Each house has a plot of corn; often there are beans planted with the corn. Sometimes there is rice in a separate field and perhaps a few banana trees. A man plants as much as the land will hold and hopes it will be enough to feed his family. In a good year there may be a surplus, perhaps enough to buy an animal, clothes or even a radio.

Zapotitlán is one of many communities taking part in Guatemala's literacy campaign, which began in 1959. The nation, with 72 per cent of its adult population unable to read or write, is the most illiterate country in Spanish America. Although a number of organizations—governmental and private—are teaching literacy, by far the largest program is one directed by the Ministry of Education, with substantial assistance from the Alliance for Progress and the Guatemalan Army's Civic Action plan.

In 1963, more than 70,000 adults wanting to learn how to read and write attended 3,268 training centers throughout Guatemala. An indication of the difficulties they encountered is that fewer than 5,000 of them successfully completed the course, which generally takes from five to nine months—although preliminary statistics for 1964 seem to show that the program is becoming more efficient and is graduating more students.

Almost all of the centers are run by volunteers, men and women—many of whom have never completed primary school—teaching under the crudest conditions, with a sense of social responsibility that is truly rare in this country. Their basic material is a series of six books about the life of a typical *campesino,* or subsistence farmer, and his family, beginning with instruction in the fundamentals. An average student finishing the course can, with a little practice, read and write a simple message.

In the past two years about 200 people who live in Zapotitlán and on the surrounding hills have become literate. In view of the fairly discouraging record of the nationwide literacy program, what effect, if any, has literacy had on the course of their lives? Was the effort worth it?

There is a thin old man in Zapotitlán by the name of Petronillo who has become something of a local hero. For a few months he attended one of the literacy classes but soon found the printed word to be so strange and unmanageable that, shortly after learning to sign his name, he quit—still a long way from what the experts call functional literacy.

One day, after he had left the class, he went to a neighboring town to sell a cow. When it came time for him to sign the bill of sale in the Mayor's office, he demurred for fear of ruining his signature (for, as he explained, this was with a pen and in the class he had always used a pencil). The Mayor promptly offered the services of his clerk, who by custom would sign such documents for illiterates at 25 cents a signature. Since the deal required two signatures and Petronillo had only 25 cents, he reluctantly took on the task himself. "Very delicate," he said, for the first one, but the second time was a pushover. And he came back feeling *"puro cuchillero,"* which roughly means "plenty tough."

Whenever the topic of literacy arises in Zapotitlán, which is more often than one might think, Petronillo's story is told and retold by everyone from the Mayor on down as an example of how important it is to be literate.

As I sat there listening to the old man tell his story with a glowing pride, it struck me as an amusing but not particularly sound reason for spending millions of dollars in an effort to make the country literate. Teaching people to sign their names may have some sort of personal, spiritual significance for old men like Petronillo, but in the complicated dynamics of social change there surely must be more important things to do first.

Many critics of the adult literacy program point to a person like Petronillo to support their opinion that literacy is of pitifully little practical value. It wasn't until some time later that the story took on a far greater importance for me.

The literacy centers distribute among other materials a series of more than 50 pamphlets published originally by the Pan American Union. Written in a simple, direct style, they range in subject from the life of Simón Bolivar to the breeding of rabbits.

One man I spoke to had read a pamphlet about the use of fertilizers and decided to try some. He bought a small amount, gave most of it to his son to use on a plot of tomatoes, and the rest he threw over a corner of his rice field. "You should see how green it's coming up," he said with an almost fierce satisfaction.

The man's wife also attended the literacy class and had read a pamphlet called "Careful with the Milk." At first, she said she didn't remember what the pamphlet advised, so I continued to chat with her husband. Gradually, her shyness faded, and she said she did remember that you were supposed to wash your hands before preparing the milk and that it should be boiled before drinking because it could have come from a sick cow.

"And do you do that now?" someone asked. "Do you wash your hands and boil the milk?"

She replied with an enthusiastic *"Sí."*

"And did you also do it before you read the book?"

With a wide toothless grin, then an embarrassed laugh, she said she didn't. Before I left she went to a corner of the dark room and brought the pamphlet out to show me. When I asked her the questions from the back page, she knew the answers thoroughly. She knew that sometimes germs that carried diseases got into the milk and that the only way to kill them was by boiling the milk; she knew that these diseases could be fatal; she knew that the milk must be covered with a clean cloth when left to cool.

To understand how literacy affects people, you must first try to understand something about the workings of the illiterate mind. For illiteracy is not merely the inability to read and write. That inability is the product of a way of life that has never required the symbols of written language. It is a way of human life governed almost exclusively by physical necessity; life in which human will is the passive object of a most pervasive and inscrutable divine will.

On one recent day a woman three months pregnant fell and began to hemorrhage. She bled for a day and died, while her family stood around, helpless. In another house a 2-year-old baby died on the same day—from a combination of many things but mostly a stomach full of worms. When I asked the father of the dead child what could be done when there was sickness in his house, he shrugged and sighed, "Ah, it is the will of God."

Didn't he know there was a hospital and doctors in Jutiapa? Yes, he knew, but Jutiapa is very far (three or four hours) and doctors are so expensive, he explained wearily, and then one never knows if the child will be cured or not; so there is all that trouble for nothing.

The man was illiterate; he was also hopelessly poor. With something more than an income of barest survival he might have been more willing to seek medical attention for his child. But would the ability to read and write have made any difference? It might well have, for the problem is not only a lack of money. It is also one of how people choose to spend what little money they have.

This man's failure to take his child to a doctor is one of many attitudes frozen in tradition, and the sum of those attitudes is inertia. Even when there is no question of money changing hands, one often finds the same entrenched resistance to change.

Recently, when hundreds of pounds of CARE cereals and powdered milk arrived in Zapotitlán for a school-lunch program, the teacher in charge could not find enough mothers willing to help in the daily preparation of the food and milk. They were too busy; they didn't have time; a baby was sick; a husband wouldn't allow it.

Why the excuses? One way to explain their reluctance: Their minds simply could not consider the advantages of their children's drinking milk. To weigh relative advantages, to speculate, to inquire, these are the methods of more sophisticated intelligences. For the people of Zapotitlán value has always been measured in the most concrete terms: how much seed gets planted or land cleared or how many loads of corn gathered.

When met with possibilities his intelligence cannot manage, a man often withdraws into the security of old and tested ways, or accepts some readily available simplification. As a result, fantastic ideas can become widely credible. One community actually refused a similar shipment of CARE foods because of a rumor that the program was a plot by the Government to fatten up the children and ship them away in cans to be eaten.

For such people literacy is a kind of cultural watershed. It marks the beginning of a vast and crucial region of intellectual activity: inquiry, reasoning, a certain quality of self-awareness. Whatever might be said for the "noble savage," there is a huge unborn portion of his consciousness—of which illiteracy is a salient characteristic—that severely limits him in the ways of the 20th century.

Illiteracy is not only the result of particular historical conditions. In a more damaging capacity it acts as a major cause of alienation in societies with a large illiterate population. For the modern illiterate recognizes a vivid and simple boundary between himself and others: the written word. And he makes inevitable associations. The literate world signifies wealth, the city, well-dressed strangers, sacks of wheat lettered CARE, almost anything that comes from outside his immediate and familiar surroundings.

In his poverty and the simplifying processes of his mind, the illiterate sees himself, however inarticulately, as something less than those people the printed word represents or suggests to him. Whenever he ventures away from his home, he sees the sign in a bus, advertisements in a store window, a newspaper; and every word is a distinct, if unconscious, reminder of his estrangement from the men who use those mysterious scribblings as naturally as he uses a hoe. Even in his own home, the instructions on a bottle of medicine render him helpless, totally dependent on what the druggist in town has told him to do with the contents of that bottle.

Isodoro Salazar lives just south of Zapotitlán in the little community of San Francisco Las Palmas, a scattering of houses on a rocky hillside. With more than five acres of land for a family of 11, he is not poor by *campesino* standards. But it is not good land. It is steep and the soil is gritty, the unloving earth of the mountainous regions where most of the subsistence farmers live. The family consumes most of what is grown, though last year they managed a surplus that brought nearly $200 at the market in Jutiapa.

Ask Isodoro Salazar why he attended a literacy class, why he gave an hour of his time five nights a week for nearly a year and made his family do the same. He will not give you one of the pat answers that appear regularly in editorials and Government manuals—that illiterates live in terrifying darkness, a most shameful ignorance sticking like a great fatal thorn in the side of Progress. What he will probably do is smile.

Why, indeed? the smile seems to say. Then, Mr. Salazar will tell one of his favorite stories, about a man who goes out to buy a ring and gets cheated because he couldn't read the numbers on the money.

In fact, the most frequent responses I have heard to the question of why literacy is important are variations of Petronillo's story about the sale of his cow. The moral of the story may not always be that the literate has a way of protecting himself when he deals with strangers. Often, it is a tale about an illiterate person who misses out on a lucrative job because he couldn't read or write. But whatever the story, it almost always contains two elements: the world outside the immediate vision of the story's hero, and the literate's successful—or the illiterate's unsuccessful—contact with that world.

Hipolito is Isodoro Salazar's oldest son. When Hipolito was 6 he put on a big-brimmed hat and followed his father into the fields, thus placing himself among the men of San Francisco Las Palmas. He is 23 today and soon will have a portion of his father's land to work for himself and for his young wife and yet unborn sons. Until two years ago Hipolito had never had a day of formal schooling. Then came the literacy class, which he attended faithfully and with apparent enthusiasm; according to his instructor, he was the best pupil.

One would expect that if the fruit of literacy had blossomed anywhere in this tiny community, the evidence could be found in Hipolito. Yet his life seems essentially unchanged. He works in the same weary routine he has always worked, no richer, no poorer; he doesn't really care about politics, as long as nobody bothers him; he has no voracious desire to read, in fact, has read little in the year since the class ended. Of what value has literacy been to him?

For one thing, he said, he now writes letters to the radio station asking to have particular songs dedicated to his wife. His brothers also write letters and every Sunday the entire family sits around the radio waiting to hear a familiar name mentioned.

Was there anything else? He went into the house and brought out a thick school notebook. On many of its lined pages were drafts of letters to the radio station and innumerable exercises copied over and over; but the bulk of the writing, over a hundred pages, was excerpts from land deeds, official correspondence, governmental decrees and scores of other pompous and solemn documents. He had copied it all out of the town archives in the

Mayor's office. Of course, he explained, with the Mayor's permission. But why? Just to practice, he said.

"And what about when you go into Zapotitlán?" I asked him. "Is it any different now that you can read?"

"Well, sure," he answered readily.

"Why?"

And I was met by a friendly, shy smile and a mumbling loss of expression. Finally, he said, "Sure it's different, a person feels different——" and as he realized he couldn't explain it any further, he withdrew slowly behind his smile. After a few moments of silence, he added, half-joking, "At least now when you go into the Mayor's office and on each desk there is a sign that says 'Treasurer,' 'Mayor,' 'Secretary,' you don't go to the Secretary when you want to see the Mayor, right?"

Two incidents that the Salazars did not consider important enough to mention may be relevant.

One of the few occasions the family has for going into Zapotitlán is the annual Independence Day celebration on the 15th of September. Until last year, acting with that almost paralyzing reticence of the isolated *campesino,* they would go only to the edge of town and there listen to the firecrackers and music of the marimba coming from the town hall. Since their literacy class they have been in the thick of two Independence Day celebrations. Similarly, even before the classes had ended, Hipolito and two of his brothers had started making daily trips to town to play basketball. Their trips continued through the summer months, when there is little work in the fields.

Is it mere coincidence, the introduction of literacy followed by these nearly imperceptible gestures toward a world beyond the enslaving routine of ancient necessities? I don't think so. For these gestures seem to fit into a larger pattern discernible in Zapotitlán, a pattern of the newly literate person turning outward toward a way of life that has become less alien to him.

In one of my conversations with Isodoro Salazar he explained to me in detail the procedure for building a well. He knew exactly how and where the well should be built, the material he would need to do it, and the kind of pump he wanted. He had read all about it in one of the pamphlets of the Pan American Union series. But why hadn't he done it? Money, he said. It would cost about $30, the pump being the big expense, and he just couldn't afford it.

Now, has literacy necessarily failed because Mr. Salazar has not gone out and built his well? Or is it not a crucial step forward that Mr. Salazar is *willing* to build a well—is even enthusiastic about the idea—and will do so if he ever has the money or if the Government ever offers him help? In this context, criticism of the program's failure to bring material benefit to the people loses much of its force, because far more important than the immediate practical application of literacy is its final effect of making a man immeasurably more susceptible to change in his life.

In the past five years the United States has given a substantial amount of financial and technical assistance to Guatemala's literacy program through the Agency for International Development. That assistance is scheduled to end next July, the primary reason being, in the words of one AID official, "a shift away from grass-roots development toward working at the ministerial level." In Washington a spokesman recently explained that AID, having created the methods and structural organization of the program, felt that Guatemala would be able to maintain the program at its present level.

The reasoning behind the AID approach to literacy is based on a theory that plays an important role in the Alliance for Progress. The theory is attractive: Create the institutional machinery of reform (in this case educational, though it has been tried in other fields, i.e., income tax), give it a certain momentum, and then let the host government carry on the work.

Whatever the merits and drawbacks of the theory, in this particular case it seems destined to fail. Not because illiteracy has actually increased in the past five years—no one ever believed that the limited United States support could have had an immediate impact on the increasing rate of illiteracy—but because any real effort to make Guatemala literate will probably not continue after the United States pulls out.

Of course, the "institutional machinery" and evidence of United States aid remains. There is a Department of Literacy, with its own stationery, printing equipment, a few vehicles, a small though experienced staff. But in almost everyone's estimate, including that of the highly competent United States adviser who has worked on the program since its inception (and who has done a remarkable job, considering the obstacles), Guatemala will not become any more literate in the foreseeable future.

There is a curious debate around the literacy program; it seems to be three-sided. There are those who say it is virtually a prerequisite to meaningful social change and therefore should be given immediate priority. Opposing this is the argument that literacy is vastly overestimated as a means of national development and that energies would best be directed elsewhere.

Finally, there is a powerful group, which includes many people in the State Department, who view literacy primarily as a dangerously volatile element extremely difficult to control, and thus, in the interest of stability, to be avoided. In this light it is not hard to understand why the program has yielded such dismal results.

For a vigorous, adequately financed campaign with functional literacy as its goal would undoubtedly awaken new needs and a new voice among people who have long been silently acquiescent. When men begin to want fertilizer and wells and books, you can never be sure what they will do to get them or what they will want next. It is not nearly as easy to control or satisfy the needs of a hundred men like Isodoro Salazar as it is to predict the behavior of a bureaucrat in the National Palace; though we might ask ourselves whether short-term predictability is a

   With all the talk about developing economies, stabilizing politi-

particularly wise objective.

cal institutions, and nurturing social responsibility in countries like Guatemala, I believe the role of literacy has been shamefully neglected and perhaps even dismissed in important places of government both in the United States and in the so-called developing countries themselves. Whether this neglect is due to the selfish designs of a few or simply the myopic vision of others, or a combination of the two, is an academic question. The neglect is a fact.

The benefits of literacy—and especially the minimal type of literacy now being taught in Guatemala—are uncertain and often intangible. Old Petronillo saved 50 cents, but more important found a new measure of self-esteem. Isodoro Salazar discovered his need for a well. His son, Hipolito, writes letters to the radio station and spends hours practicing his handwriting in an old notebook.

Mere pastimes, it may be said, new diversions in an ancient and dull routine. But the next time Hipolito rides a bus and sees the sign that says, "We are not responsible for objects left on this bus," it will no longer be an unintelligible scrawl, no longer the password that has excluded him from the common discourse of those around him.

Surely it does not require a visionary's foresight to recognize the importance of such a change. It is a man breaking through, a little bewildered but alert and unafraid of considering new possibilities.

As I left the house of Isodoro Salazar, he said, "Bring us back something from your land."

"Like what?" I asked.

"Ideas," he replied, "but something we can do with our hands."

That is not the request of an illiterate man.

The Negev:
Challenge and Hope

by Seth S. King

BEERSHEBA

IN THE BOOK of the Prophet Ezekiel are the words: "And the desolate land shall be tilled, whereas it lay desolate in the sight of all that passed by. And they shall say, This land that was desolate is become like the Garden of Eden; and the waste and desolate and ruined cities are become fenced and are inhabited."

The land Ezekiel meant is the land on which so many of Israel's chances for survival and economic independence now hang. To some Israeli officials this wedge-shaped region is "The South and Negev." Others just say "The Negev."

But by whatever name it goes, it is the only sizable piece of undeveloped land left in this tiny country. It makes up more than half the nation. It is Israel's Land of the Big Sky, and, compared to the rest of the nation, it has more potential crop area, more potential mineral deposits, the worst climate—and by far the most problems.

Within its modest limits—it is not quite 150 miles long and, at its broadest, barely sixty miles wide—the Negev duplicates the terrain characteristics of large parts of the western United States. In the north, the rolling plains look like western Kansas.

From the *New York Times Magazine,* March 2, 1958, copyright © 1958 by The New York Times Company.

At Beersheba the land changes into a semblance of western Wyoming's sparsely covered rangelands. A few miles farther south it turns into a crumpled desert wilderness for which even Nevada could apologize.

When Israel was born, almost ten years ago, most of the Negev was wasteland. Today, a lot of it still is wasteland and a good part of it will have to stay that way for a long while. But on the rest of it there is impressive evidence of the frantic race the Israeli Government is now running against time and immigration.

Within the past three years a whole system of interlocking villages has been planted in the rolling short-grass areas north of here. A crescent of small towns, with Beersheba as the middle, has been staked out from the coast north of the Gaza Strip across to the shores of the Dead Sea.

A new asphalt highway has recently been completed from Beersheba to the infant port of Elath at the head of the Gulf of Aqaba. In Elath itself the first phase of harbor development is nearly ended, and, until cargoes in greater quantities start coming over the new road, a badly needed period of breath-catching is in progress.

The feverish pace of this activity has been dictated by the mounting pressure of Israel's new arrivals and the need to provide homes and jobs for them. During the past three years the inflow of Jews has increased from 33,000 in 1955 to more than 80,000 in 1957. In proportionate numbers these waves of newcomers have rivaled anything seen in the frontier days of the American West. But there the comparison stops.

There has been nothing spontaneous about the growth of the Negev. There have been no great discoveries of gold or oil and there has been nothing else to make a man want to drop what he was doing and rush into this area. But the immigrants have to be put somewhere, and the Negev offers the best of the limited possibilities.

The planners who decide these things have established other "development areas" in addition to the Negev. Other farms and towns are going up in the mountains of Galilee north of Haifa and in the rocky corridor that runs from the coastal plain up to

Jerusalem. Since 1955 between 60 and 80 per cent of all the new immigrants have been sent directly from their ships to development areas. The majority has come to the Negev.

By necessity, the major agricultural development has been restricted to the north, although even there irrigation water has had to be piped in and a carefully calculated crop schedule has had to be followed. If developed by individual farmers, most of this land could yield modest grain crops and support a limited number of cattle or sheep. But farming of this kind, with its large tracts and small population, was a luxury that couldn't even be considered. Instead of large single-family farms, Israel has had to set up cooperative settlements, with each man getting no more than ten acres and the whole being worked on a group basis.

Five cooperative villages of eighty to ninety families each are grouped around a rural center which provides elementary schools, a clinic and basic shopping facilities. In turn, the rural centers focus on an urban center, with a high school, a small hospital, major repair shops for farm machinery and, most important, processing plants for the crops.

The only example of this system so far is in the Lachish region, where Joshua defeated the Canaanites and Samson maneuvered against the Philistines. Fifty-eight villages and two rural centers have been built there and three more rural centers are going up. The urban center is Kiryat Gat, with more than 6,000 new settlers. A cotton gin and a peanut processing plant are already operating. A spinning mill is nearing completion and plans have been drawn for a sugar beet factory, a grain mill and a corn silo.

The industrial development of the Negev has similarly been governed by stern limitations. New plants and towns have had to be created near the raw materials they will use. And they have had to be placed near the meager and costly roads now available.

The planners started at Ashdod Yam and Ascalon, the old Philistine cities on the coast north of Gaza. Then they turned to the more populated areas west of Beersheba, where cotton, peanuts and sugar beets could be grown and fed into processing plants. East of Beersheba there was nothing but space and a road. But there was need for an upland town to house workers who could not live and work successfully near the potash plant on the steaming shores of the Dead Sea at S'dom nor in the vacant desert near the phosphate deposits at Oron.

To the south of Beersheba there was the road to Elath. At Mitzpeh Ramon, on the lip of the great depression called the Wadi Ramon, there were deposits of flint, clays and gypsum. At Timna near the site of King Solomon's copper mines were deposits of copper ore.

So the planners stuck pins in their maps and started towns where they appeared to be needed: Sderot and Ofakim west of Beersheba, Dimona between here and the Dead Sea, and Mitzpeh Ramon and Timna to the south.

Dominating the new towns and villages is ancient Beersheba, which likes to call itself "The Capital of the Negev." For centuries this oasis drowsed in the desert sun. It was little more than a trading center for the nomadic Bedouins and an administrative way-station on the back road to Egypt. In 1949, when the first Israeli civilians came down to take over the area from their conquering army, they were a community of 250.

Today the lines of rough, new houses and apartment buildings are climbing over the sandy landscape in all directions. There are now more than 35,000 people living and working here. There will be at least 3,000 more in the next three months. Today there is a ceramics factory, a grain elevator and mill, and a chemical insecticide plant. Beersheba is now linked to Tel Aviv by a railroad and is the rail loading point for the potash and phosphates that come in by truck. It is still the weekly market center for Israel's Bedouins, 13,000 of whom occupy a large reservation northeast of here. But it is now also the shopping and trade center for the settlements scattered around it. It is a vital community that is still in too much of a hurry to bother about frills. Like the land around it, it is still raw and ugly.

The demands the Negev has already made on the enterprise and stamina of Israel's planners are monumental. But they are no greater than the demands the Negev makes on those who agree to live here.

The Jew from North Africa, from Egypt or Persia or Eastern Europe usually sets foot on his Promised Land at the port of Haifa, whose modern apartment buildings climb up into the coolness of Mount Carmel's forests. But three or four hours later, when he jumps to the ground from the truck that hauled him here, he is engulfed by something entirely different.

If it is summer, and summer is ten months long here, the heat waves dance about him through the dust clouds. If it is winter he is cut by cold winds or buffeted by sheets of blinding rain.

If he and his family were brought to Israel by the Jewish Agency, as most immigrants are, then he has agreed to come to the Negev in return for more agency help. He has agreed either to become a farmer in a cooperative settlement or to live in town and work in a plant or a mine.

At Haifa he and each member of his family were given $1.50 for pocket money. If he is lucky, when he arrives in the Negev there is a two-and-a-half-room house of concrete blocks or plywood waiting for him. Inside it are beds and mattresses, a table and a kerosene cooker, a broom, a mop, and food for eight days. If he is not so lucky he will have to move into a tin shack until his house is ready.

For the first year, the newcomer has been promised from twelve to fifteen days of work each month on "inspired" projects—on new roads, on construction jobs, in the fields. For this, he gets about $3.50 each day, meaning that at best he can expect a salary of $52 a month.

If the dreams of the planners are fulfilled, a town immigrant will have a steady job by the end of that first year. But his wages will be carefully controlled by the Government. Depending on his skill, he can expect to work a five-and-a-half-day week and be paid about $25 in salary.

The immigrant who goes to a cooperative farm rather than a town spends his first year in much the same way. In his second year he should get some income from his crops and the animals the Jewish Agency has provided for him. To supplement this, he may get "rounding out" labor on public works, which should bring him $35 a month. After that, theoretically, he and his settlement must provide for themselves.

If Israel were at peace with her Arab neighbors, all this would be enough of a problem. But added to it is the constant possibility of violence.

Those who live in settlements along the Negev's borders must spend part of their time off protecting their fields and livestock from Arab marauders. The man who drives a truck through the lonely stretches south of Beersheba has a gun in the seat beside him. The worker who journeys daily from Dimona to the Dead Sea can recall, if he chooses, the times vehicles along this road have been ambushed and their occupants shot up.

For his harsh and uncertain prospects, the man who chooses the Negev is given some special consideration by the Government. Until he has a full-time job, his taxes are waived. He is given at least a half year of free medical care after he arrives. His children's schooling is free. His rent is no more than $9 a month. If he has any small cash to start with he can buy his home for a down payment of $150. If he agrees to work at S'dom or Timna or some other difficult spot he gets a salary bonus.

If he is lucky enough to live in Beersheba, he has access to the movies, to a small swimming pool and to a few modest restaurants. In Ascalon or Ashdot Yam or in the nearby settlements he has miles of Mediterranean beaches—if he can find a way to get to them.

But elsewhere he has little to look forward to once his day's work is done. In the new towns the last things that go up are the shopping and recreation centers. There is little public transport available and not much of any place to go if there were.

Above all, the man who brings his family to Israel has, either by choice or necessity, turned his back on his old home. The Government of Israel will not prevent him from leaving, but to move from one job to another in a planned economy is not easy and to quit Israel entirely is usually impossible.

There is only one problem he is certain to avoid—there is no anti-Semitism in the Negev.

Anyone who travels from Kiryat Gat to Elath, who sees Beersheba, Dimona and Ascalon, can easily be caught up by what is rising around him. But with each step ahead in the Negev, Israel has brought along a heavy load of further problems.

Most of the industries now built or under construction have been started with the Government loaning most of the initial capital and sharing in the direction. In some instances, the Government has had to subsidize them to bring their export prices down to competitive levels.

Despite the continuous increase in population, the Negev is still desperately short of trained labor. The majority of the immigrants have never before worked in either agriculture or industry.

The expansion of agriculture in the Negev is nearing its limit because of the shortage of water. The only major source left is the Jordan River. Even if the Arab nations should suddenly agree to joint use of this water, it would take Israel at least three years to complete the tunnels and pipelines to bring it here.

Most of the Negev's established farm settlements are still not self-supporting, even though some are nearly eight years old.

The mineral ores that have been found are generally of low grades; they are expensive to mine and are located far from any cheap transportation.

But despite all this, the men who are laboring so mightily to make the Negev bloom are confident they will succeed—if the money can be found to keep their schemes alive.

Israel's budget during the current fiscal year is out of balance by $350,000,000. To bridge this gap and keep going, Israel has to depend in part on the industrial equipment she is now getting from West Germany as reparations. For much of the remainder she looks to the United States, either for foreign-aid money or for the contributions of American Jewry.

Israel's agricultural development is in the hands of the Jewish Agency, the action group of the World Zionist Organization. Most of the agency's funds, last year about $80,000,000, come from the United Jewish Appeal in America. For much of her industrial development money, Israel depends on the sale of State of Israel bonds. Jews in the United States have been the heaviest buyers of these bonds ($50,000,000 in 1957).

There are now indications that the rush of immigration may be slowing down. The Jewish Agency is planning for a total of about 50,000 this year—30,000 fewer than last year. This is still a staggering number for a country as delicately balanced as Israel. But it could mean a breathing spell, of sorts.

Whether or not this happens—and there is nothing as unpredictable as Jewish immigration—the Negev will continue to occupy the attention and energies of Israel's leaders.

Not long ago Premier David Ben-Gurion, an old-time, Bible-quoting Zionist pioneer himself, said that the worst enemies Israel had were not the Arab nations, but the great desolation in the Negev and the concentration of Israel's population in the narrow coastal strip of northern Israel.

A few days later he told Israel's Knesset (Parliament): "If we thoroughly mobilize our scientific potential and pioneering initiative, and if the entire nation backs these to its fullest, it will not be impossible to convert the South and Negev into a densely populated and blooming center for hundreds of thousands, perhaps even millions, and thereby fulfill the prophecy of Ezekiel."

Why Nigeria Is "Different"

by David E. Lilienthal

THE NEWS from the Congo, Angola, Kenya, the Union of South Africa naturally leads many Westerners to think of Africa as a place of bloodshed, chaos, racial bitterness, warring tribal factions —indeed, as a threat to the continued existence of the United Nations. But it would be a grave error to concentrate solely on the problems and crises of the new Africa, and thereby to ignore its affirmative, hopeful opportunities.

Africa is a land of great opportunities, and in their realization lies the best hope of ameliorating the problems. Among the countries that represent this hopeful aspect is Nigeria, the most populous nation on the continent.

There are two chief reasons for optimism over Nigeria:

First, the progress Nigeria has made in the art and practice of responsible government. For this, some of the credit must go to enlightened British leadership in the years preceding Nigeria's accession to independence within the Commonwealth last Oct. 1. Under British and mission-school tutelage, Nigerians spent a generation in building their own trained and competent civil service.

The second is the fact that Nigeria's leaders are ambitious not

From the *New York Times Magazine,* June 11, 1961, copyright © 1961 by The New York Times Company.

for political dominance over the rest of tropical Africa, but for the development of their own country's vast resources. Chief among these is the Niger River; in the fullest use of the waters of that great stream and its tributaries lies the key to the economic and political future of this huge land and its more than 40,000,000 people.

To understand Nigeria's achievements, even this early, in self-government, one must recall the kind of nation it is. Not unlike America, Nigeria is highly diverse—not only geographically but religiously (about half the population is Islamic; the balance is either Christian or has traditional West African religious beliefs), ethnically (there are some 250 distinct tribal groups) and linguistically (scores of dialects are spoken). In addition, there are scores of tribal leaders whose secular or religious authority has ancient and deeply honored cultural foundations.

Welding these diverse forces into a single nation is a task that would exact the highest statecraft of a people with centuries, not merely decades, of experience in political democracy. The Nigerians have chosen federal union as did America's Founding Fathers almost 200 years ago. There are three "states": the Eastern, Western and Northern Regions. (The Federal Parliament recently voted to carve a fourth, the Mid-West Region, out of the Western.) Each region, and the Federal Government, has its own duly elected Parliament, Prime Minister and Cabinet, its own administrative service, its own judiciary.

An evolving instinct for accommodation—the heart of democratic self-government—has been evidenced in many ways. For example, a distinguished Nigerian, Sir Abubakar Tafawa Balewa, was recently elected Federal Prime Minister. He is a Moslem from the Northern Region, a section almost as different from the Western and Eastern Regions as New York is from Argentina or Morocco.

His defeated opponent, Dr. Nnamdi Azikiwe of Eastern Region, an extraordinarily popular man, thereupon accepted the honorific post of Governor-General—i.e., the Queen's representative and Head of State—thus voluntarily placing himself outside politics for an indefinite period.

The opposition is now headed by Obafemi Awolowo, scholarly,

precise, a kind of Woodrow Wilson in Yoruba robes. This is no "tame-bear" Opposition, yet the decorum and content of debate in Parliament compare favorably with those of many legislative bodies I have observed in other nations—my own included—where such institutions have a much longer history.

As in Britain, Cabinet Ministers are chosen from men who have been elected to Parliament. Thus they must be active politicians as well as administrators. They include men of exceptional talents. For example, the Minister of Economic Development, Jaja Wachuku, is widely admired in Britain and in the United Nations, as well as at home, for the range of his capabilities. The Minister of Mines and Power, Mallam Maitama Sule, strikes me as being among the best-informed and most clearheaded public servants I have ever met.

Another measure of capacity for self-government is the quality of the ministries' nonpolitical administrative offices—the "permanent civil servants," as they are called in the British parlance used in Nigeria. A few still are Britons, like E. G. Lewis, the far-sighted Permanent Secretary for Economic Development. Most are Nigerians.

One day in Ibadan, capital of the Western Region, I was invited to attend one of the regular meetings of the dozen or so permanent secretaries of the region, all Nigerians. They spoke of their several responsibilities   education, health, economic development, etc.—with admirable brevity and clarity. The questions they put to me had an engaging and almost startling directness and candor (this directness is the rule, I found, among Nigerians of all classes). As one who has spent most of his adult life in public service, I can testify that this group knows the business of government.

But self-government requires more than competence and dedication at the top. In the final analysis, it calls for certain qualities among the rank-and-file of the people themselves. On my trips throughout the country I saw happy people who treat each other —and their visitors—with friendly smiles and gentleness and natural, simple courtesy. These are among the very human qualities that make the trying tasks of self-government manageable.

As important as Nigeria's demonstration of an evolving capacity to govern itself is the top priority its leaders have placed on development of its natural resources. Here is where, in Nigerian eyes, the Niger River and its tributaries figure so conspicuously.

The Niger—the "black river"—is one of the longest in the world. It rises on the northerly slopes of the mountains of Guinea, near the great bulge of West Africa, and flows in a sweeping arc for 2,600 miles through the Republic of Mali (until recently the French Sudan of Foreign Legion fame), past the fabled city of Timbuktu, through the new Republic of Niger and across Nigeria to the Atlantic Ocean.

Its silt-laden waters for part of its course are truly black—not brown like the Missouri or the middle Mississippi. Before they reach Timbuktu, they sprawl out into a chain of shallow lakes and marshes, called, oddly, the delta of the upper Niger. For miles, they flow through desert, with sand dunes on either side. For stretches, they churn through labyrinths of rocks and rapids.

Across the Northern Region of Nigeria, the river courses slowly and majestically between low banks. The flat, treeless savanna stretches away on both sides, sere in the dry season. Tributaries—the Benue and the Kaduna—join the mainstream and the Niger flows more broadly. In flood, it spreads implacably across the scrub land and through the rain forest of its lower reaches, before it breaks up into the twisting channels and sodden mangrove swamps of its vast final delta.

For some years, both before and since independence, detailed hydrologic and engineering and economic studies have been made of the lower Niger's potentialities. I read these reports during my recent stay. In tone, their impersonal massing of facts and estimates could have been concerned with any underdeveloped river anywhere. They took on life when Minister Sule, the gleam in his eyes reminding me of Senator Norris in the early days of the T.V.A., told me what he and his colleagues conceive as their meaning to Nigeria:

> Electricity at low cost is the heart of our plans for the industrial development of this nation, and the raising of our peoples' living standards, throughout the cities and villages of this land. The power from the Niger is our answer.

Electricity means pumps for wells in villages where women and children now carry all drinking water on their heads for long distances, refrigeration to provide better use of food and better health, light for the new readers produced by the spread of education, local industries in rural villages now wholly dependent on farming.

The dams and reservoirs that development would bring would mean water for thirsty land, providing ample forage for cattle now gaunt during the long dry season of the north; flood control for downstream farmers, assuring them their crops will not be washed away; a navigable waterway opening great reaches of what is now back country to barges and even ocean-going vessels.

These changes could within half a generation transform the lives of Nigerians and—conceivably—of their neighbors along the Niger's upper reaches.

Engineers' plans call for a first dam at a site known as Kainji, 100 miles north of Jebba. The Kainji dam, a project estimated to cost somewhat less than $200,000,000, ultimately would have a capacity of nearly 1,000,000 kilowatts. It would be only the first step in a chain of water-control structures of the entire lower Niger system.

The concept of full development of the lower Niger River is no longer a dream. A detailed Federal Ministry of Development presentation is expected this month. Such problems as financing and organization—very difficult but solvable—are yet to be fully worked out, but the turning of the first shovel could be only months away. By 1966, if these first steps are well done, Nigeria will have taken a seven-league stride forward.

There are formidable obstacles to be overcome, of course. The task requires a high degree of coordination and management. Even the first steps require substantial amounts of capital above what Nigeria has available—probably as much as $150,000,000 of external financing. The estimates for succeeding stages are not yet complete, but the sums will be large.

Where will Nigeria turn for such help as it feels it needs—technical, managerial and financial? I do not think the assumption is far-fetched that Nigeria and the West, each in its own interest, would prefer that the aid come from the West rather than the Soviets. Both Nigeria and the West hold similar basic political ideas. And large as the sums will be, they will be less than the amounts that will be spent just to keep a modicum of order in the Congo, for example.

Furthermore, these capital outlays will be productive. I do not mean as a *quid pro quo* for "friendship" (that myth is happily about exploded), but productive in a more meaningful sense, productive for the people of Nigeria.

The direct physical benefits to Nigeria of the Niger development are by no means the only ones; there are indirect, non-material benefits of the greatest significance.

Undertaking a task so large, one that calls for so many skills both of modern technology and of social change, sets up a goal, a "national purpose," that can provide an authentic unifying force for a new nation. The challenge itself already has stirred national pride, and pride can be one of the most creative aspects of nationalism.

Moreover, the river's development invites understanding in the minds of Nigerians and of their African neighbors, of the interdependence of peoples, tribes and nations. This is indeed the beginning of political wisdom, and perhaps the best hope for ultimate peace in that troubled continent—or in the world, for that matter.

A demonstration of initiative by Nigeria in developing the lower Niger may well encourage later development programs by some of her sister new nations upstream. If this occurs, there may be an opportunity for the resulting benefits to be shared, just as Canada and the United States have agreed to share the benefits of future Canadian upstream development of the Columbia River. Thus, the Niger, as an international river, can furnish a politically stabilizing force among new nations.

Does the story of Nigeria hold the answer for the world of tropical Africa? Certainly not, but Nigeria does throw some light on possible steps toward the solution of tropical Africa's problems.

For one example, I suggest that Nigeria demonstrates there can be no real independence until, step by step, other new nations equip themselves with *their own* trained civil-service administrations. Nothing of this sort can be built up overnight, of course, but an intensive start can and should be made.

The second major lesson Nigeria may have for others in Africa lies in the focusing of her attention on her own problems and potentialities. The Niger River plan illustrates one significant way of drawing a nation's people together through a mutually shared need for national cooperation.

The third major lesson—or potential lesson—is more for the West than for Africa. It is that we should more and more concentrate on opportunities, be less preoccupied with week-by-week emergencies of the newly developing world. Nigeria is a good example of such an opportunity.

Change Comes to Africa's Villages

by Barbara Ward

THAT THE POLITICS of tropical Africa today is marked by a continuous turbulence is not really surprising. Every problem of transition confronts the continent in its most violent form—authoritarian colonial rule has to give way overnight to largely unfamiliar democratic processes; racial attitudes born of superiority and dependence have to be painfully readjusted; tribes must form nations; their leaders must adapt themselves, whether they like it or not, to the pressures of the cold war. It would require super-human wisdom to ride out this upheaval without shipwreck here and there.

Yet, of all the problems of transition, the deepest, the most enduring and probably the most difficult does not lie on the surface of politics. It is to be found at the very foundation of the new states in the effort to take the African village—where 70 or 80 per cent of the peoples of Africa still live—out of its millennial communal and tribal past into the modern world of general education and dynamic farming.

Just how far the village has to go can best be judged not in abstractions but in a concrete image of the village itself. First of all, in spite of tribal differences, in spite of the spectrum of

From the *New York Times Magazine,* November 19, 1961, copyright © 1961 by The New York Times Company.

climate and vegetation running from the arid rim of deserts through parklike savannah country to the dense, green, matted walls of the rain forest, the villages have a family resemblance. Mud huts stand in small compounds, roofs and wall tops thatched with straw or sorghum stalks or the big leaves of plantains— with an increasing incursion of stained and rusty corrugated-iron roofing in townships nearer the cities and the ports.

Mud walls, mud compounds, mud underfoot, all baked in the sun or slimy with tropical rain, make the village a splash of chrome or gray in the green ring of shade trees or the all-encompassing green of the forest. At the doors of the huts, women pound millet or Guinea corn or cassava for the family meal while the men sit under the trees and talk and smoke and talk again. Somewhere in the center, hidden behind a thick hedge or a laterite wall, is the place of the fetish. In Moslem villages, a tiny baked-mud mosque takes its place. The house of the head-man or the chief stands out by reason of the extra carving above the lintel of his door or the dignity of a large Victorian armchair in his living room. And in and out of the compounds and the alleyways run little black goats while scraggy, squawking hens peck millet from the dust.

One would say: "This has not changed in half a millennium." But everywhere the signs of change are there. In many of the villages a plain, square, concrete community hall stands upright among the sagging huts. It has been built by the villagers themselves. The market economy is reaching out to them. They have their village stores where women traders conduct transactions which vary from a hundredweight of firewood down to the transfer of a single cigarette.

Imported canned goods are displayed on trestle tables beside wood stoves roasting local plantains—the African equivalent of the hamburger. The "mammy wagons," open trucks using extravagant titles as trademarks ("God Deliver Us," "Never Say Die," "Don't Trust a Lovely Woman") roar up the village street, depositing visitors and taking on a load of passengers and yams for the near-by market. Even if the forest is all around and trees block the view beyond the first turn of the road, the wider world is pouring through and eroding the old isolation.

The economic basis of the village is beginning to change, as well. The starting point is still traditional farming in which the land is held by the village group and no one outside the clan may claim a share (although some tribes are more lenient than others in allowing strangers to rent a temporary strip). Within the group, families have the use of individual holdings and this use, but not any form of ownership, is heritable.

Whether the surrounding area is forest, savannah, or semi-arid land, the farming family's usual practice has been to clear no more than the three or four acres needed for food crops, grow yams and Guinea corn and cassava for four years and then, as the soil's fertility petered out, move on to another four-acre plot, leaving the vegetation to flow back over the old site. In fifteen years or so, the soil is restored.

The system seems confusing to the outside observer. So much land appears not to be in use at all. Forest and farm overlap in ways repugnant to tidy Western concepts. And some aspects are confusing even to the Africans themselves. There are few complete and adequate surveys; endless litigation arises over the delimitation of clan lands. Family plots, fixed by tradition, become unbelievably complex as the family grows and subdivisions occur. A village can become a patchwork of interlocking farm and fallow where no farmer can change methods or rotation without the agreement and cooperation of everyone else.

But the system has had signal virtues. Above all, it has kept a vegetable cover over Africa's friable soils and neither tropical rains nor tropical heat has washed or baked the earth into sterility.

The system is also incredibly durable. In fact, it is the special order which man has lived for by far the longest part of his history; civilization is a newcomer compared with a hundred thousand years of tribal life.

Yet change is on the way. Nature may have isolated the African farmer. But it certainly did not deprive him of the power to seize opportunities once he could see them. Wherever new openings entailed only small amounts of capital (no village community can produce massive saving) the farming communities have taken them up with purpose and vigor. Truck gardening is increasing near the cities. Where the growing of cash crops does not demand elaborate organization or plantation lines, the peasant farmers provide the bulk of the crop.

Cocoa in Ghana and Western Nigeria is grown on small farms in the forest. Ninety per cent of Nigeria's palm kernels are picked from wild palms. And there can be little doubt that many more villagers would have entered the timber trade if the initial cost of equipment had not been so high, and if the European middleman had been more ready to help. It is not dour conservatism but lack of capital that keeps the more enterprising farmers from changing the scale of their operations.

But the chief key to change in Africa today lies in the schoolhouse. In more and more of the villages, the passer-by will see a green clearing with a couple of insecure football posts stuck up in the middle and, around it, a square of low mud buildings, white-washed, roofed with thatch or corrugated iron, veranda posts painted black, cannas growing scarlet and yellow in the corners. Here the children in khaki shorts and shirts or tidy mission dresses of butcher blue chatter and race and cheer the passing cars with extravagant gaiety, or sit in the shade frowning over their reading books.

In the dark little classrooms they are quiet, attentive scholars. They try to learn their letters and figures with an almost alarming concentration. So much turns on the outcome, so many family ambitions, so many personal hopes. And they feel the cold breath of failure when their teacher says: "If you don't learn better than that, you'll have to stay on the farm."

And here begin the reasons why, although there is change in the villages of Africa, there must be more. Some of the compulsions are shared by all developing lands. More food must be grown if towns and industries are to expand. Farmers must earn more income if they are to buy the goods from an expanding industries sector. And, with or without industrial growth, traditional farming cannot indefinitely support a steadily growing population. As land runs short, the subdivisions increase, fallowing is cut, a fatal depletion of the soil sets in.

This pressure is not yet tropical Africa's main problem. But the shape of things to come is already visible in some areas. Around Owerri, in Eastern Nigeria, the fallowing time is already too short to allow the soil to recover. Trees and bushes are stunted, streams run down raw, red gulleys where the bones of the land stand out like the limbs of a starving man; eroded sheets of the clayey laterite earth appear in the clearings and on them nothing grows at all. No sight is more grim than this slow murder of the soil—our planet's "flowery earth-rind" upon which the continuance of life itself depends.

But in Africa the overwhelming need for rapid change starts not so much in eroded fields as in the tidy white buildings and noisy compound of the village school. All through the continent, education is seen—rightly—as the door to the future. "Universal primary education" is a symbol of statehood. Politicians must promise it to parents. The timetable is under constant pressure for revision—to enlarge it, to speed it up, to provide the schooling without fees. But the boy who leaves school no longer wants to work in the village where perhaps 80 per cent of the opportunities for a livelihood are still to be found.

The isolation, the oppression of forest life, the endless struggle with hoe and machete against recalcitrant vegetation, the closed-clan system, the authority of the elders—all these make up an environment stifling to the young mind that has learned something of the world beyond. The boy is up and away to the city.

In colonial times, when education covered perhaps 5 per cent of the population, his school-leaving certificate would secure him an apprenticeship in the town, or open the way to the lower rungs of the bureaucracy.

Today, such doors are closing fast. The number of school-leavers multiplies with the end of each school year. The opportunities for absorbing them in the towns do not. Already in Eastern Nigeria there may be as many as 300,000 school-leavers looking for work. Four years from now the figure may have grown to 700,000—or 40 per cent of the employable men. Estimates for Western Nigeria are not much different. There is talk of 900,000 unemployed school-leavers by 1967. No one can doubt that a social and political explosion on an incalculable scale may be in the making.

What can be done about this vast exodus from the villages?

The answers are, of course, as wide as the whole strategy of development. At one end of the scale is large-scale industrialization. But modern industry does not in the short run match its heavy capital cost with any heavy increase in employment. For example, an oil refinery that may be built at Port Harcourt in Eastern Nigeria should cost about $30 million. But it will provide only 350 jobs. This is an extreme example, but even medium-sized industries may require as much as $2,800 in capital for each worker taken on.

Another series of answers lies in stimulating small-scale and workshop production, replacing imports with local goods and introducing more efficient methods into traditional trades. Firms like Sears Roebuck in Latin America have shown what marketing organizations can do to stimulate the production of local consumer goods. The big European importers in Africa—Britain's United Africa Company, the Swiss Union Trading Company, the various French firms, S. C. O. A. and C. F. A. O.—have a big part to play here.

Even so, on the analogy of other lands, industrialization, large and small, would not do much more than absorb the future increase in rural population. The present numbers, including the present flood of school-leavers, cannot be wholly absorbed in the cities. Means have to be found to keep them, productively, on the land. And so development policy has to double back on its tracks and return to the problem of the village.

One of the possible methods of change is found not only in Africa but all through the developing world. It is to persuade the villagers to consolidate their holdings in economic plots and to provide them with the credit, the fertilizer, the improved seeds, the pattern of crop rotation, the insecticides, the storage and the marketing facilities which make intensive farming safe for the land and profitable for the farmer.

This pattern has proved possible in Kenya and in Southern Rhodesia. There, native holdings have begun to be as productive as highly capitalized European farms. But the basic reason for the improvement is the same—the very large input of capital which made the consolidation of holdings and the provision of services possible. Moreover, the crucial change in Kenyan and

Rhodesian land tenure was imposed by authoritarian European governments. Change by persuasion will cost no less and it will take much longer.

For this reason, African governments are looking for other models. One is to tempt the educated sons of farmers into new farm settlements as soon as they leave school. In Nigeria, new lands have been cleared in the bush by Government bulldozers. Here, on each new settlement, about 200 school-leavers, with a year's training in a farm institute, work together to get the land ready for farming.

Each boy can look forward to owning freehold about a 20-acre plot on which he will farm according to modern methods, with a proper rotation, fertilizers, imported seed and some farm animals to make mixed farming possible. Each plot will have its cash crops, too, and the settlement provides good housing, water, light, roads and community services.

Conditions and earnings should begin to compare with those of urban life. The boys are, in fact, pioneers of the belief that better living is possible on the land and even though the capital cost for each farmer may be as high as $8,400, a town family will pay as much today to make a son into a lawyer or a doctor. Equal expenditures may give a professional stamp to farming and also create a lasting asset in the shape of better land.

This is the argument and the boys seem cheerful enough as they drive the tractors—symbols of emancipation—out to the fields of Guinea corn or feed their N'dama cattle on the husks. Moreover, last year perhaps 40 per cent of the school-leavers in Western Nigeria applied for openings in the farm settlements— the first sign of the tide of young opinion turning back to the farm.

Some of these farm settlements will be dedicated almost wholly to cash crops and, while each boy will own his own plot, the settlement itself is to be run on the lines of a plantation. A general strategy of planting and development will be adopted and individual farmers will thus gain the advantages of modern methods of cultivation and of larger-scale operations.

The archetype of such experiments is the successful growing of cotton by peasant proprietors on individual plots in the vast irrigated estate of the Gezira in the Sudan. Such a combination of private ownership of land with a collective strategy of planting and marketing seems to combine the most productive features of both types of farming and many Africans wonder whether the idea of the cooperative plantation may not prove a master idea in tropical agriculture. The Chagga tribe in Tanganyika has shown that its communal tribal system of landholding could be adapted for the extensive production of coffee as a cash crop. May there not be here an alternative method of modifying village agriculture—one which, by persuading the community as a unit to become producers of cash crops, gives the farmers all the gains of large-scale cooperative enterprise?

But whatever the approach—community development, new farm settlements, cooperative plantations—one thing is clear. All methods, without exception, demand massive investment of fresh capital. To give only one example, Eastern Nigeria would need to spend perhaps $20 million a year to coax even a quarter of its school-leavers into new settlements. Yet the region's whole annual development budget is not much above $60 million and the agricultural estimates have to cover all the other interrelated needs of village life—water, power, extension services, roads—while $10 million and more has to be found for the recurrent costs of education alone.

This is the final universal dilemma of village development. Villages produce barely any surplus capital because they are not developed. But they cannot develop until they find the capital. The consequences are to be seen all around the world—in thrusting cities, growing ports and brisk industrial enclaves surrounded, engulfed, held back, weighed down, even stopped in their tracks by the drag of a vast, unchanging, stagnant countryside.

Yet there could be a really effective speeding up of rural change if, in the next decade of sustained economic development, the Western donor nations were prepared to put a wholly new emphasis upon capital assistance to the farms and villages in developing lands. In the past, the countryside has, of course, gained from outside aid. Road building, the construction of dams and extensions of electric power all help, directly or indirectly, to raise rural standards and a good deal of technical assistance has been made available to agricultural extension services and community development.

But what has been lacking has been any large-scale, multiple-sided, consistently thought-through program for accelerating rural development in *all* its facets. In the Indian subcontinent, governments are feeling their way toward such a concept—in India's "special project districts," in Pakistan's plans for agricultural corporations charged with the task of planning over-all development for specific areas. That such an approach would be applicable in Africa has been shown by the success of the Swynnerton Plan in Kenya in which heavy doses of capital and competently integrated planning were used to resettle Kikuyu farmers on economic holdings and to give them the stock, the credit and the extension services needed to make a success of the new methods.

If, now, a similar systematic concentration of forethought, capital and technical skill were applied to farming in other African regions, there could be a corresponding adoption of more dynamic techniques and the creation in the countryside of a new kind of life for the farmers.

The opportunity is more than economic. Political and social instability is the price paid for stagnant agriculture and the uncontrolled drift of semiliterates to towns where no work—and the political agitator—await them. In the end, we return to the point at which we began. There can be no halt to the turbulence of African politics without some restoration of social cohesion at new levels of skill and choice. The village still holds the key to this cohesion. Restore it there, and Africa regains a foundation upon which to build up securely and productively its new, adventurous, post-colonial, post-tribal patterns of life.

Mexico Follows a "Solo Camino"

by Keith Botsford

MEXICO CITY

SOMEWHERE AT the back of my mind there is the title of a dreadful travelogue seen in my childhood: "Mexico—Land of Paradox." Commonplace though it is, the phrase is perfectly adapted to the Mexican presidency.

As I write, a modest, capable lawyer who, like most Mexican politicians has come up the hard way through the ranks—Catholic, calm, colorless, without any pretensions to intellectual or physical distinction—is touring the provinces in a "campaign" which is exactly like one of ours—in everything but reality. His name is Gustavo Diaz Ordaz, and he is the candidate of the Party of the Institutional Revolution, or P.R.I.

The P.R.I. is only one of several parties in Mexico (for appearances' sake, a Federal law encourages the continued existence of others), and Diaz Ordaz is not even the only candidate, but everyone in this country of nearly 40 million inhabitants—the most modern and most ancient, the toughest and the most temperamental of the republics south of the border—knows that he will win next July's election and that, short of the swearing-in, he is the next President of Mexico.

The Mexican presidency is an institution baffling to anyone except a Mexican, yet the system has worked for close to 50

From the *New York Times Magazine,* April 26, 1964, copyright © 1964 by The New York Times Company.

years, giving the country a unity and stability precious in Latin America. Constitutionally, the presidency in Mexico, as in the United States, is but one among three separate and equal branches of government. Actually, a Mexican President has at his disposal as much absolute power—though for various reasons he chooses not to flaunt it—as any dictator in Latin America.

The legislature is a rubber stamp. The judiciary is both overworked and lacking in self-confidence. The executive is both enormous and incredibly far-reaching. More than 80 ministries, departments, agencies and other dependencies reach nearly every sector of Mexican life, from the armed forces to the petroleum industry, from social security to small businesses to Indian affairs. They are under the President's direct control. He not only makes the budget, he also spends the money. For the six years of his term, he decides what shall be done, by whom, when and how—without anyone to say boo to him.

Within the lines laid down by over-all P.R.I. and Mexican national policy, his control is total as is the adulation—so dear to the Mexican public—which surrounds him. (It is said that Lázaro Cárdenas, when he became President 30 years ago, wished to avoid this total immersion in sycophancy, and appointed a court gadfly to tell him the truth rather than what he wanted to hear. It is also said that by the end of his term Cárdenas, too, had succumbed: The voice of the gadfly was stilled.)

A typical day for a Mexican President runs from 10 A.M. to 10 P.M., with a break for the traditional Mexican lunch from 3 to 5. He will meet daily with his own staff, and at regular intervals with department heads, ministers and the directors of such organizations as the petroleum monopoly and the national bank. Full Cabinet meetings are rare. At least once a month, he will pay a ceremonial visit to some part of the country; these tours help keep him in touch with the nation and with the state governments. And in the course of a month he will receive 100 or more individuals or groups with petitions or grievances—for, as head of the nation, he is rather like a tribal chieftain, the court of ultimate resort for anyone unable to get satisfaction from the regular agencies of government.

With such power, it is not surprising that each Mexican President leaves his personal mark on his administration. Thus Cárdenas (1934–40), who nationalized the oil industry, distributed more than twice as much land to Mexican peasants as all other presidents since the Revolution put together. Avila Camacho (1940–46) shifted the country from Cárdenas' "socialistic" and agrarian leanings and began its transformation to an industrial nation.

Miguel Alemán (1946–52) was responsible for the roads, the dams, the irrigation projects, University City and thousands of other tangible public works—all of which proved eminently profitable to the country's business interests (and the President's associates). Adolfo Ruiz Cortines (1952–58) will be remembered chiefly for his efforts to eliminate graft and corruption, and for taking the first steps toward economic planning.

Adolfo López Mateos, President for the past six years, has steered a middle course—on the one hand, nationalizing electricity and a portion of the mining industry, building up the social-security system and resisting pressures to adopt a tougher attitude toward Cuba; on the other hand, providing incentives to the growth of private investment and stabilizing the economy.

Mexicans say jokingly that to every handsome President there succeeds an ugly one, but it is true that among the Presidents just mentioned no two in a row represent the same tendency. Rather, the excesses of each are corrected by his successor. Yet through the middle there is a very clear line, and each President has moved closer to that middle line.

One reason for this is that, though his power is absolute, a Mexican President chooses to operate within well-defined limits. Two factors help to explain why: history and the P.R.I.

We tend to forget, after some 50 years, that Mexico has been the scene of one of the major revolutions in history, one of the few that completely changed the structure of a country. Out of this revolution came a new class and though its allegiance today may be more verbal than real, this class still depends, politically and economically, on the revolution and the institutions that grew out of it.

In the early days, when Mexico was hardly a nation, the President could rule only by playing off rival war lords, one against another. He had to be stronger, wilier and more ruthless than his rivals. The key to Mexico's emergence as a true nation was the foundation in 1929 of a party which would embrace all the tendencies within the revolution and work out their differences inside the party, while agreeing on how and by whom real political power could be wielded. This was the P.R.I.

Once the P.R.I. was founded, the presidency was able to develop from *caudillismo* to the institutional stage, to the point where it now is a structure that will operate and survive regardless of who holds the office. There remain, however, anomalies in the system. The most curious is the process by which Mexican Presidents are selected, the notorious *tapado*.

"*Tapado*" means, literally, "bottled-up," concealed, and that is what Diaz Ordaz, for instance, was until uncorked a few months ago before an expectant but unenthusiastic public.

The *tapado* is a professional's game. The public has no voice in the matter. The result is that most presidential candidates are faceless when nominated, and the role of the "campaign" is to get them known.

No one knows the exact process, but there is general agreement that the final decision as to who his successor shall be belongs to the outgoing President. He does not, however, act in solitary splendor. His decision must reflect the feeling of a majority of his party, a delicate equilibrium among all the tendencies within the P.R.I. To determine who might be acceptable, the President canvasses widely: in the party, among former Presidents, the ministries, the armed forces, labor and even among the other parties.

It is easy to see that the result of so much delicate negotiating is necessarily rather colorless, odorless and tasteless. Obviously, a candidate acceptable to *everyone* cannot depart very far from a sort of unwritten norm.

There are a hundred arguments against the *tapado,* of which the strongest is that it saps the political process at its base. But equally, the P.R.I. can present arguments in its favor, of which the most telling is that of "unity" and "stability." An open fight for the presidency could break the party into a hundred splinters, and then Mexico would be back with its sister republics of Latin America, in a political never-never land. Undemocratic the system may be, but it does reflect Mexican reality, and it does reflect the P.R.I.

The P.R.I. is unlike any other political party. First, it is completely unideological. It thinks in terms of bridges, hog production and a firm hand at the helm, not in terms of ideas. The world outside Mexico hardly exists, and foreign relations consist of banalities in favor of peace, disarmament and motherhood. Consequently, it has concrete and tangible results to offer the people, and at the same time it has avoided the ideological battles to which so many parties in Latin America have succumbed.

Second, it is an agglomeration of tendencies. It seeks to incorporate *everybody,* including such seeming incompatibles as business and labor, church and anticlerical groups. It can do this because its "revolutionary" bias is not very clearly defined, and by no means practiced consistently.

Unlike Venezuela's *Acción Democratica,* for instance, which tried to remain pure and thus drove its dissidents into the opposition, the P.R.I. absorbs, promotes and keeps a watchful eye on those who might form a potential opposition.

In some areas the P.R.I. can claim 97 per cent of the electorate as members; in others, less. It all depends on the efficiency of the local machine, and ultimately means very little— votes, not membership, create the party's power. (The P.R.I. has its activists and its passive base; other Mexican parties have their activists, every six years, but they have no base.)

Third, the P.R.I. is organized throughout the country in every imaginable form of substructure. Wherever two whitewashed houses shine under the hard, bright Mexican sun, one seems to bear the emblem of the P.R.I. The Mexicans, great joiners, all have a home somewhere in the P.R.I., in one of the agricultural, industrial or professional sectors, in the women's organization, the youth organization, the manufacturers' organization and so on. Thus, though different groups may have different tendencies, tensions are worked out on a series of levels, avoiding open struggles for power.

It is the P.R.I. which answers one of the most important questions about the Mexican presidency: Why is the office, with all its power, not abused?

The various tensions within the P.R.I. and its responsiveness to these pressures, even at the base, help to keep the President within bounds, just as a basic respect for democratic forms enables the party to avoid evolving into a totalitarian bureaucracy imposed on a voiceless mass. As the heir to the Revolution, the party helps determine policies, even as in consultation with the outgoing President, it helps nominate the new Chief Executive. Thus, beforehand, the President is limited by the general tendencies of the political machine that puts him in office, and these tendencies—again, as distinct from totalitarianism—are based on pressures from the electorate manifested within the P.R.I. They are not imposed; they are a basically middle-of-the-road consensus.

Diaz Ordaz, for instance, even if he wishes to, cannot go far in restoring communal agricultural property to private ownership; it is difficult to imagine him denationalizing any part of the public sector of the Mexican economy, or desecularizing Mexican education, despite the fact that he will be the first openly Catholic President since the Revolution; he cannot with impunity abandon the Mexican tradition of nonintervention in hemispheric affairs, though many think he will try; he cannot alter the social-welfare programs or abandon what his predecessors have begun. In other words, the Mexican Revolution has its tradition, and it is only within that tradition that the presidency can operate.

This is far from saying that the President is a stooge of the Establishment which has put him in office. Obviously, the powers-that-be choose a man in their own image, but the moment he becomes President he becomes also the head of the Establishment. To the extent that he possesses force and imagination, he can make significant shifts in its image.

It can be asked whether the Mexican people like this situation; the question is not particularly relevant. In the first place, despite substantial progress in the 50 years since the Revolution, it is doubtful whether more than 10 or 15 per cent of the population is actually interested or involved in the electoral process. In spite of compulsory registration, according to a recent estimate only 31 per cent of those eligible vote. Secondly, it is unlikely that a real consciousness of political power can develop out of elections that are a foregone conclusion.

The average Mexican has been accustomed throughout history to being ruled. He is grateful for small mercies. The P.R.I. is a great step forward from the Indian kings, from the Spanish Empire and from the dictatorship of Porfirio Díaz.

The nation is not very demanding. A few tangible signs of progress, however slow, satisfy it. Besides, countries in the early stages of development like Mexico respond as much to rhetoric as to achievement, and the present Establishment offers a revolution and nationalism, two potent psychological satisfactions. Anyway, the opposition—limited to a very small urban, educated part of the population—has offered no meaningful alternative to the P.R.I.

On the right, there is the P.A.N. (*Partido Acción Nacional*) representing private enterprise and, more particularly, the church; on the left, a multitude of small and powerless parties whose leaders, such as Vicente Lombárdo Toledano, prefer to make their peace with the P.R.I. rather than preach in the desert. Under the new electoral law, designed to create an "opposition," there may be a slightly increased number of non-P.R.I. Deputies (they now number six out of 178—with none in the Senate), yet the opposition will still be token. The P.R.I. monopolizes the issues as well as the Government.

But how long can the present system last? The affairs of state become more complex as a nation develops. To handle with efficacy the multitudinous problems of planning, the interplay of investment, and of the private and public sectors of the economy, of agricultural and industrial development, of population pressures and a hundred other social and cultural factors, is now beyond the capacities of any single politician.

The Mexican presidency is clearly going to have to evolve beyond its present enormous concentration of authority in the hands of the Chief Executive. No man can continue to decide everything in a country growing as fast as Mexico.

Similarly, Mexico cannot for too much longer remain isolated in a sort of provincial limbo, with such vague slogans as *"Un solo camino—Mexico"* ("A single path—Mexico") as a substitute for thought on the international scene, particularly in regard to hemispheric affairs. Within the nation, the President can still be a friend to everyone; but it is not so easy to be everyone's friend in the international family.

What can one expect then, from the Mexican presidency in the future? First, greater continuity and more emphasis on technical planning; second, the assumption of more serious responsibilities on the international scene. Both of these developments require an informed electorate.

The P.R.I. is an extraordinary organism, and the presidency in Mexico has been exercised with dignity and a good measure of loyalty to the people. The final question, however, is whether the day when the Government can no longer be run by the professionals *for* the public without the latter's active participation can long be postponed. The answer to this question lies within the P.R.I.

How Life Has Changed in a Cuban Sugar Mill Town

by José Yglesias

THE EXECUTIVES of the United Fruit Company's largest sugar mill in Cuba lived on La Avenida, a street lined with regal coconut palms along the blue-green Bay of Nipe in Oriente Province. Their old-fashioned Southern homes were cared for, in every case, by a cook, a cleaning man and a gardener, paid out of a monthly company allotment. At the railroad crossing behind La Avenida and at the start of the avenue near the sugar mill, there were always guards to keep out Cubans who were not on specific errands.

Now the pavement is cracked, the gardens unkempt and the white paint almost gone; three houses have burned down. Luis Chao, the Chinese who worked for the company administrator, stands on the long porch of the Visitor's House and exclaims, "Bad, bad, bad, they do not know how to live here!" For in 1960, when the sugar mill was nationalized, the poorest of the poor from the *batey*—the Cuban name for the town around a sugar mill—were moved into La Avenida. The largest families from the neighborhood called Brooklyn took over the street,

From the *New York Times Magazine,* July 23, 1967, copyright © 1967 by The New York Times Company.

two to each house. They have made it their own: little Negro children play ball on the street, and their parents now have elbow room to keep chickens, goats, cows and pigs. The calm of that street—like the hierarchy of the old company town—is gone forever.

La Avenida is now called Katanga. United Fruit's name for the mill, Central Preston, was changed to Central Guatemala at a nationalization ceremony in 1960 at which Jacobo Arbenz, the deposed President of Guatemala, was the guest of honor. Most of the 6,000 people in the town of Guatemala live in its two other neighborhoods, Brooklyn and New York (their names remain unchanged). New York lies on the other side of the railroad from La Avenida. The railroad, like everything else in the town, was once private property, built by United Fruit to bring in the cane from its own fields, and here in the best houses near the administration building lived the Cuban office workers; in lesser houses away from the offices lived the skilled mill workers. Brooklyn also has two sections: on one side of the railroad there are two-family houses of three rooms each; on the other, barracks-like buildings (the *barracones*) composed of some 20 rooms, each measuring 10 by 10, one family to a room. New York was overwhelmingly white, Brooklyn Negro.

The town and the mill lie on a finger of land poking north into the Bay of Nipe along the northern side of Cuba on the Atlantic, 15 hours by bus from Havana and three hours from the eastern tip of the island. Inland begin the mountains of the Sierra del Cristal, which end in the south at Guantánamo where, in 1958, nine months before Batista's fall, Raúl Castro opened the second front of the insurrection. Except at Nicaro and Moa, further east, where nickel and manganese are manufactured, this northern section of Oriente—the province known as the cradle of Cuban revolutions—is a dense, green, undulating sea of cane.

The Bay of Nipe is 14 miles long and 8 miles wide, but United Fruit's 300,000 acres made it almost a private lake. On the wall of one of the ground-floor offices of the administration building there still survives a blueprint map of the area drawn by the company's engineers, and here and there around the bay are little pockets with the laconic statement: "Owned By Others." In 1959, with the Agrarian Reform, the company lost ownership of the sugar cane fields; in 1960, the mill itself was nationalized. The Americans on La Avenida packed up and left; by the time of nationalization, the administrator of the mill was a Cuban who had been an assistant in the accounting department; today he is exiled in Miami.

There are 152 sugar mills in Cuba, each with its own *batey,* and life in each is very much like that in Guatemala, orbiting about the production of the mill and the seasonal nature of sugarcane production. Oriente towns differ from those in other provinces in that harvesting and milling, which start in January, go on into July; in other provinces not as rich in cane, the mills begin to halt in April. But Guatemala has its unique features: Americans brought to the town amenities not found in others. True, many of these comforts were restricted to Americans, to lure them to overseas jobs, but Cubans with jobs could enjoy them, too—the shops filled with American goods, the hospital, the bakery, the houses in the New York section. Today the consumer goods are no longer there, but everything else is. On one of my trips by car to Guatemala, the Cuban doctors with me— who were seeing it for the first time—kept saying, "Charming, charming!"

Like other Cuban towns, Guatemala's government is called the *Administración,* but it is concerned mainly with community services rather than political activities. Guatemala is part of the municipality of Guaro, a nearby town, and has the equivalent of a mayor in Rilde Paredes, a short, wiry man of 30 who lives in the worst part of Brooklyn and gets about on a motorbike. He is appointed to his job by the Party (the Communist party, today the official Government party), but for the last two years his appointment and the work plan for the town have had to be approved by an *asamblea*—a meeting to which all the townspeople are called—held once or twice a year, depending on whether the winter assembly will interfere with the harvest. (This policy of the last two years is called "decentralization," a departure from the paralyzing, vertical rule of the Havana ministries which made local initiative impossible, so that even the construction of a neighborhood park had to be referred back to the capital for approval.) The sugar mill is owned by Minaz, the sugar ministry, and Paredes' relation to it, like that of all officials, is to be helpful in meeting its production goals. Paredes doesn't seem to enjoy any special prestige, for when he took me on my first visit to the mill, the guard at the gate, an old friend of his from the Brooklyn district, apologized at length but didn't let us in until he got approval by telephone from Orden Público, the town police, which as part of the Ministry of the Interior is responsible for plant security.

Though the social realities of the town have changed—there are no more private clubs for Americans or Cuban office employes, no more limitations on the use of the hospital (mill employes only) or of the pool (La Avenida residents only), no more racial discrimination—the concern for the Central, the towering mill, remains, though with heightened ideological overtones. A story about Roberto Henderson, the only top executive of U. S. origin who returned to Cuba after having left with the others, is typical. At a meeting of the executives in 1960, he alone objected to the angry statement of the administrator that the Cubans wouldn't be able to make sugar without the Americans. Henderson insisted that no American had ever made sugar at the Central; that had been the work of the Cubans. This proud part of the story done, the narrator usually adds, with the Cubans' love of piquancy, that it was Henderson's Cuban wife, not he, who had wanted to leave. (The argument continued in the States, where they were divorced. But in the end, Henderson won; they were remarried and returned to Cuba.)

The Central is one of the giant mills, with a capacity for grinding 15,400,000 pounds of cane a day, enough to fill approximately 450 railroad cars. But whether the Central is efficient is a subject of debate, and the position taken is usually—though not always—an index to the politics of the speaker.

In the United Fruit era, the mill turned out daily as many as 13,000 bags, each holding 250 pounds of sugar. Today the Central averages about 8,000 such bags a day. Revolutionaries do not deny these facts, but they have answers and explanations. They point out that the company limited the production period to three months; now the harvest lasts at least six months, and thus the total production figures are higher. They say that the grade of sugar produced now is much finer than the crude brown sugar La United (pronounced "you-nye") manufactured and that the equipment of the mill is old and does not work at maximum efficiency.

There is general agreement, however, that the main problem derives from the cane fields, not the mill. La United had 14,000 cane-cutters in the fields, all experts and backed by their wives and children to help gather and pack the cane in the railroad cars that shuttle between field and mill. Overseers would halt the cutting periodically to make certain that there were empty cars ready to take what was cut. Thus, when the cane reached the mill, it was still fresh; and since cane-cutting was piecework, this could be done without cost to the company.

Now, with full employment in Cuba, full-time *macheteros* are not readily available and volunteers must do much of the cutting. And since they must be used when they are available, the cutting has to be done without the periodic delays that would insure the cane's freshness when taken to the mill. The cane often lies in the fields a couple of weeks after cutting, its juice drying and its acid content rising.

One afternoon I came to the railroad crossing, and there were no cars waiting their turn to enter the mill. "Where are they?" I said to the flagman, who was squatting with a friend at the crossing. He shrugged with disgust. One of the three milling belt lines had had to shut down temporarily.

The flagman's crony, a retired machinist, got up. "It is the usual inefficiency. They cannot do anything right."

The belt line started up again in a couple of hours, but the flagman and his friend, eager to talk to someone new, went through a thorough denunciation of every aspect of Cuban life. "I tell you, if some ships appeared in the bay right now, they would sink from the number of people who would try to leave on them!"

Such frank talk did not surprise me; it can make a Cuban unpopular, but it is unlikely that he will be arrested or lose his job. Orden Público in Guatemala had only five full-time men; its equivalent of the police chief was a young man of 24 who seemed to spend every afternoon playing ball; much of the guard duty at the mill was done by the volunteer militia. In a town where everyone knows everyone else, your ideological position—as well as everything else about you—is well-known. The head of the Ministry of the Interior for the entire region had admitted to me that counterrevolutionary surveillance was a minor part of his job now; and the Committees for Defense of the Revolution, organized on a block basis to wipe out counterrevolutionary activity, now listed "vigilance" as only one of the 17 "fronts" on which it was active.

Convinced political opponents have left (none that I know of was killed or jailed), are waiting to leave or are defeatedly aware they cannot organize to turn the Revolution away from Communism. This last is probably the only point on which, say, the local head of the Ministry of the Interior and the *disgustados* —the unhappy—agree. In any case, the authorities seem to have no great concern on this score. During the three months I spent in Cuba I didn't observe anyone assigned to watch me, but revolutionaries would proudly say: "Everyone is watching, and you can be sure that you will be reported to Orden Público if they think you are carrying messages—or bombs—for the C.I.A." When I repeated this to an old colleague of Hubert Matos (the insurrectionary leader jailed in 1959 for his opposition to the course of the Revolution), a man now living and working quietly near Guatemala, he sadly nodded.

Curiously, all this has made for a more relaxed public life in Cuba. Guatemala has no loudspeakers in the town square, but Mayari, the nearest city-sized town, does; yet what one hears— and only during the day—are simply the regular radio programs, mostly pop tunes, and they can, in any case, usually be heard blaring from the home radios that Cubans like to turn on loud. Castro gave five radio talks during my stay, and not as many people remained up past their normal bedtime as they did in the early days; they heard the rebroadcasts the next day or read the full text in the papers. This doesn't mean that the propaganda arm of the Party, the Committees for Defense of the Revolution, the trade unions—all mass organizations, in fact—do not organize to blanket town and country in support of national campaigns. While I was there, the harvest was all-important, and newspapers, posters, announcements during station breaks reported its progress and urged Cubans to go to the cane fields and cut cane in their off-hours.

The nature of the political climate in Cuba was such that I

could engage in relatively free-wheeling discussions without fear
that I, or those I talked with, would be thought conspirators.
Thus, for example, I did not hesitate to continue the conversation begun with the complaining flagman and his friend at the
railroad crossing.

The talk turned to the subject of the harvest. "They say there
used to be more *macheteros* cutting cane in the old days," I
suggested.

"They say, they say!" said the flagman. "They say they are
planting more of everything all over Cuba—where is the food?"

His crony waved a hand irritably. "There are more cane-cutters
now—the whole country is cutting cane, the shops are closed all
the time, but they cannot do anything right!"

"They do not know how to cut cane. The *macheteros* are all in
the army," said the flagman.

"But the army is cutting cane," I said.

"Why should they cut cane," he answered, "when they do
not get enough to eat?"

"But the *campesinos*—the peasants—are still here, and they
know how to cut cane," I said.

The flagman got red with anger. "The *campesinos* are sons of
whores!"

The flagman earns $4 a day and his crony, the retired machin-
ist, gets a pension of $2.50 a day. The machinist would have
got less than half that before the Revolution, but there was no
rationing then, and the stores were full of goods; also, one could
buy at lower prices from *campesinos* and fishermen. The rationing is strict but honest; prices at the Government stores are more
or less the same. But the *campesinos* sell their chickens and
vegetables at three times the store price. The best meal at Guatemala's restaurant or cafeteria costs as much as $3.80, or what the
flagman earns in one day. However, it is usual for a family to
have several earners now, and for some of the children to be
away from home at a live-in school where absolutely everything
they need is supplied free.

Nevertheless, the housewife spends an enormous amount of
time shopping and keeping an eye peeled for the vegetable truck
that supplies her store. And the best thing even a revolutionary
can find to say about the food situation—as did one member of

the Federation of Women on her way home after being disappointed at the vegetable stand—is, "We get along. We have to sell what we produce to pay for all the building and development the Revolution is doing."

The ration book allows the following per person: rice, four pounds a month; lard or oil, one pound every 21 days; beans, three-quarters of a pound a month; butter, two ounces a month; malanga, a potato-like vegetable, two pounds a month; coffee, one and a half ounces a week; milk, one bottle of fresh a month, a varying number of cans for children up to the age of 13 and four cans for adults over 65; tomato puree, one-half can a month; salt, one-half pound a month; onions, one pound a month; one chicken a month per family; and one-quarter pound of meat a week. Any food not mentioned here is unrationed, including bread and sea food. And during the harvest, workers at the mill, who work seven days a week, can get extra provisions.

In Havana the regular ration of meat is three-quarters of a pound a week, three times as much as at Guatemala; the rationale is that people in the big cities can raise neither pigs nor chickens, nor get easily to the farmers who sell them. It is legal to sell a chicken or a pig for consumption, but not parts of either, and the buyer cannot buy for resale.

Not everyone complains about the rationing, however. Mrs. Juana Poyato, now living in the better section of New York, called me up to her porch to have coffee. I had met her at the mill the previous night and had stopped to talk because it was a surprise to find a woman—particularly a gray-haired woman—working in the mill. Her job was to keep the *guarapo,* the cane juice, flowing, and she had to wield long, heavy brooms on her 7 P.M.–to–3 A.M. shift. She is 56, has 11 children and until recently lived in one of the three-room, two-family houses of Brooklyn. "We were 15 persons in all," she said, "and now look at my palace!"

I asked her about the rationing. "I do not know if it is bad— I tell you frankly—because I always had it bad. How can I tell you I do not get ham when I never had ham? You know when I had ham? One of my sons used to work for the Americans in their garden, and when they had ham and had sliced off all the meat from the bone, they would wrap up the bone and give it to him and say, 'Here, give it to your mother.' I would throw it in a pot with water and vegetables—and beans if there were any— and hope it would fill my children's stomachs."

Later that day I stood on the steps of the pharmacy on the town square to photograph the charming park, which had been completely made over since the Revolution, and I soon found myself in a conversation with the pharmacist. It was a surprise to find that he had been the pharmacist there for 30 years, since someone with such a position seemed the likeliest candidate for the trek to Miami. (Unlike other towns in Cuba, the only private enterprises at Guatemala are the barber shops; United Fruit owned everything, and the *Administración* simply took over.)

Whenever I would point out that he personally could not be doing as well now, he would tell me about some practice of the old days that he despised. When I said he must at least have eaten better, he countered, "In this life you have to be human. What was the use of eating well when hundreds around you were starving?"

I asked him, then, what he liked about the Revolution. "Everything," he said. I threw up my arms. "I shall tell you what I like," he said. "I love construction, and when I see the construction of houses and schools—oh, wait until you get to Levisa near Nicaro and see them building a whole new city!—when I see our great projects, I am thrilled. What did we spend our time doing before? And remember, I do not blame La United for anything; I blame the Government. Why, we spent our time juggling for position. To get out from under the *barracones* [the barracks-like structures, which were built on four-foot stilts]— yes, people lived under the *barracones* in Brooklyn and put up cardboard and sacks to make walls! To try to get out from under the *barracones* into the 10-by-10 rooms. To try to move from Brooklyn into New York and then to get a house in the better section or to get a house on a street that was lighted, for there was always some little thing that made someone superior or inferior to you."

The next morning, on my last day at Guatemala, I squatted on the stoop of a kiosk in Brooklyn, and talked to the man with a wooden leg who ran it. A Negro and a young mulatto from the *barracones* joined us. No one lives *under* the barracks any more, but they are still there and almost as crowded as before. Besides the houses in New York and La Avenida, which emptied after the Revolution, the authorities have built only some 175 new units (75 more should be completed this year); and though the Government plans to demolish all the *barracones,* only three have been torn down. I was told that at least two more might have been demolished when the tenants moved out, but the authorities did not act fast enough and new tenants had rushed in.

Most of the *barracones* are 60 years old and consist of 10 rooms back to back with 10 others; there are public latrines and showers nearby and also sinks for washing clothes. Around the buildings are cement drains for rain-water; everything else, including the streets, is dirt. There was a strike in the forties that brought electricity to the barracks, but it was not until the Revolution that running water became available inside the rooms. The kiosk man and his friends told me all this, for all three had been born and reared there.

"Remember Sanchez," said the Negro. "He was one of the company guards who used to police the area and run out people living under the building. Well, he retired and the company threw him out of his house like they did everyone who retired or the families of those who died. Yes sir, he ended up living under a *barracón!*"

Everyone at the barracks has added a ramshackle porch to his room, but that is all the expansion that can occur. The young mulatto with us sighed: "Oh, how I wish there would be an end to these *barracones."*

I asked if there was a rat problem, and the young mulatto leaned away from me to get a better look at a man naive enough to ask such a question. Then he laughed.

The kiosk man said, "I got bit on my one ankle last night."

The mulatto had found two in his traps that morning, and a chicken of a neighbor's had had her crop eaten while she slept on her nest.

"We keep all our food in bottles," said the Negro. "Peña was saying the other day that his damn goose could not hatch her eggs and then he took a closer look and found the eggs were all perfect, empty shells. It is a marvel how they can suck out an egg through a little pinhole!"

It made them all laugh.

The young mulatto looked at me. "You know, there are still many filthy people about," he said. "Sometimes you go into the showers and you find dung there." He sighed again: "How I wish we could see the last of the *barracones!*"

I asked about the food. "We manage," one said, and the others nodded: the sign of good revolutionaries.

When I left them, I went over to the Party headquarters. It was closed, and I waited with a 52-year-old woman named Luisa Durán, who was worried about a scholarship for which her youngest daughter had applied. The argument she had with the Party Secretary was the last political discussion I heard in Guatemala and the most interesting.

"I fear my daughter is not going to get the scholarship," she said to him, "for she is not one of the lucky ones."

"I am surprised she did not get one last fall," said the Party Secretary, "there were 700 from here who did."

Luisa shrugged, so he turned to me. "I saw you in Brooklyn, but I could not stop. You know we are going to eradicate all those *barracones.*"

Luisa gave an unbelieving smile. "When it comes to housing, it is still the same here as before the Revolution."

I asked her why. "Let me not talk," she said. "What is the use?"

The Party Secretary urged her.

"Listen, I have been here before," she said, "and I have been to the administration office innumerable times. I wish Fidel would come here, I would tell him. I am not afraid, for I do not lie. I am a revolutionary, an *old* revolutionary, a Communist of the old Socialist party, and I tell you it is a shame what they have done to my old man that he is still living in Brooklyn." She had told me she had four children, her husband was retired and they lived in one of the three-room houses.

"But that is just our problem," said the Party Secretary, "that we need houses for everyone and that it takes time. Now at least we can say that everyone has hygienic conditions."

"Hygienic?" she said, and gave him a disgusted look. "You want to see the house I have lived in for 26 years? And do not talk to me about gastroenteritis! A new word they have given us with the Revolution. It is vomiting and diarrhea, and all it is is bad digestion. I know, you are going to tell me that having a pig causes gastroenteritis. Let one of those little doctors come and tell me that, and I shall tell him he lies!"

"Let us not argue about that. It is something the scientists tell us, and you and I have to accept it," said the Party Secretary, not too enthusiastically, for he had been a *campesino* until five years ago, and it must cost him a great effort not to raise a couple of pigs around the house.

"All I can tell you is the Revolution does not care for us old folks," said Luisa. "My old man is retired three years with a miserable $38 a month when he worked all his life and earned two retirements."

The Party's man said he could not be getting that small a pension if he had been a stevedore. "I know, I know," said Luisa. "He retired before they passed the law increasing them. I tell you, if you are an old man, they do not care about you. I was a Socialist before you were, and you have to have been a Socialist in those days to know how hard they were."

"So it comes down to the fact that you want to move to a better house," he said. "But people who are in worse conditions get precedence, you know that."

"You know who gets the houses," she said disdainfully.

I said there were large families on La Avenida.

"That was at first," she said in a kind tone because I was a newcomer. Then she gave the Party man an accusing look.

"It is true that we have to give the technicians some of the new houses," he said.

"Aha!" said Luisa.

"They are people who live in their own homes in Havana, and we want them to come here with their special knowledge. We cannot offer them the worst we have!"

"Where do you live?" Luisa asked, with narrowed eyes.

It turned out that the Party Secretary lived in the emergency prefabs built for people who had lost their homes in Hurricane Flora in 1963. He has a two-bedroom house with tiny living room and kitchenette. It gave Luisa pause; then she said, "How many are you?"

"Eight," said the Party man.

"Then you must know those houses are no good," she said. "I would not live there."

"You would not live there!" said the Party Secretary. "You must have had privileges in the old days. You say you had no trouble getting treated at the hospital—what about the people from the country who did not have the kind of relationship you had with Dr. Ortega that got you that privilege?"

"Listen, I do not lie," said Luisa. "I was a Socialist long before you, and I do not lie. The only time I lie is when I see a Negro and I call him a mulatto, or when I see a mulatto and I act as if I saw nothing. Dr. Ortega never failed to treat me or to give me medicine when a ship had not come in."

"And how long were the periods when ships did not come for sugar and there was no work for stevedores like your husband?"

"There was one time when a ship did not come in for three months and 20 days," Luisa said. "But Dr. Ortega and Raspail at the grocery treated me well. Raspail gave us credit; now, if you do not have 20 cents you get nothing."

"I do not ask you to lie," said the Party man. "I ask you to say that the *campesinos* could not get credit you did or treatment at the hospital."

"What if I told you that the *campesinos* always got treated free at the hospital?" said Luisa.

The Party man colored and got angry for the first time. "I will tell you about my sister. We brought her on our backs in a hammock because she was so sick we thought she was dying and because there was no ambulance, nothing at all with which to bring her across country. And when we got to the hospital, your Dr. Ortega—who is so kind and is now up North [in the States] —said, lay her down there, we cannot admit her unless you pay $175 now! And we ran around like madmen borrowing the money."

"But she got treated?"

"Yes, and we sold every animal we had to pay for it.

"Now tell me," he went on, when he had calmed down, "you have four children, one girl married in Havana and working in the hospital, one son working, one daughter a teacher and one applying for a scholarship?" He turned to me. "You are going to see how much money is coming into that house."

Luisa protested that the daughter and son who were married could not help support them, and the teacher only cleared $86 a month.

"Isn't your son in the militia?" said the Party man. "I think I know him."

He was; so were her daughters.

"And you, you would carry a gun, right?"

"If they came, if they invaded? I would cook for the soldiers; I am too old to fight."

It made them happy with each other. I asked Luisa just what her house was like, for I hadn't yet been in that part of Brooklyn. "Come with me, and I will show you," she said, aggrieved again.

It was a miserable place. There was a narrow porch, which four people would crowd, separated by a low wooden railing from a porch belonging to the other half of the house. Each room was tiny; a bed took up most of the living room. But it turned out her married son lived in the other half of the house, and the daughter who taught was moving away soon to be near the place where she studied nights. Then they would be only three— a glorious situation compared with the *barracones*.

"I told the Party official right to his face," Luisa said to Mirda, the daughter who taught. "We have been treated very bad."

I asked Mirda if she felt the way her mother did. She was wary and said no. I asked if she liked the Revolution. She said yes. "I have not had the experiences my mother has, and I like this. It is what I know."

Luisa looked away from her and said to me, "Old Socialists to them are people to hold tight in their fists."

"Well, Mother, it is your present stance that counts," Mirda said. "Not what you were."

"You are very fresh, Mirda," her mother said. "Some day you will grow old and not count in production."

"And when I do, they should throw me aside."

As I was leaving, Luisa said, "If you are a writer, you must live in Havana?"

I said I lived in New York and that I was a North American, and I could see that, though this interested her enormously (I had to answer the usual questions about what the United States Government would do to me when I got back), Luisa was disappointed that she had been talking to someone who could not help her get out of Brooklyn.

I said good-by and left. At the end of the dirt street stood a tall Negro in dungarees. He kept waving to me and calling, "Well, sir, well, sir, do you remember me?" in a sweet Jamaican English. I said I did, but he could see I wasn't sure. "I met you at the mill the other night, and my name is Roland H. Miller."

Mr. Miller came to cut cane 46 years ago and stayed. "But first I saw almost all the world working on a ship, and I fought for the British Empire in the Arab lands. That was at the beginning of the First World War. And for the last 30 years I have been driving the railroad cars."

I asked him how old he was.

"I am 73 years today," he said, and burst into laughter. "I am already retired two months, and I am still drawing my salary until the pension comes. Isn't that fine of the revolutionary Government?"

I said I was leaving on the next bus and asked if I could take his photograph. He threw his shoulders back and posed, then peered when I wrote down his name. "The name is Roland H. Miller," he repeated. "It is a name Fidel knows."

I looked surprised, and he explained. "I knew Fidel and Raúl and their old man, too. I worked for him when they were boys, and look what a wonderful man Fidel has become. I am retired at higher pay, and I can keep my house. I can keep my house! They will not throw me out, think of that! Isn't that a fine thing? Say it is a fine thing, mon."

Part 4

HOW CAN WE HELP ...AND NOT HELP?

THE DEVELOPED NATIONS have sent aid to the underdeveloped countries in recent years, but the transfer of real wealth has hardly been all one way. Over the years the rich have probably taken much more than they have given. Colonialism and economic imperialism operated for at least a half-century. The developed countries gained through international specialization. More recently, wide fluctuations in the prices paid by wealthy nations for international commodities, such as copper and coffee, have more than offset the amount of aid received by several less developed nations. And when the United States engages in foreign "dumping" of its own surplus agricultural commodities, thereby depriving some underdeveloped country of its all-important export market, it should not expect much gratitude for its assistance. In addition, the foreign investments of developed countries have reaped enormous returns through the exploitation of natural resources in underdeveloped regions. If we are to be honest with ourselves, we must admit that we have done precious little in return up to now. More often than not, narrow self-interest and political expediency have guided our policies of assistance to poor nations.

When our motives have been of a higher character, a lack of preparation and a failure of vision have led to other difficulties. While Barbara Ward emphasizes the need for much greater foreign assistance, including long-term loans, the Streits point out the need for more careful planning and caution in the selection of projects to be assisted. The Helmand Valley project proved to be a burden for Afghanistan, just as Egypt is now experiencing severe difficulties with its agriculture as a result of the billion-dollar Aswan Dam project. As William Vogt points out, good intentions are no substitute for accepting responsibility for the results of our actions.

Senator Fulbright, long an advocate of substantial revisions in U.S. foreign aid policies, draws attention to the often neglected dimension of human pride. Pride is perhaps more important in less-developed countries, where it is one of the few luxuries the people can afford. Fulbright's three-point program would go far toward removing most of the serious abuses in our present aid program. And it would help to eliminate the political stigma that is now attached to so many of our efforts abroad, good or bad. This would also serve to make our aid more effective, perhaps relieving some of our own sense of frustration.

The underlying moral in each of these articles is clear. We have an obligation to provide economic assistance, and a great deal more of it. But we must put even greater emphasis on the qualitative dimension of aid.

Economic NATO
for One Billion

by Barbara Ward

EVER SINCE the Atlantic nations formed their alliance nearly ten years ago, there has been recurrent talk of reinforcing its purely military provisions with constructive economic policies. "Action under Article 2 of the North Atlantic Treaty" has been a magic formula repeated at meeting after meeting of the treaty powers. Occasionally a subcommittee or a working party or "Three Wise Men" are actually asked to make concrete suggestions. The air seemed particularly thick with such plans last Christmas when the shock of the sputniks was still substituting genuine alarm for the old routine atmosphere.

This year, too, parliamentarians from the NATO countries have discussed the issue. No doubt it was canvassed in the corridors at the Commonwealth Economic Conference in Montreal last month, and again at the recent World Bank and Monetary Fund meetings at New Delhi. President Eisenhower has instructed Treasury Secretary Robert B. Anderson to begin negotiations looking toward the creation of a new lending agency to be called the International Development Association. If talk were policy, by now there would be as much economic as strategic substance to NATO. Yet the Emperor has hardly an economic

From the *New York Times Magazine,* October 19, 1958, copyright © 1958 by The New York Times Company.

garment to his name and the chances of continued nudity must be rated fairly high.

One reason is, of course, that the prosperous core of the Western world—North America, Western Europe and the white member states of the British Commonwealth—seems once again to have weathered an American business recession with unexpected success. Besides, Western confidence does not rest on reviving American activity alone. The expanding internal market of Western Europe has shown a strength and resilience which confirms all over again the wisdom and success of one great former act of economic strategy—the Marshall Plan.

One reason the pressure in Europe itself for a joint economic strategy today is something less than urgent is that the Continent still lives on the momentum inherited from the Marshall period. Large-scale investment, freer flow of men and capital, the communities in coal and steel and atomic energy, the coming common market—all these elements of strength are rooted in the Marshall Plan and would have been inconceivable without it.

This is not to say that there are no economic problems common to the Atlantic world, but even while economists shake their heads over the immediate crises of deflation or inflation—or of both together—there is no mistaking the confident ring in their voices when they speak of an American national income doubled by 1965, or of European standards of consumption reaching trans-Atlantic levels by 1970.

Thus the Atlantic nations, which already consume 70 per cent of the world's income for 16 per cent of its population and share among themselves—with the addition of Japan—nearly 70 per cent of the world's trade, face the gratifying economic prospect of becoming wealthier still. Is it surprising that the need for new ventures and new policies receives on the whole a sluggish response?

There simply remains 84 per cent of the human race. If we leave out the areas now controlled by communism, nearly half of humanity lives outside the golden circle of Western wealth and among them the prospects are different indeed.

In the past decade, during which vast political changes have occurred all around the world, involving the virtual disappearance of the old Western colonialism and the emergence of Communist outward pressure seeking to take its place, we have become little by little more aware of the economic realities of this new political era. The whole world is now involved in a revolution which was begun, elaborated and, if not perfected, at least consolidated in the West—the revolution of technical modernization. Education, health, science, productivity, research, agricultural advance and industrialization are all elements in this revolution and all have one thing in common—they require capital.

A generally accepted estimate is that an annual productive investment of 12 to 15 per cent of national income is required to transform an economy from static agriculture with marginal trading into a modern, dynamic economy in which capital accumulation begins to sustain itself. This is a species of "sound barrier" through which nations must pass if they are to modernize; and whatever the virtues of older, stabler cultures, and however raw and crude the first results of the modernizing process may be, more than a billion people have no choice but to attempt the flight through the "sound barrier." If they do not, it is not stability that lies ahead but the decay and misery attendant upon population relentlessly outgrowing resources.

This is as much a fact about the contemporary world as the sputniks' orbits or supersonic speed. From Patagonia to Cape Comorin, in the highlands of East Africa or the paddy fields of lower Burma, in teeming slums and rural shanties, nearly half of humanity lives with the problem not of how to grow wealthier but of how to stave off deepening distress.

In per capita income, many of the lands of Asia, the Middle East and Latin America are worse off than they were in 1939. The share of underdeveloped areas in world trade is falling. Nor is there any way in which this disintegration will check itself unless positive decisions are taken to reverse the trend.

The need to modernize is inescapable. The peoples of the world will do it, one way or another, and if it is not accomplished with Western backing it will be driven through by totalitarian means, with forced saving and iron discipline at home and Communist aid and guidance from abroad. China has already reached the steel targets set for India in 1961. This kind of comparison will be crucial for Asia.

Nor can we suppose, if 84 per cent of the human race turns to totalitarian methods, that the prosperity and commerce of the Western enclave will be very secure. Just when the Western nations' dependence upon external supplies in increasing, they may find area after area compelling them to accept the vagaries, bans and blockages of Communist trade policy. And what scale of defense establishment would be needed to repel Communist pressure from every quarter of the globe?

These are not remote contingencies. They are possibilities written today into the underdeveloped peoples' condition of passion and despair. And for this condition the West must take some measure of responsibility.

There are three main ways for the underprivileged countries to secure the capital they need for modernization: (1) Internal savings. (2) Increased earnings through foreign trade. (3) Capital loaned from abroad for local development.

Internal savings are essential, but the poorer the country and the greater the pressure of population, the harder it is to save. Saving, after all, means postponing consumption, and if you are near the lower margin of consumption already, postponing it further may mean quite simply that you do not survive.

In many underdeveloped lands, medicine has arrived before modernization. The death rate falls before the economy expands. New mouths consume extra production before it can be set aside for new investment. During India's first Five-Year Plan, at least half the added production vanished down new little Indian throats.

It takes Draconian discipline to wring annual savings of 15 per cent from peoples living at the very margins of existence. In fact, the evidence so far suggests that it requires totalitarian leadership and control.

This fact makes all the more decisive the other sources of potential capital—expanded trade and foreign investment. At this point the direct impact of Western policies begins to be felt. Yet it cannot be said that the Western nations show much realization of the actual effects of their present pattern of trading and lending.

Western tariff policies do little to encourage the expansion of underdeveloped economies. Some primary products such as tea and coffee are very heavily taxed as luxuries in the West. Others

—including some minerals and dairy products—are restricted to protect local Western producers.

Attempts to encourage local industrialization by smelting or refining ores on the spot are discouraged by fixing higher Western tariffs for worked up materials. One of the main competitive manufactured exports of Asia—textiles—is rigorously controlled in Western markets. Yet in Lancashire a textile worker can find another job at better wages in engineering, while the mill worker in Ahmadabad or Hong Kong has the sole alternative of unemployment and semi-starvation.

Underdeveloped areas are by definition highly dependent upon their exports because a strong local market does not yet exist as an alternative. Yet it is precisely the exports of primary producers —such as tea or rubber or manganese or tin—that feel the full force of any fluctuations in Western prosperity. In the 1957 recession there was a 13 per cent fall in the general price level of raw materials and some metals fell by much more. The loss of income to primary producers over eighteen months probably exceeded $3 billion—about three times the aid extended to underdeveloped areas in the same period.

If, during times of sharply falling prices, the underdeveloped nations are to maintain their imports—imports of machinery, for instance, such as road equipment or port installations or other essential means of modernization—they must dig into their reserves of foreign currency. But these are what they usually lack, since they tend in good times to spend up to the hilt to advance their urgent plans of development.

Foreign investment has sparked much of the world's past development and, in a century in which economic growth has become one of the central political issues, it might be expected to do so once more and on a comparable scale. But this is not the case.

In Britain's heyday as industrial leader of the world, it exported on an average 7 per cent of its national income in foreign investment, and in the process set many lands, including America, on the road to more rapid economic advance. Today, the United States, the new leader, would need to export two whole Marshall Plans a year—or roughly $28 billion—to equal this scale.

Nor do present foreign investments go in the main to underdeveloped areas. American private investment in its best postwar year has risen to about $5 billion, but at the most $1 billion found its way to the emergent territories. Direct governmental aid has tended to concentrate on military assistance. Economic aid to the underdeveloped areas in any strict sense is probably less than a billion dollars a year.

As a result, the right kind of capital is not always available. Even in the laissez-faire years of the nineteenth century, a great deal of borrowing was undertaken by governments, not by private enterprise, so that they could build roads and harbors and public utilities and establish services such as education, which, though essential, do not produce an immediate revenue. But governments today cannot float loans easily in the capital markets of the West. The colonial grants advanced by Britain and France tend to end when independence is reached. The emergent lands thus find it difficult to raise just the kind of money they need most urgently—money for basic development without which foreign private investment is hard to tempt in.

Mining and plantations will usually attract the foreign investor, but they do not account for more than a quarter of the capital needs of modernization. There is virtually no mechanism for the rest, yet this is the key to rapid development.

If one wants a case history of the results of all these gaps and incoherencies and uncertainties in the pattern of world development, one need look no farther than India today. That India's survival as a great democratic experiment in Asia is a Western interest needs perhaps no underlining. But the economic implications of this political fact are apparently not so obvious. The second Five-Year Plan was drawn up on virtually the lowest capital assumptions compatible with giving some slight increase in well-being to India's growing millions. But, from the start, it assumed that the gap between domestic savings and export earnings and the actual capital needs of the plan could be covered by some foreign lending and assistance.

But after 1956 trouble began. India's export income from primary products such as tea, jute and manganese fell heavily. Its efforts to increase textile exports met Western quotas and restrictions. At the same time, Western suppliers of capital goods, whose order books had emptied in the recession, began delivering machinery ahead of time. Foreign payments rose as foreign earnings shrank. In spite of assistance from America last year and a steady release of sterling balances held in London, India this summer faced the risk of default unless some $350 million could be found before next March.

Some short-term remedies were subsequently worked out in discussions in Washington. But is it not pertinent to ask how a nation whose development is essential to the survival of freedom in Asia could have been left to cope, from hand to mouth, with the immediate consequences of Western recession and with the long-term facts of its own desperate poverty? One can only make an ironic comparison between the West's spasmodic interest in India and the detail, drive, elaboration, capital and technical aid with which Russia has nursed the totalitarian experiment in China.

There is no secret about the policies which could reverse this dangerous trend toward dislocation, deepening misery and ultimate explosion in the world's underdeveloped regions. They have been fully and widely discussed, their practical implications studied and both scale and methods laid down with a fair measure of agreement. Two such policies are concerned with trade, two with international lending. There are others, of course, but these four points are the core of any effective long-term program and could be the basis of a new economic policy in NATO.

The first concerns *measures to counter fluctuations in primary prices*.

Many primary producers favor the idea of agreed upper and lower limits to the movement of international prices for raw materials. The difficulty about such policies is that they tend to isolate particular commodities from genuine changes in the market. If prices are fixed too high, they encourage overproduction or the use of substitutes; if too low, the primary producer loses the export income needed for local development.

For this reason, there is some advocacy for an idea put forward in a United Nations report on the international implications of full employment. According to this plan, a country hard hit by fluctuations in the normal demand for its basic products would be able to receive trading credits to tide it over the worst of the crisis. These credits would enable it to maintain its basic imports and would prevent slackening of demand in one area from spreading through the whole system.

This plan, however, is really one particular aspect of another, wider policy: *measures to increase the working capital available for international trade.*

Various methods have been discussed, but by far the simplest and most straightforward is to increase the currency reserves available to the International Monetary Fund. Its core of hard currency has never been more than about $2 billion, only one-third of the world's normal dollar gap on ordinary commercial transactions. Five times that figure would barely be sufficient. If nations increased their contributions in proportion to their existing gold and hard currency reserves, this method would have the added advantage of injecting into the world system more dollars, marks and Swiss francs—the currencies in shortest supply.

The load which this increased working capital might be expected to carry would depend upon the effectiveness of the two other policies, both designed to increase international lending. The first concerns scale; the second, institutions.

Although 12 per cent of national income is the minimum investment needed for "breakthrough" into self-sustaining growth, most underdeveloped areas today are proceeding at a level of only 7 or 8 per cent. The missing 4 or 5 per cent is the gap external assistance needs to fill.

The job could be done comfortably by an annual allotment of, say, $4 billion to international development. This sum is, in very rough terms, the equivalent of about 1 per cent of present national incomes in the West. Hence the proposal has been made that *the countries with more than $750 annual per capita income should put aside 1 per cent of their national income for international development.* In practice, most of these countries are included in NATO and its associates in Europe and the Commonwealth.

The last point—the instruments through which loans and grants for development should be made—must remain flexible. Some assistance will doubtless continue to be bilateral, from government to government. Yet the experience of the World Bank and other international agencies suggests that the most efficient way of setting the proposed capital to work is *to increase the sums available for lending by the World Bank, say, to $1 billion a* *year and to set up a new agency, affiliated with the bank, for long-term, low-interest loans to governments.*

Such an agency might have between one and two billion dollars a year at its disposal and still leave the West with a billion dollars for other forms of aid, including bilateral aid, without departing from the formula of 1 per cent of national income.

Senator Monroney's imaginative scheme for an International Development Association financed largely by the Western powers and lending money to governments for forty years at 2 per cent has already received powerful support in the Senate, and has thus more chance of receiving crucial American backing than the alternative of a special United Nations development fund.

These, then, are some possible lines of advance in the world-wide economic crisis that confronts the NATO powers today. No wishful thinking is going to withdraw half of humanity from the present risk of steady impoverishment. No Western protests about "squandering our hard-won wealth" are going to make the transfer of 1 per cent of national income an unbearable burden. It is less than the British spend on drinking, smoking and gambling; much less than American expenditure on television, movies, magazines and sports. It is barely a twentieth of what is spent, year after year, on arms.

The question is, in short, purely a political one: since we have the means to counter a demonstrable crisis, shall we, in fact, do so?

The wealthy West as a whole confronts a situation comparable to that of 1947 when America alone was faced with the political question of helping Europe in its hour of desperate necessity, and gave the spectacular and triumphant answer of the Marshall Plan. Self-interest demands that the West act.

Yet is self-interest, however enlightened, the last word in Western policy? Great principles of equality and justice and compassion have always been at work in Western society, making it the most continuously active leaven for true betterment mankind has ever known. Justice and pity helped to transform the early rigors of industrialism into modern welfare capitalism. Are those same forces to sleep while the rest of mankind plunges onward into the industrial age?

It would be a strange, stunted philosophy that limited its effectiveness to physical frontiers, and hitherto the Western spirit has claimed its principles to be valid for all mankind. Now that claim is being put to the test in what could become the most exhilarating challenge ever offered to free men. Surely we cannot fail. Surely our generosity and vision are equal to the task.

Foreign Aid? Yes,
but with a New Approach

by J. W. Fulbright

DIFFICULT AS the effort might be, it would be salutary for Americans to try to imagine exactly how they might feel as recipients of economic aid—and all that goes with it—from foreign countries.

How, for example, would the management and employes of the bankrupt New Haven Railroad feel if they were placed under the tutelage of a mission of, say, German transportation experts —who, for all they might do to show us how to run a railroad, would also be living purveyors of the message that "we Germans know how to do something you Americans don't know how to do"?

Or consider how a Texas rancher might feel as the pupil of a group of agronomists from Colombia assigned to teach him how to grow coffee. Would he be humbly and touchingly grateful? Or would his gratitude be tinged with a touch of rancor toward his benefactors because his pride was injured by the feeling of being a suppliant and a recipient?

Imagine, to take another example, how the recent flood victims of Oregon and California might have felt, having lost their homes and possessions and perhaps members of their families, if

From the *New York Times Magazine,* March 21, 1965, copyright © 1965 by The New York Times Company.

they were then asked to participate in little picture-taking ceremonies with beaming foreign ambassadors dispensing food and
blankets labeled "Gift of the French People" or "Gift of the
Russian People." If we can imagine ourselves in this position,
I think we might agree that it is not an altogether heartwarming
experience to be confronted with a gift of food whose label
seems to convey the message that "the soup which you are about
to consume is a charity from the great and generous and affluent
people of someplace or other."

Several years ago, during a visit to a country which was then
receiving American aid, I attended an informal supper with some
local officials and American diplomats. One of the Americans
favored us with an explanation of the costs and logistics of an
impending disaster-relief mission in which American supplies
were involved. As he warmed to his subject, I noticed our hosts
becoming increasingly preoccupied with their soup. The American official was clearly well-informed on all the details of our
mission of mercy, but the local officials did not seem to appreciate it.

I do not think they were ungrateful for our relief supplies.
I think what they failed to appreciate was the strong and clear
suggestion that they were our wards and we their patrons, that
they were benighted and we were blessed, that they were incom-
petent and needy while we were rich and happy and very tender-
hearted besides. They did not seem to appreciate this at all, and
I did not appreciate it either. In the course of a recent trip to
Yugoslavia, I had the honor to decline to participate in an air-
port ceremony at Zagreb, where American planes were arriving
with bedding supplies for victims of a major flood.

These are extreme examples of what might be called extreme
bilateralism in relations between a rich country and a poor country. They are by no means representative of how most of our
aid is extended and received but they do, I think, illustrate the
psychological problem that is inherent in every manifestation of
direct American assistance to underdeveloped countries.

It is a problem of pride and self-respect, which has everything
to do with a country's will and capacity to foster its own development. There is an inescapable element of charity in bilateral aid,

and charity, over a long period of time, has a debilitating effect on both the recipient and the donor. It fosters attitudes of cranky dependency or simple anger on the part of the recipient and of self-righteous frustration on the part of the donor—attitudes which, once formed, feed destructively upon each other.

There have been abundant manifestations in recent months and years of the negative attitudes that are bred by the client-ward relationship. In the face of repeated threats by the United States to "reconsider" its involvement in the Vietnamese war, the politicians or generals who happen to be in power in Saigon at a given moment simply threaten us with their own collapse and it usually brings us to heel.

Because we do not like President Nasser's Congo policy, we threatened to cut off surplus food products (which are assumed to give us some leverage on the recipient's policy), and Nasser, as a matter of personal and national pride, told us we could take our aid programs and jump in the lake. Few Americans admired this response, even though it has the ring of something like "millions for defense but not one cent for tribute."

The complement of these jaundiced attitudes abroad has been the development of no less jaundiced attitudes in the American Congress. Year by year, the debate over foreign aid has become more rancorous and protracted as Congressmen have failed to see the promised breakthrough to self-sustaining economic growth in the underdeveloped countries, and instead have seen American generosity rewarded with turbulence and insults and ingratitude. The result of this feeling of frustration has been an accelerating war of attrition against foreign aid, interrupted in 1964 only because the Administration conceded much of the issue in advance by submitting a drastically reduced request.

In addition to reducing the size of the foreign-aid program—or, more precisely, the part of the program that pertains to economic development as distinguished from military assistance and special categories intended for short-term political objectives—Congress has fallen into the habit of using the annual foreign-aid debate as the occasion to air extraneous grievances ranging from Ecuadorian views on American fishing rights to the mistreatment of Jews in the Soviet Union. Few of these issues have any direct bearing on the problems of economic development in under-developed countries, which is what foreign aid is supposed to be about.

The ill-tempered debates which these extraneous issues foster in Congress have had two principal consequences. First, they have produced an avalanche of proposals and a number of successful efforts to write unwarranted restrictions on the President's authority in foreign affairs into the foreign-aid bill. Second, they have insulted and offended, and complicated our relations with, a growing list of foreign countries which do not understand, and cannot be persuaded, that the fulminations of Senators are not the official policy of the United States.

If foreign aid had ceased to be a useful instrument of American policy, the problems connected with it could easily be resolved simply by abandoning the program. I believe, however, that, despite all difficulties, American foreign aid has been largely successful and that it will continue for the indefinite future to be an essential instrument of American foreign policy. The question that I wish to raise is not one of foreign aid as such but of a particular approach to foreign aid. I believe that our present approach—which combines various kinds of aid having diverse purposes in a single package, and administers them for the most part bilaterally—has been useful and productive in the past but is no longer adequate to meet the changing needs of American foreign policy in a changing world.

Nor do my reservations about the present program have anything to do with its management and execution. Mr. David Bell is a talented and highly competent administrator. The Agency for International Development (AID), which he heads, is staffed both in Washington and in the field by able and dedicated public servants, many of whom bring not only technical competence to their jobs but an extra measure of devotion necessary to withstand the barbs of Congressional criticism and public mistrust. Nor is there any reason to believe that there is more waste in our foreign-aid program than in any other governmental function; there may indeed be less. The question then is of our approach to foreign aid.

We must broaden and deepen our understanding of the profound transformation that is taking place in the less developed nations of Asia, Africa and Latin America and recognize, as a group of more than 50 American development experts recently pointed out, in a statement published by Indiana University, that the time horizons in our thinking about aid have been too short and that: "We are dealing with the development century and not the development decade."

The continuing need for the rich countries to assist the poor countries is a matter of both political and moral compulsion. It is difficult to see how the world's less developed nations can overcome their enormous social and economic problems without generous assistance from the more favored nations, and it is difficult to see how the rich countries can expect to be secure in their affluence as islands in a global sea of misery. But beyond the social and economic and political and strategic reasons for the rich aiding the poor is the simple motive of humanitarian conscience.

This is, I think, one which commends itself to most Americans more than they may care to admit. During and immediately after World War II, our idealistic impulses led us into some costly errors and many Americans since then, including some distinguished statesmen, have been expending a great deal of energy on efforts to show how tough and mean and hardheaded they are. The foreign-aid debate in the Senate often sounds like a contest as to whether it is more coldly self-interested and hard-boiled to grant aid or to deny it.

I think we could take a long step toward resolving the present debate over foreign aid by expunging from it the vocabulary of puerile toughness in which we have come to take such tiresome pride, and which, I believe, is fundamentally alien to our national character. It would do us no harm to recognize that there is a moral as well as a political and economic case for foreign aid and that there is nothing wrong with human decency as a motive in our foreign policy.

Of all the changes that are needed in our foreign aid, the most important is a change in our own attitude. In the long run, no policy can be sustained by the sole force of cold-blooded self-interest. We do not provide social security to the unemployed simply because it helps to quiet them and makes the possessing classes more secure in their affluence, although social security undoubtedly does contribute to that end. We do it because it seems decent and proper, because we feel some sense of responsibility. If we are at all sincere in our aspiration to achieve a world community of nations, we must bring something of the same spirit to our modest efforts to assist the poor nations in their struggle for a decent life. We must recognize that aid is a humane as well as a practical program, that, as Woodrow Wilson said of the League of Nations, there is a "pulse of sympathy in it" and "a compulsion of conscience throughout it."

The difficulties with foreign aid which we are now experiencing are attributable to the fact that the authorization of American aid has become deeply involved in Congressional politics and controversy, while the disbursement of our aid has involved the United States too deeply in the politics of too many countries. A new approach is needed. To this end, I propose the three following fundamental changes in our foreign aid program.

1. Put economic aid on a long-term basis

Congress should cease its annual reviews of foreign aid and place the program under long-term authorizations. The case for doing so is both familiar and persuasive, and just about everybody involved with foreign aid agrees to it—except Congress.

A long-term authorization would not, of course, remove the foreign-aid program from direct Congressional authority; the funds authorized would still have to be appropriated annually. It might be possible, however, by putting the authorizing legislation, which sets maximum amounts and is intended to govern policy, on a three-year or four-year basis, to insulate the program from transitory waves of emotion.

A long-term authorization might have the effect of reversing the pernicious tendency to write binding restrictions into law in response to some transitory irritation such as an insult from Nasser or Sukarno or a vote in the United Nations that displeases us. Such annoyances are genuine enough but they are often forgotten very quickly as events move on, while the legislative proscriptions to which they gave rise remain to govern—or to frustrate—policy.

Economic development is a long-term process which does not lend itself to the one-year legislative cycle of the American Congress. The conventional short-term approach greatly impedes planning by the aid recipient while the donor is denied the opportunity to offer incentives to recipients to make necessary internal economic reforms. There has been a tendency in the experience of AID and its predecessor agencies to hasten to commit funds as the end of a fiscal year approaches with the result that recipients may be pushed into premature commitments.

The Foreign Assistance Act of 1961, which in my opinion was the best aid bill we have ever enacted, provided long-term authorizations both for the Alliance for Progress and for development lending to Asian and African countries. The Congress, most unwisely, has been tampering with these legislative provisions ever since, so that we are in effect back on a year-to-year basis.

The very nature of the economic development process requires the casting of foreign aid in a new time perspective. The Congress of the United States could make an important contribution to this end by adopting foreign-aid authorization bills of four or three or, at least, two years.

2. Don't confuse economic and military aid

My second proposal is the separation of the economic and military components of foreign aid—or, more exactly, of those forms of aid which pertain to the economic development of underdeveloped countries from those which pertain to the maintenance of armed forces, supporting assistance for security purposes and political loans which are really designed to influence a country's posture in the cold war or the outcome of its next election.

The distinction, in any case, is not merely a legislative one; it is an operative distinction of great importance, pertaining to functions which are quite distinct and not always even compatible.

The fundamental distinction between economic and military-political assistance—and it could hardly be more fundamental—is that one is designed to alter a status quo and the other is usually designed to preserve it. The relationship between the two is that politico-military assistance is intended, or should be intended, to buy time for the more fundamental purpose of developing the nation.

Military assistance is administered by the Department of Defense with the Secretary of State and the administrator of AID acting as policy coordinators. Military and economic assistance are thus overlapping in operation and merged in legislative authorization, giving rise to the constant possibility that recipients will suspect—perhaps rightly—that conditions attached to one form of aid are in reality intended to advance the purpose of the other. I believe that the two functions should be separated to the greatest possible extent, because of the vital importance, *for purposes of economic growth,* of maintaining the economic integrity of economic programs—both in the mind of the recipient and in the policy of the donor.

The same considerations apply with even greater force to those forms of aid which are designed to have nothing more than short-term political effects. I have no firm opinion, frankly, as to whether the United States has any business—or can be expected to gain in the long run—in trying to buy a vote in the United Nations or influence the election of a government. But even if we grant that political bribery is a necessary part of foreign policy, it is perfectly clear that it has nothing to do with economic development, that it is much more nearly a proper function for the C.I.A. than for AID.

As a Democrat, I do not make a habit of supporting my positions on issues with Republican campaign materials. In this case, however, I find myself impressed with a cogent case made in a 1964 publication of the Republican Critical Issues Council for separating economic-development aid from aid for short-term political purposes. The latter, says the Republican task force on foreign aid, should be provided from a special emergency fund at the disposal of the President: "It should not be confused with economic and technical assistance directed toward what we believe is foreign aid's appropriate role in achieving constructive longer-range purposes."

A corollary to the need for separating development assistance from military and short-term political assistance is the need for even greater selectivity—although this principle has in fact been accepted and to a great extent implemented by Presidents Kennedy and Johnson.

The United States nonetheless maintains aid programs in about 90 countries. Few of these contribute appreciably to economic development or to our security. Many are token programs designed to maintain an American "presence," which I take to be a euphemism for the exertion of one form or another of political leverage.

It is an open question whether an American aid "presence" gains any more leverage than it gives. Recent events in Egypt and Indonesia, where we have carefully cultivated our "presence," suggest that when a nationalist leader is feeling angry toward the United States he is unlikely to be deterred by a token or even a substantial American aid program and, further, that a threat to cut off our aid is far less likely to restrain a proud nationalist like Nasser than to goad him into further statements or actions hostile to the United States.

I was recently visited by the American Ambassador to an African country who expressed the view that the best way we can maintain friendly relations with the smaller African countries is by maintaining no "presence" whatever in them except normal diplomatic representation.

There is often far more to be gained by a conspicuous American "absence" from a country than by an American "presence." It is just about inevitable that any small and weak but proud country will view any great power that snuggles too close as a threat to its dignity and independence. I think we would be wise indeed to respect that feeling by vacating those many American "aid" missions whose function is not aid at all, and certainly not development aid, but merely the maintenance of an irritating and unnecessary American "presence."

I think that the President—the President, not the Congress—would be well-advised to terminate aid programs, such as that in Indonesia, which contribute nothing to economic development and exert far more leverage in arousing the ill temper of Congress than in influencing the political behavior of the recipient. If we take these steps, we may find that we have saved some libraries, some embassy windows, a small amount of money and a large amount of good will.

3. Make economic aid an international affair

My third and, I believe, most important proposal for a new approach to foreign aid is that we cease to administer our economic development assistance on a bilateral basis. Let us instead place most, or all, of the funds made available for this purpose at the disposal of the international lending agencies, notably the World Bank and its affiliate, the International Development Association.

The fundamental difference between bilateralism and multilateralism in foreign aid is psychological. The one carries a connotation of charity, of patron and ward, of arrogance and humiliation; the other has the more dignified connotation of a community organized to meet its common and rightful responsibilities toward its less fortunate members. The one is appropriate to a world of nation states with unlimited sovereignty, the other to a world that is at least groping toward a broader community.

Unlike any single nation, an international agency like the World Bank is capable of entering into an *institutional* relationship with the recipient of its aid. It is true, of course, that the international agencies draw most of their resources from the same countries that provide bilateral aid, but, as the former president of the World Bank, Eugene Black, has pointed out, "the act of generosity is one stage removed, and this is quite enough to draw its sting."

Greatly as they want our aid, the poor nations of the world want our respect no less. Above all, they need the self-respect that will enable them to go forward confidently in building their own societies. I believe we can help to make this possible by multilateralizing our aid. And in so doing, we will also be advancing our own security by the cultivation of stable and mutually respectful relations.

By the reckoning of the Johnson Administration, 85 per cent of United States development loans in Asia and Africa will be committed under international arrangements in the next fiscal year, and, it is pointed out, most United States aid to Latin America is provided through the international channels of the Alliance for Progress. This is fine as far as it goes, but that is not really very far toward true multilateralism. The arrangements referred to consist largely of procedures of consultation and coordination, while final decisions about kinds and amounts of aid and the execution of programs remain bilateral.

The kind of multilateralism which is needed is one which will vest in an international agency such as the World Bank full authority to determine, *according to objective economic criteria,* who will receive aid and the amounts, kinds and conditions of aid. The United States and other donors would, of course, reserve to themselves final decisions as to the amounts of money they were prepared to contribute to the international agency, although it would be useful and proper for the international organ to suggest equitable contributions by the participating countries.

Specifically, I suggest that all development loan funds now administered by our Agency for International Development be turned over to the World Bank's International Development Association (I.D.A.) to be used for long-term low-interest development lending for programs that cannot be financed by conventional loans. This is precisely the purpose for which our development loans are intended and precisely the purpose for which the I.D.A. was set up.

I think that the assignment of these funds to the I.D.A. should be accompanied by an effort to persuade other countries to do the same thing, or at least to increase their contributions to I.D.A. I would not, however, make this a condition of our own contributions, because I believe it is in our interests to channel our development lending through an international agency whether others do so or not.

It should be understood that while the Bank and the I.D.A. are independent international agencies, the influence of the United States on their policies is considerable because decisions on loans are made by votes weighted according to contributions. As the largest single contributor, the United States has the greatest voting power. In channeling its development loans through the I.D.A., therefore, the United States would be renouncing exclusive control, with its attendant disadvantages, while retaining great influence on the disposition of its contributions.

The fundamental and, I think, inescapable limit on bilateral aid programs is that, however well and honestly they are administered, they cannot escape political pressure—or, what is just as bad, the suspicion of political pressure.

The problem was succinctly stated by Eugene Black in an address to the Board of Governors of the World Bank shortly before his retirement as its president. "Economic priorities are inevitably confused," he said, "when economic objectivity is lost—and economic objectivity is not easy when aid is influenced by political ends."

As to the Bank and the I.D.A., Mr. Black pointed out that they have the great advantage not only of being economically objective but of being *known* to be so. "Because they are known to have no ulterior motive," he said, "they can exert more influence over the use of a loan than is possible for a bilateral lender: They can insist that the projects for which they lend are established on a sound basis, and—most important—they can make their lending conditional upon commensurate efforts being made by the recipient country itself." This is not to say that bilateral lenders cannot and do not attach requirements of self-help and internal reform to their loans but only that it is easier for an international agency to insist on certain conditions being met without offending nationalist sensibilities and without arousing suspicions that the conditions have a political rather than a development purpose.

In addition to its salutary effects on relations between donors and recipients, the multilateralization of aid would contribute to the same domestic ends that I described in connection with my proposal for multi-year legislative authorizations of foreign aid. Without compromising the ultimate authority and responsibility of Congress, the channeling of our development loans through international agencies would remove the most important, most promising and most politically vulnerable part of our aid program from the pressures of partisan politics, special interests and transitory political preoccupations.

Even if all development lending were placed under the I.D.A. and the Inter-American Development Bank, other forms of foreign aid would remain under bilateral administration. Military assistance, agricultural assistance, supporting assistance for short-term political or budgetary purposes, the use of the President's contingency fund and various forms of technical assistance would continue to be administered by the United States Government. They would, however, be clearly identified for what they are— programs whose objectives are largely political and military and only partially or indirectly economic.

The emergence of the majority of the human race from poverty, and the assistance of the privileged minority in bringing that about, may one day be remembered as one of the bright chapters in human history. Economic assistance may become at the same time an instrument of hope for a better life in the poor countries and an instrument of peace and community among all countries.

This is a distant vista, to be sure, but a journey of a thousand miles must begin with a single step. I believe that America can take that step now by committing itself to a renewed effort in the field of foreign aid and by recognizing that economic development is a distinct and necessary objective of our policy which can best be advanced by separating it from lesser objectives and that this separation in turn can most effectively be achieved by transferring the management of our development aid from national to international auspices.

It can be argued that it is inappropriate for America to commit itself to such a program until and unless others do. For myself, I should be proud to see my country take the lead in a policy of intelligent example.

Lesson in Foreign Aid Policy

by Peggy and Pierre Streit

KABUL, AFGHANISTAN

THE HELMAND VALLEY Irrigation Project, the largest American-financed and -constructed development in Asia, was conceived in 1950 as a boon to the people of Afghanistan. Since then, this boon has become a bitter burden that seriously threatens the Afghan economy and presents the United States with a critical problem in a politically strategic area.

The history of the Helmand Valley Project is timely and valuable for two reasons. First, most of its problems are encountered again and again in underdeveloped countries. And, second, the American techniques of foreign aid, employed with dubious success in Afghanistan, are being used elsewhere in the Middle East and Asia.

American foreign aid policies are now undergoing critical reappraisal in Washington. To a large extent the story of this important but little known project can help make future aid programs more effective.

Afghanistan is a landlocked country, bordered on the north by Russia, on the west by Iran and on the east and south by Pakistan. Her geographical position has long isolated her people,

From the *New York Times Magazine,* March 18, 1956, copyright © 1956 by The New York Times Company.

both physically and culturally, from the social and technological developments of both East and West.

Recently, however, with the awakening of the Middle East and Asian countries, Afghanistan has begun to seek economic development of her potentially rich land, primarily by harnessing the waters of her turbulent Helmand River. This river has its source in the Hindu Kush Mountains and then winds for 800 miles through southern Afghanistan into Iran.

Before World War II, the Afghan Government hired Japanese technicians to begin work on a large canal designed to tap waters of the Helmand for cultivation. Work, interrupted by the war, was resumed shortly thereafter, this time with the help of the Morrison-Knudson Company, an American construction firm hired by the Afghan Government. By 1949, however, the Afghans had vastly increased the scope of their plans. They now envisioned the Helmand River Project as providing a firm water supply, hydroelectric power, flood control, improvement of old river land and development of approximately 500,000 acres of new land. Here the Afghans hoped to settle a large percentage of their two million nomads, whose perennial wanderings represent a severe drain on the Afghan economy, if not a complete loss.

The Government of Afghanistan turned to the United States Export-Import Bank for assistance in this vast undertaking. In requesting a loan, it sought aid only for the construction of major works—the dams and principal canals. The Afghans undertook to do the rest—to bring the water from the main canals to the land, to prepare the new lands for cultivation and to settle the nomads. In 1950, on the basis of these assurances and the fact that Afghanistan had a tidy dollar reserve accumulated during the war years, the bank granted a loan of $21.5 million for the development of the Helmand Basin. The loan stipulated that an American construction company should do the work, and Morrison-Knudson, already on the scene, was hired.

M-K brought to Afghanistan the efficiency of American private enterprise. It acquired its equipment, from nails to 25-ton trucks, from the United States in record time and was able to work steadily without the onerous handicap of having to apply to Congress each year for funds. It utilized the full talents and capabilities of local Afghan labor by establishing a training program, thus substantially reducing costs. Construction costs were held to American standards despite the fact that all equipment had to be shipped 8,000 miles. Two large dams and the irrigation network were completed months ahead of schedule.

Where once there was parched, brown Afghan earth there are now two fresh, blue lakes, and cranes and ducks are nesting where only the desert fox could live. For the first time farmers can rely on a steady supply of water from the Helmand. Last year, a drought year, these waters saved a large part of Afghanistan's fruit crop. And whereas in the past farmers have barely been able to reap one crop, they now almost doubled their produce with two yearly plantings. But as Morrison-Knudson's work progressed, the portent of a major economic and political crisis began to appear. It became sharply and tragically apparent that the persons who granted the loan, like the Afghans who accepted it, had failed to evaluate the country's ability, economically and socially, to handle the problems created by such an extensive undertaking.

It became apparent that the Helmand Valley Authority, the Afghan organization created to take over the operation and maintenance of the irrigation network, to prepare the new lands for cultivation and to settle them, had no trained men to assume these responsibilities. Furthermore, the inadequate Afghan educational system offered little hope of obtaining these men. At the time H. V. A. was to assume operation, it had one trained engineer and one trained agriculturist, both fresh from foreign schools and with no practical experience. The Afghan Government gradually realized that the operation of hydraulic valves, the determination of proper water distribution and the maintenance of a tremendous network of canals was a highly complex job and that misuse of equipment and canals could seriously damage or destroy both.

Furthermore, it also became clear that the newly settled nomad-farmers had no conception of the proper use of either land or water. Men who for centuries had used the most primitive agricultural methods and had thirsted for water did not understand the importance either of leveling the land or of leaching it of its salt content. Suddenly endowed with an abundance of water, they drowned their land, raising its salt content to the point of ruination. This land can be reclaimed, but the process is expensive and until the Afghan farmer learns how to use his newly acquired treasures, reclamation will be useless.

Some of the newly developed desert lands have also proved of inferior quality and unsuited for cultivation unless very expertly handled. By ill fortune, the very first tracts to be settled and cultivated have been particularly difficult. Though extensive soil surveys ordinarily precede an irrigation project, these surveys had not been considered feasible in the case of the Helmand because of their complicated and time-consuming nature. Thus, nomads, lured from their old life by promises of a new one of ease and plenty, have been settled on lands that offer a hard and meager existence. Some of them have already abandoned the valley to return to their ancient nomadic wanderings.

Despite these ominous developments, the Afghan Government, having used up its first loan, turned to the Export-Import Bank for another to push the project through. In 1954, the bank, primarily to safeguard its initial investment, granted the country a second loan of $18.5 million. To date, however, there has been no decisive improvement in the Helmand Valley Project, and the very magnitude of the unforeseen difficulties has created a major political crisis in Afghanistan.

Under the terms of the loan, Afghanistan has paid all local construction and operation costs as her share of the project expenses. These have amounted to about one-third of the Afghan yearly budget of approximately $24,000,000—or what to Afghanistan is the staggering sum of $8,000,000 a year. Thus, an overwhelming sum has been and is likely to continue to be spent on an undertaking which so far has yielded no revenue and which is not likely to yield any soon.

In consequence, the Helmand Valley Project, which was to have been a boon to Afghanistan, has today placed a dangerous strain both on the Afghan economy and on the nation's morale. Some Western observers in Kabul reason that recent Afghan-Russian trade agreements and the Afghan acceptance of a $100,000,000 Soviet credit represent a partial attempt to mitigate this plight. If this is so, the United States may have unwittingly and indirectly contributed to driving Afghanistan into Russian arms.

The current state of Afghan fears and disillusionment over the outcome of the Helmand Valley Project is indicated by the fact that no word of it is being published in the local newspapers and by the further fact that no key figure in the present Afghan Cabinet has journeyed the 400 miles from the capital to see the project. American observers guess that top Afghan officials are afraid to associate themselves too closely with such a precarious enterprise.

There are persistent rumors that the Cabinet is considering dropping the development as too big to handle. But strong pressures so far have prevented this. The Afghans have invested too much money to permit their withdrawal. And to abandon the settlement project is to lose face with and control of the nomads, an eventuality Kabul dares not risk.

In their distress over the failures of the project, the Afghans, not unnaturally, have laid much of the blame on those most closely associated with it. These are the Export-Import Bank, which the Afghans somehow feel made an injudicious loan, and the Morrison-Knudson Company, which the Afghans rightly or wrongly hold responsible for the development of some of the inferior lands. But to Afghan eyes these two organizations are synonymous with the American Government. This conviction was further strengthened when the International Cooperation Administration, the foreign aid arm of the United States Government, began work in Afghanistan in 1952.

Hence, whether Afghan logic is valid or not, in the eyes of Afghanistan, as well as the Middle East and Asia, the good name of the United States is now vitally at stake in the Helmand Valley —and at a time when the Soviet Union is entering the foreign aid field, not only in Afghanistan but throughout Asia.

In the International Cooperation Administration, both the Afghans and the Americans had hoped to find some solution to the grievous problems of the Helmand. But I. C. A.'s operation in Afghanistan has been limited to technical assistance—to providing the country with American personnel having the technical know-how to advise the Afghans on their economic and social problems. And its budget in Afghanistan has been a comparatively small one—approximately two million dollars in 1955.

In view of the significance of the Helmand Valley Project, both to Afghanistan and to the United States, it might have been expected that I. C. A. would have placed all its limited resources and its total personnel emphasis on this development. I. C. A. officials believe, however, that Afghanistan vitally needs help in many other fields as well. Thus, besides the Helmand Project, I. C. A. has embarked on long-range national programs in approximately sixteen fields, including education, agriculture and natural resources, industry and mining, public health and sanitation, rural development, public administration and community development.

These programs, I. C. A. officials claim, will eventually redound to the benefit of the Helmand Valley by providing a broad reservoir of educated personnel upon which the project can ultimately draw.

Critics of this approach protest that I. C. A.'s work in Afghanistan has been spread so thin that results are and will be negligible. They believe that the broad national programs mentioned above are too indirect to benefit the Helmand Valley in any but a remote way. This, they feel, is particularly true of I. C. A.'s educational program. These critics hold that the crisis in the Helmand calls for fast and specific action which I. C. A. has not taken. They feel that if the project is to be saved, a thorough survey of its technical and personnel needs must be made and immediate steps taken to meet them.

What direct assistance I. C. A. has provided in the Helmand is also vigorously criticized, and by its own employes, on the grounds of inefficiency, mismanagement of personnel and general program disorganization. The discontent and frustration of many I. C. A. technicians now working in the valley is reflected in the following extracts from the final reports of two men who have recently left the Helmand:

> . . . The high rate of the intestinal diseases, caused mostly by the contaminated water they were forced to use, no other being available, indicated that this well-drilling program was a definite need if there was to be any improvement in the health of the villagers. The well-drilling rig was ordered early in 1954, and arrived in Afghanistan in July of 1955; the four-inch well casing arrived in late 1954. The pumps

and other well supply equipment have not arrived as yet [October, 1955]. Small size galvanized pipe, to be used to extend water lines from proposed concrete water tanks, has not arrived. Due to the complete lack of materials, the water supply improvement has not been carried out as planned.

. . . The well-drilling rig is at present being assembled by A. C. U. [Afghan Construction Unit], but no crew experienced in its operation is available. The well-drilling operator originally requested probably will not be on hand for the training of a crew of workmen. Therefore, a scratch crew used by M-K in the drilling of a few wells will be hired. No arrangements have been made by I. C. A. for paying the crew, maintenance of the machine or cost of operation.

. . . I suggest that work on the hospital be continued to completion as soon as possible. This is one construction project of two that is visible evidence of F. O. A. [I. C. A.] work in Afghanistan, the other being the swimming pool at Lashkari Bazaar."

. . . My assignment was as an agricultural economist to advise on problems of land use and those social problems ordinarily associated with the settlement of newly developed land. The cooperating agency was unable to find a counterpart [an Afghan to be instructed by the American technician] for me until quite recently; so that very little of my time has been devoted to my professional field, and accomplishments are few.

. . . On this tour of duty living conditions, for me, have been satisfactory and my personal relations with Americans, Afghans and Pakistanis have all been harmonious and pleasant, but the amount of visible accomplishment has been very disappointing, my advice has not been sought in any important matter and that volunteered has been rejected in nearly every instance. The course of events will reveal whether or not the advice was good. . . .

I. C. A. faces overwhelming problems in Afghanistan, and particularly in the Helmand Valley. It must work with an almost illiterate people, overcome the language barrier, cope with Washington bureaucracy and meet many bitter and accumulated problems inherited from a project it had no part in creating. Where responsibility rests for the existing confusion and inefficiency is open to question. But the fact clearly remains that the help Afghanistan needs she is not getting, and the Helmand Valley has profited relatively little from I. C. A.'s presence there.

Could the United States have been spared the crisis it now faces in Afghanistan? Four agencies have been involved in the Helmand Valley Project, yet it does not seem that full responsibility can be attributed to any one of them.

Undoubtedly the Afghan Government overestimated its ability to cope with such a massive project. But having been long isolated from the rest of the world and having no previous experience with large-scale developments, Afghanistan can hardly be blamed for her lack of knowledge.

The Morrison-Knudson Company did recognize some of the inherent hazards of the undertaking. But M-K, as a private organization, had responsibility only for a construction job and not for its economic and political consequences.

The United States Export-Import Bank, in granting the first loan, dealt with the project primarily as a banking venture. It could not fully examine the consequences of the loan, nor did it feel called upon to assume responsibility for them.

The American Embassy in Afghanistan was extremely small when the initial loan was made. It had no staff to make extensive appraisals of the project. Furthermore, Afghanistan was then far outside the pale of the primary preoccupations of American foreign policy. At the time of the second loan, the die had been cast—American interests appeared so deeply involved in Afghanistan that there was little choice but to continue with the project.

In short, there was no single agency charged with the responsibility for investigating the long-range consequences of this giant American-financed venture.

What has been learned by five years of bitter experience in Afghanistan?

One lesson seems clear: a prerequisite of future extensive economic development projects in Asia and the Middle East is a thorough evaluation of the economic and social tolerance of a given country for a given project. One thing that must be guarded against is doing too much too soon. Furthermore, it seems apparent that over-all authority and responsibility for this work and supervising the projects as they progress must be vested in a suitable agency.

It should also be recognized that the techniques of American foreign aid which were effective in Europe, where the foreign aid program was born, do not necessarily apply in Asia. In Europe trained technicians existed; all they needed was up-to-date technical advice. In Asia these trained technicians seldom exist, and American technical advisors find themselves with no one to advise. Thus, American foreign aid policies must be revised to permit American technicians to operate projects until the nationals of the assisted country have had sufficient time and training to utilize American advice. This indicates that an economic development project has little practical use in Asia unless it is supplemented with a training program geared to produce the personnel needed to operate it.

The United States must also accept the fact that its prestige will inevitably be at stake wherever any American organization, public or private, engages in development projects in this part of the world.

And, finally, the United States Government and the American people must reconcile themselves to the fact that the much needed foreign aid program in underdeveloped countries of Asia and the Middle East is a Herculean task, long range in nature, fraught with frustration and criticism, with results that, by American standards, are bound to be agonizingly slow.

Perhaps the most important lesson the Helmand Valley Project can teach is that the United States still has much to learn about helping others to help themselves.

We Help Build
the Population Bomb

by William Vogt

IN 1960, THE LAST YEAR for which census estimates are available, some 70 per cent of the world's population, or about 2.1 billion people, lived in underprivileged countries. Since their populations are growing much more rapidly than those of the industrialized nations, by the end of the century about 80 per cent of the world's population—4.6 billion souls—will inhabit underdeveloped areas if current growth trends continue.

Most inhabitants of these less-developed countries now live in desperate squalor. But as the population grows their misery will grow, too.

The explanation for this appalling prospect is one of the most cruel paradoxes of our time. We of the prosperous West, especially Americans, though moved by humanitarian intentions, are chiefly responsible for building a pyramid of misery. We have slashed death rates in underdeveloped countries to about 17 per 1,000 without making compensating reductions in birth rates, which remain at approximately 43 per 1,000. The ratio, if sustained, will double the populations of these countries within 27 years.

Thus, we have speeded an unprecedented increase in the num-

From the *New York Times Magazine,* April 4, 1965, copyright © 1965 by The New York Times Company.

ber of people—and in the spread of poverty. Literally hundreds of millions of men, women and children are suffering pain, hunger, sickness and fear. The U.S. Department of Agriculture estimated in a 1963 publication that 56 per cent of the world's population did not receive sufficient calories. Today, the number of undernourished people is about 1.9 billion—400 million more than in 1940.

The goodwill and philanthropy of the U.S. Government, private foundations, groups such as the World Health Organization, CARE, UNICEF, the Food for Peace program and many others have combined in a massive attack on death rates. Many of the billions of dollars we have spent on economic aid to underdeveloped countries have had the same effect. Diseases that once ravaged wide areas have been eliminated and it is fairly easy nowadays to check an epidemic of malaria, cholera or smallpox. Such humanitarian skills are relatively simple and cheap to apply. But to feed, house and educate the people who have been added to the swollen populations of underdeveloped countries—65 million more people in the world each year—is an infinitely more difficult and costly task.

Compounding their plight, we have deliberately, cold-bloodedly withheld birth-control knowledge and equipment from poor countries, as we have withheld them from the poor and uninformed in our own country. As recently as March 4 the State Department announced that the United States "will not supply any contraceptives" as part of its foreign aid, which includes, of course, nations where tens of millions exist on less than 15 cents a day.

In short, our policies have condemned more people to worse misery, in the name of charity. We knowingly set off the population explosion we lament. We did it by violating one of the cardinal principles of applied ecology—by expanding populations beyond the carrying capacity of their environments. Humanitarians should consider that point. For while we save an infant from death through disease, we have also preserved a lingering life of pain.

But hungry and sick as they are, people in underdeveloped nations are not too hungry or sick to reproduce.

President Johnson, in his State of the Union message, pledged to help contain the population explosion. The U.N., more than

10 years and 100 million babies after its first attempt to limit India's population was blocked by a spinster health minister who would approve only the rhythm method of birth control—useless among peasant masses—is sending another team to the country. Unfortunately, it cannot save from the most abject misery the approximately 10 million people added to the population each year.

It seems to me that because such children and parents are alive, trapped in dreadful poverty in many parts of the world, we have a responsibility to them. And though we like to think we are generous, we have been spending less than one-quarter of 1 per cent of our gross national product on nonmilitary foreign aid. That aid equals one-quarter of our outlay on alcoholic beverages.

Obviously, we have grossly miscalculated the impact of our philanthropy on human populations. To correct the disastrous consequences of our policies we must immediately take two preliminary steps. The U.S. should give active assistance to birth-control programs overseas, even though this recommendation would almost certainly be impossible to carry out if the Roman Catholic Church continues its opposition.

At the same time we must vastly expand our economic foreign aid.

Beyond these preliminary steps, there is more we can do to reduce the dimensions of impending catastrophe:

A union of the world's best minds—anthropologists, agronomists, economists, physicians, educators, financiers—ought to develop a blueprint to solve the problem of overpopulation.

Our Government and the United Nations need specialized demographic units to watch, forecast and interpret population changes. The units should be represented in the highest policy-making councils. If it is clear that such programs as malaria control and free school lunches will increase the population beyond the probable capacity to provide for them, we should either withhold the aid or accept the responsibility—at whatever cost to ourselves—of supporting the additional people in a decade or two.

We should provide active help in all aspects of birth control as freely as we now help to build steel mills or hydroelectric projects in foreign countries. Birth control is no panacea, but living standards are even more likely to rise with some limitations on the size of the family than with high-powered development loans. In several underdeveloped countries, notably Korea and Taiwan, there has been encouraging acceptance of birth control by peasants. The Ford Foundation has generously financed field trials of birth-control experiments, but the need is far greater than even a wealthy philanthropy like Ford can meet.

We can continue to follow our present path, increasing population pressures in much of the under-developed world. This is the way to disaster.

We can withdraw behind our golden moat and try to ride out the greatest storm ever to sweep over the human race. I doubt if many of us would willingly make this decision.

Or we can make our aid programs truly helpful by including the one element—population balance—without which all the other economic factors are useless.

Whatever we do will inevitably change the destiny of hundreds of millions of people, as we already have. They—and we—face one of the greatest dilemmas in the history of civilized man. It has probably never been stated more clearly than in a sermon by the Rev. Duncan Howlett of the All Souls Unitarian Church in Washington, D.C.:

> In the last ten years we have increased human hunger by feeding the hungry. We have increased human suffering by healing the sick. We have increased human want by giving to the needy. . . . The truth of it comes as a shocking discovery, for we have all been brought up in the Christian tradition in which caring for the least of our brethren has been counted the highest virtue. . . . If we are to export life-giving goods and knowledge, we have the moral obligation to export the population-controlling knowledge we also possess.

Dr. Howlett's logic is inescapable. So is the arithmetic of human population.

Part 5

PROSPECTS FOR THE FUTURE

THE PRESSURES building in the world's underdeveloped regions have an enormous explosive potential. Fundamental social and economic transformations are inevitable if the transition from inertia and despair to dynamism and hope is to be accomplished. These transformations can take a wide variety of forms. We must be more willing to recognize that there are many ways to become modernized, and that not all of these will be compatible with our own prejudices. It is also important to realize that in some instances the political, social, and economic straitjackets worn by numerous poor nations will not yield easily or quietly to the pressures for change. The people of the underdeveloped world want peaceful transitions to a better way of life, but they will insist on transitions, peaceful or not. Further, they will insist on restructuring their societies along lines compatible with their own beliefs. We can accept this and become their allies, or we can become their enemies.

Guatemala, as Alan Howard shows, is one of those underdeveloped countries with a modern veneer, limited to Guatemala City. Elsewhere, Guatemala is downtrodden and hungry. It is also seething with anger and frustration and ripe for revolt.

Conservative elements in politics and the military continue the effort to slow needed reforms.

Since Barnard Collier's article on Eduardo Frei, Chile has had another election. This time the avowed communist sympathizer Salvador Allende won on a platform of socialist reform and nationalization of foreign-owned copper interests. A few years ago he probably could not have taken office without violence. This time, to its credit, the United States appears to have accepted this blow to its anti-communist Latin American policy with dignified grace, if not warm enthusiasm. Significantly, Chileans have accepted their own election with calm.

With the Guerrillas in Guatemala

by Alan Howard

THE OLD MAN pushed himself away from the tree he was leaning against and stepped forward to address the quietly waiting group. He rested the stock of his rifle on the ground and began to talk slowly in a dry voice.

"I remember the year 1927, when I worked on the railroad line," he said. "They paid us 34 cents a day. In order to get to work on time I had to leave my house at 2 in the morning and would not get back until 10 at night. . . ." He spoke a little longer about those days, before most of his listeners were even born; then he told them about a recent trip to the coast for the cotton harvest.

"The pay wasn't bad, 75 cents a day, but it cost 40 cents for food. And there was the problem of the women who worked in the fields. They had to leave their infants under a tree because of the sun. One day the company fumigated the plants, and some babies died." He paused, his broad lips set apart in what looked like a stiff grin but was not. "Even then," he said, "the company would not suspend the fumigation."

This was a political education meeting of a guerrilla patrol

From the *New York Times Magazine,* June 26, 1966, copyright © 1966 by The New York Times Company.

in the mountains of Guatemala. The subject under discussion was "Exploitation."

This nation of nearly five million people is two very distinct countries. There is the capital city: supermarkets and traffic jams, tasteful new buildings and busy commercial life, and—beyond the urban slums that eat into the city from all sides—the wide, shaded streets of the suburbs and the drably adequate housing projects of the growing middle classes.

But drive out of the capital in any direction, beyond the suburbs, and within minutes you have crossed the frontier into another Guatemala. Here 70 per cent of the population lives in small rural communities, working tiny plots of land that yield just enough for survival. Here the chances against a child's completing even a primary school education are more than 1,000 to 1. Here, in a country with one of the highest mortality rates in the world, a man's principal link to the national economy is as a cheap source of labor for the few hundred families that own most of the good land.

This other Guatemala is a land of the forgotten and the futureless, inhabited by men like the one who spoke at the guerrilla meeting. It is a country pregnant with revolution.

For most of its 150-mile length the highway from Guatemala City to the Caribbean coast runs through a river valley in the shadow of the Sierra de las Minas, a range of wooded mountains that is the base of a small guerrilla army. From time to time its men will ambush an army patrol along the highway—the main artery of the nation's economy—or stop and destroy a truck carrying oil, foodstuffs or some other basic commodity.

Until fairly recently even Guatemalans who lived in the capital did not know much about these sporadic guerrilla activities; very little news filtered through from the countryside. They knew, though, that to certain parts of the *oriente* (eastern) region one went at one's own risk. In the city you occasionally heard a bomb explode in the distance; the next day the Government would announce that it had been the work of "terrorist bandits" who would soon be apprehended. But they rarely were.

Then, last December, a series of spectacular kidnappings by the guerrillas startled the capital into awareness and set the Government on edge.

The victims were three wealthy businessmen and the object was to raise ransom money, chiefly to finance the purchase of badly needed weapons. The businessmen were released and the guerrilla treasury was richer by some $250,000.

The National Palace issued a series of denials that internal security was threatened—amidst insistent rumors of an impending coup. The kidnappings took place just as a Presidential election campaign was getting under way. In the months that followed, as the campaign gained momentum, it seemed that almost everyone was talking about the guerrillas.

The Presidential candidate on the far right, an army colonel, charged that the Government had lost control of "the entire eastern region of Guatemala" to the guerrillas. His first official act would be a massive campaign to destroy them. The Government candidate, another army colonel, promptly disputed the charge. Both men, however, agreed that the guerrillas were agents of an international Communist conspiracy.

A third candidate, Julio Cesar Méndez Montenegro, a civilian who eventually won the election in March and who is due to take office Friday, did not have much to say about the guerrillas during the campaign. His silence, coupled with his running-mate's talk of a possible pact with the guerrillas, helped to feed an already widespread suspicion among the military that Méndez was too far left for comfort.

Méndez ran on a platform of political liberty. He denied "any political ties whatsoever with communism," and promised a "government of the people, by the people, for the people" and progress in all sectors of Guatemalan society. Méndez seems to be genuinely liked among the middle and lower urban classes and others who see his Revolutionary party as the heir to the popular October Revolution of 1944 (which ended 13 years of repressive military rule) and its still-unrealized goals: the right of labor to organize, political democracy and freedom, land reform. As the former dean of the University of San Carlos Law School in Guatemala City, long a center of leftist activity, his credentials among many socially concerned intellectuals are highly respected.

But although Méndez talks about social reform, he has yet to put forth a concrete program. If and when he does, his real troubles will begin. For in order to carry out the changes implied by his adherence to the ideology of the October Revolution he will have to overcome the opposition of powerful military leaders who consider such ideas perilously close to communism.

Guatemala has been ruled by a military Government since 1963, when a group of colonels seized power in a bloodless coup. After some jockeying for position, the man who emerged on top as Chief of State was Col. Enrique Peralta Azurdia, the leader of a relatively moderate military faction. He pledged free elections and to the surprise of many observers they actually took place on March 6.

In the weeks following the election, rumors were thick that a military *golpe* (coup) would nullify the results. There was also so much talk about shiploads of U.S. Marines standing by off-shore, reminiscent of the Dominican intervention, that the American Embassy felt it necessary to deny any knowledge of such plans. (Contrary to the rumors, the U.S undoubtedly applied what pressure it could to discourage the diehard element in the army from seizing power.) Since then, Méndez seems to have reached an accord with the army, for the time being at least, by giving it a free hand in chasing down the guerrillas. But what his future policy will be remains a question mark.

A state of siege gives police the power to search and arrest without a warrant and hold suspects incommunicado. Many military patrols cruise throughout the city and civilian cars must travel at night with their interior lights on.

The Guatemalan Army is a well-equipped force of about 12,000 men, supported by the U.S. with more than $2-million annually and a small team of military advisers. But since 1962, when it found and destroyed entire rebel units, forcing the guerrillas to dismantle their organization and melt back into the city, the army has been continually frustrated by the swift and elusive movements of its enemy.

In the latest rebel attack on May 17, 12 soldiers were killed in a guerrilla ambush. Also last month, the guerrillas resumed their kidnappings. Three men were snatched: the Government information chief, the Chief Justice of the Supreme Court and the Vice President of the Congress. Unlike the motive for last December's kidnappings, the aim this time was to take hostages for 28 persons seized by the regime as suspected rebels.

In an interview three days after the election, the outgoing Guatemalan Chief of State, Colonel Peralta, was asked: "How is it the guerrillas are always able to get away after an attack?" He replied: "Many people protect them. Besides, they disguise themselves as priests and even as women."

Luís Augusto Turcios Lima, the 24-year-old leader of the Rebel Armed Forces (F.A.R.), would certainly agree with the first sentence of Peralta's reply. For Turcios maintains that his movement is growing steadily only because it has won the support of great numbers of peasants who comprise Guatemala's "second nation."

Turcios, a thin, intense young man, had recently returned from the First Tri-Continental Congress of Havana when I met him not long ago in the Sierra de las Minas.

Making contact with the guerrillas was harder than I had expected. The rebels knew I was coming—I had received the name of an underground leader in Guatemala City while I was still in New York—but since the Government intercepted the message that gave my time of arrival, I was shadowed from the plane to my hotel by police. But the rebels knew I was being followed, and it was only after two weeks of being trailed and two more weeks of shuttling from house to house that I was finally able to get away unobserved with a guide who led me to Turcios's camp in the mountains.

He talks in rapid bursts, with a tone that usually sounds half-angry. His English is poor so we spoke in Spanish. "The purpose of the congress was solidarity," he said—"to coordinate the anti-imperialist struggle."

In fact, its practical effect in Guatemala was probably divisive. By recognizing Turcios as the *comandante* of the rebel forces, the congress banished a group led by his former comrade-in-arms, Marco Antonio Yon Sosa. The result has been a definite, though perhaps temporary, setback to the revolutionary movement in Guatemala.

The two forces, Yon Sosa's *Movimiento* 13 *de Noviembre* (M-13), which has not been heard from for several months, and Turcios's F.A.R., have the same ultimate goal: a Socialist Guatemala. But they disagree on strategy and the speed with which a Socialist state can be constructed after the existing Government is toppled. An American official in Guatemala defines the difference simply: Yon Sosa has not "sold out to the Communists; he's his own boy."

This interpretation probably arises from the fact that the Guatemalan Communist party supports Turcios's group and has an influential voice in its leadership, though Turcios himself is not a Communist.

During the Havana congress, Fidel Castro offered support—arms and men—to Turcios, but the *comandante* says he refused the offer. Turcios insists that he intends to keep F.A.R. unencumbered by any foreign commitments whatsoever. "One thing I guarantee you," he said. "We depend on nobody—not for arms, not for *anything*. We have done it all ourselves."

Most officials here privately concede this is probably true. Cuba is undoubtedly a source of inspiration and a practical example, but there has been no evidence of funds passed to the rebels from foreign sources.

Turcios's most vivid impression of the Havana congress was his meeting with Vietnamese delegates. "They are the bravest people in the world," he said, "and the masters of guerrilla warfare. We have learned much from them. Wait and see what we do to the first American units that come here."

When Turcios speaks of the Vietnamese, and he often does, the words have a special intensity that is absent from his more abstract remarks about solidarity and Socialist theory. For though he has suddenly found himself in a position of political leadership, Turcios is essentially a soldier fighting for a new code of honor. If he has an alter ego, it would not be Lenin or Mao or even Castro, whose works he has read and admires, but Augusto Sandino, the Nicaraguan general who fought the U.S. Marines sent to Nicaragua during the Coolidge and Hoover Administrations.

Turcios began his military career when he entered the *Politécnica,* Guatemala's West Point, at 15; since he was two years younger than the minimum age for admission, he needed special permission. He graduated second in his class. "Bad marks in conduct kept me from first," he said with a smile.

After graduation he was sent to Fort Benning, Ga., for training in the élite Ranger course. Did he like it? "Sure, I liked it," he said. "We had the officers' club, 15-ounce Texas steaks, good clothes, the best equipment. Plenty of money, too; every month I sent $150 to my mother. What worries did I have?"

After finishing the six-month course, Turcios returned to Guatemala in early 1960 and went on active duty. Then, on Nov. 13, he took part in an unsuccessful coup staged by a group of younger army officers that has turned out to be the seed of the current rebel movement. His reasons for joining the revolt were, he said, "the traditional ones of younger officers: fed up with corruption, desiring structural changes in the army; nothing really different"—with one exception. The presence of Cuban exiles training in Guatemala for the Bay of Pigs invasion gave the revolt a highly nationalistic tone.

"It was a shameless violation of our national sovereignty," Turcios declared, "And why was it permitted? Because our Government is a puppet."

Turcios spent four months in exile after the revolt, then returned to Guatemala. Politics was still uppermost in his mind, and in a series of meetings with leaders of the country's leading political parties he sought "to find out exactly what they stood for." It was at this time that he first met the Communists, who made a tremendous impact on Turcios. "They were different from the others," he said. "They really cared about the people."

So, in July, 1961, began what he calls his "close collaboration" with the Communist party. The first guerrilla movement was formed then, only to meet disaster less than a year later when the army captured and killed a number of rebels. "We have learned from our mistakes," Turcios said. "The first guerrillas failed because they thought mainly in military terms and not enough in the political."

He dates the beginning of the new F.A.R. to early 1963, about the time he met a young law student named César Montes. Together with two other men, they began making contact with *campesinos* in the Sierra de las Minas region. Fresh from the failure of the earlier guerrilla force, they talked with the peasants and organized them in groups, but did not form military units until they were certain of peasant support and an assured chain of supply and information.

A precise estimate of the number of rebels and the extent of their control today is difficult. As Turcios explained, "We want it to be a surprise." Nevertheless, there are probably no more than 300 full-time guerrillas under Turcios's command, and one American official puts the figure at under 100.

I witnessed one example of guerrilla methods while visiting Turcios's rebel camp. One afternoon a man appeared and was introduced to me as the head of the resistance unit in a nearby town. From his clothing and speech he could not be distinguished from any other peasant who lived in the area. His job, he explained, was to organize the "irregulars"—*campesinos* who are called upon for a specific mission when the guerrillas need them and who are back at work in their fields the following day. He was responsible for distributing weapons, making sure they were well hidden and teaching his men how to use them properly.

"Then your people are trained to fight?" I asked.

"Trained?" He thought for a moment. "Not exactly. But they know how to shoot."

The rebels' weapons range from World War II vintage guns to the most modern equipment. Many are American-made. Turcios said that approximately 80 per cent of the weapons are seized or stolen from the Guatemalan Army.

When it comes to discussing specifics and the ideological complexities of the revolution's program, Turcios often lets César Montes do the talking. Montes is a co-signer of the F.A.R. statements that issue from the mountains. He has a captain's rank and officially is second in command, but it is difficult to imagine him in a subordinate role.

Montes is 24 and a member of the Central Committee of the Guatemalan Communist party. A man of explicit and thoroughly Marxist vision, he generates much of the movement's ideological energy. "A revolution cannot be exported," he said—"not a true revolution. It grows up out of the needs of the people. Our movement cannot be destroyed until those needs are satisfied."

Montes described one of the most urgent of those needs as land reform. "But you cannot simply turn over great tracts of land to the people and say, 'Go ahead, it's all yours,' " he added. "Nor can you collectivize land in an area where there is a long tradition of small property owners. In fact, when you talk about a program of national land reform you are actually talking about many dif-

ferent regional programs, each fitting the distinct needs and pe-
culiarities of a particular region of the country."

Because the revolution is "anti-imperialist" as well as agrarian,
one of its major aims is the nationalization of large foreign holdings such as the United Fruit Company and the *Empresa Elec-
trica,* a subsidiary of the U.S.-controlled Electric Bond and Share
Company. Asked about indemnification, Montes's reply was crisp
and bitter.

"Haven't you Americans taken enough already?" he snapped.

F.A.R. leaders are convinced that social revolution can take
place only through armed struggle. This is a key area of dis-
agreement between them and a "conservative" faction in the
Guatemalan Communist party who view the guerrillas mainly as
a wedge to obtain future parliamentary influence for themselves.
The guerrillas, for their part, refuse to compromise with political
elements outside their movement. This friction was apparent in
the mildly equivocating tone of Montes's remarks about a possible pact with President-elect Méndez and his Revolutionary
party:

"I have a great deal of respect for Méndez," he said. "He was
my professor in law school and I believe he is an honest and
intelligent man. But the army will never allow him to carry out
the profound reforms our country needs."

Unlike Montes, Turcios is not caught in the currents of ideological dispute within the Communist party. He thus could talk
about alliances with his characteristic bluntness. "No pact," he
declared. "Not unless they want to come out here and fight beside us."

The rebels concede that they have neither intention nor hopes
of seizing power in the near future. Their aim is to build a resistance base in the countryside and a safe refuge by developing
a highly conscious mass of *campesinos.* "The more time we have
to prepare the people now," Montes explained, "the less difficult
will be the transformation to socialism later."

The guerrillas work within a framework that includes many
shades of the left. A resistance organization operates in the
capital and other major cities with the aim of procuring arms,
funds and supplies, distributing propaganda, carrying out at-

tacks against police stations and other missions of sabotage. In two recent incidents, grenades were tossed at the building of the country's leading newspaper, La Prensa Libre, and an attempt was made to blow up the tomb of the conservative, anti-Communist former President, Col. Carlos Castillo Armas.

In part because many leftists have been driven underground in recent years, the guerrillas seem to have developed a broad base of collaborators among workers, students and intellectuals, and even among younger army officers.

A university professor's explanation for his sympathy for the revolutionary movement was more or less typical: "I have no particular aversion to Marxism. We sit down and talk with the Communists and sometimes we convince them they are wrong on a particular point and sometimes we admit our mistake. The important thing is that we want more or less the same thing for our country—to be free to make our own decisions, which has not been the case with any of our Governments since 1954."

The year 1954 keeps turning up in any discussion of Guatemalan politics. The Government of Jacobo Arbenz Guzmán—who allowed a number of Communists to reach influential positions—had tried to apply a land reform law. It was grossly mismanaged, however, and in the discontent and confusion it stirred, the conservative Castillo Armas succeeded—with the help of the C.I.A. and the acquiescence of the Guatemalan Army—in overthrowing Arbenz in 1954. In the next few years Castillo Armas launched an anti-Communist crusade.

Political repression was eased somewhat in 1958 with the election of Miguel Ydigoras Fuentes, but when he was ousted five years later in a *coup d'état* by the present military Government there was established more firmly than ever in the public mind a distrust of the army and a deep skepticism about the ability of a civilian regime to survive its displeasure.

Unless the army blunders in some spectacular way, the focus of guerrilla activity will remain in the countryside, where the movement's successes and failures must be counted. The process of organizing and arming *campesinos* for full-time duty usually begins with a tactic called "armed propaganda."

The night before we left the base camp for an armed propaganda mission in a nearby village, a briefing was held to review the procedure.

The village would be secured militarily. All inhabitants would be required to attend a meeting at which several rebels would talk on different themes: reform, exploitation, the people's army, security measures. During this initial contact with the community the rebels would seek out the village leaders, hoping to make them the nucleus of a Local Clandestine Committee—a tightly organized unit that, in its most advanced stage, acts as the final political authority of the village.

Often, the rebels win over the local Government official to their cause. If they fail, the rebels try to persuade him to remain neutral. And if he actively opposes rebel authority, he will probably be executed. In the past year the rebels had executed, by their own count, 13 men in the region and scores of police and army officials in other areas who had allegedly tortured and killed rebel partisans. The army usually retaliates by rounding up a number of suspects, jailing them for interrogation and eventually releasing them. Torture is more or less standard practice and sometimes a suspect doesn't come home.

During the briefing Turcios sat in the rear of the group, listening to the questions and discussion.

"This is the most important part of the meeting," he said. "We would like everyone to take part and criticize, especially the *campesinos*. It helps to incorporate them into the struggle. If you only knew how hard it was in the first guerrilla unit we formed. Not one of them would criticize me. It was always '*Comandante* this, *Comandante* that.' It went on every night for nearly two months. You understand, I stood for authority, the church, the Government, the *patrón*. Finally, a bunch of them got together; *hombre,* they really let me have it, cut me to pieces. If you only knew how good that made me feel. To see them, in that moment, break free after centuries of slavery."

On the day after this briefing, the unit separated and I went with one patrol on its armed propaganda mission. The leader, Tito, was a former army officer like Turcios, but the others on the patrol had various backgrounds. Danilo, who completed his fourth year at the university as an agronomy student, works closely with one of the cooperatives in the area; Christina, a nurse from the city, had just joined the guerrillas; Rogelio was a *campesino* and a survivor of the first abortive guerrilla movement.

We climbed up the mountains most of the day. By dusk we had passed through the pine groves that cover the midpoint of the peaks and entered Lechero, a code name for the village that was our destination. Lechero consisted of 30 houses—huts, really—scattered along a narrow plateau. Most of the men were still in the fields when we arrived so the rebels were greeted by the women. They were cautious, but the children ran to the edge of the muddy yards of the huts and waved.

The guerrillas posted sentries and set down their packs around a grassy mound where the two crude roads of the village ran together. Tito stopped the first people who came by and asked if they had heard of the rebels. They had heard of them, vaguely, but they had also heard rumors of what the army does to people who help the rebels.

The villagers were clearly afraid. Strangers with guns could only mean trouble and they obviously wanted the rebels to leave. Tito told them the men would not go until it was over. The group realized that the longer the rebels stayed, the more dangerous it was for the village. A little later the patrol broke up into pairs and went from house to house, informing the people of the meeting.

It had been dark for some time when dull spots of orange light began to appear on the slopes above the road. The lights drifted downward, in clusters, then joined to form a scattered line that slowly descended on the mountainside. The line vanished for a few minutes, then reappeared suddenly around the corner of a nearby house as about 40 men of the village approached with burning sticks of kindling in their hands. They dropped the sticks into a pile and sat down on the smooth grass to hear the rebels explain why they had come.

The rebels spoke on subjects they had discussed before during hundreds of similar talks. They recounted some of their own experiences, talked about poverty, suffering and the indifference of the Government. They said they had joined the guerrillas because the people needed an army of their own.

The meeting did not seem to be going well. The villagers listened quietly, but it was unusually cold and many hugged their arms and moved in place to keep warm.

Tito spoke last. He apologized for keeping them out in the cold so long and suggested they move closer together around the fire. The rebels moved in among the group and Tito started to speak, kneeling in the center of the rough circle. "This is how we must be," he began. "Together we are warm. You have heard, the war is coming and we must prepare. . . ."

The mood of the meeting slowly began to change. Tito did not cite statistics—the mortality rate, the illiteracy rate, the per capita income for peasants of about $90 a year. Instead, he talked about the great expanse of idle land, about the abuses of the rich and the many white coffins of children. After each point he made, the men of the village said, *"Si, es cierto."* "Yes, that's true." At first the chorus was little more than a murmur of acknowledgment, but as Tito neared the end of his talk a few voices rose louder than the others; it was always the same phrase, *"Si es cierto,"* but now spoken in a new tone, no longer timid, reaching into the unmistakable register of defiance.

"A Revolution Without the Execution Wall"

by Barnard Collier

SANTIAGO, CHILE

A SKINNY DOG from Chile and a fat dog from Argentina met in a mountain pass on the border between the two countries and, both having climbed nearly 12,000 feet straight up, stopped to rest.

"You seem to have suffered a rough trip," said the beautiful, sleek Argentine dog, noting that the Chilean dog's ribs were visible through his sad coat.

"Yes," snapped the Chilean dog, "I am not nearly so well nourished as you. But I am told that in Argentina there is more than enough for all and therefore I am headed that way."

"Ah, yes," said the Argentine dog proudly. "In Argentina we have filet mignon three times a day if we like. We have the great wines from Mendoza. And one can satisfy almost any craving in Buenos Aires. It is the Paris of South America. Lord, the girls in their Dior frocks and Dior shoes, their perfect coiffures, their delicious . . . I'm sorry, I get carried away."

"Well, I must be off," said the Chilean dog. *"Adiós."*

"Adiós," said the Argentine dog, and he trotted off toward Santiago.

From the *New York Times Magazine,* February 19, 1967, copyright © 1967 by The New York Times Company.

"Wait a minute!" shouted the Chilean dog after he had gone a few strides. "Why on earth, after all you've told me about your country, are you going to *Chile?* Tell me, *hombre!"*

The Argentine dog turned around. "I'm going to Chile," he replied softly, "to bark."

It is an old European fable, adopted by both Chileans and Argentines for different effect. But it illustrates better than all their proud patriotic phrases just how special the Chileans feel in relation to some of their South American neighbors.

Take Argentina, for example, they say: it is now run by the military and the extreme right wing of the Catholic Church, and neither brooks much backtalk. Brazil is controlled by a once-docile military which now has a messiah complex. Paraguay is ruled by Gen. Alfredo Stroessner, who wears jackboots and stands for no nonsense and never has. The military in Peru last tossed out an elected president five years ago, and though it now seems pleased with President Fernando Belaúnde Terry's economic miracle, it still lurks in the background.

Can countries like these hope to lead Latin America in the 20th century? ask the Chileans. Can Western nations without full political freedom presume to worldwide prestige? Can they avoid the inevitable bloodshed provoked by frustrated rights and abridged freedoms? Can they hope to achieve what Chile is going to achieve because of its uniqueness, its free political spirit?

Obviously not, answer the Chileans. So with the nth degree of conceit, Chileans are convinced that the eyes of the world are focused on their peculiar-looking country for news of its social and economic experiment.

The man who is President of this self-preoccupied country of 8.5-million people is Eduardo Frei Montalva, 56, who sees himself—as, indeed, many others also see him—as perhaps the most accomplished "statesman" in all Latin America. Sometimes, it seems, President Frei (pronounced Fray) relishes more his picture of himself as Latin America's voice and conscience than he does the irritating business of simply being the leader of a single country constantly in a state of hypertension.

Frei loves the international scene. "The world in general recognizes the effort that is being made in Chile," he told his people not long ago, "and the most outstanding figures in the world come here to express their warm interest and respect, and even their enthusiasm, for what is happening here."

And when the world's great cannot make it to Chile, the Chilean President and statesman is more than happy to go to the world's great—to London to visit the Queen, to Rome for sessions with Aldo Moro, to Paris for talks with de Gaulle. Or to Washington to see President Johnson.

But this last he has not yet done, and when an invitation came recently for a state visit to Washington on Feb. 1 and 2 he very badly wanted to go. Junketing around Europe does no harm at home, but a trip to the United States is something else again: that is where the money and the power are.

To complete his personal portrait of the statesman, President Frei needed the ride in the bubble-top Lincoln down Pennsylvania Avenue, the lovely state dinners and the scores of Chilean reporters sending back to Santiago every trivial detail. Frei knew he was going to get these things and he is vain enough, his friends and his enemies agree, to find it difficult to expect less.

Then, alas, on Jan. 17, two weeks before he was to leave, the Chilean Senate astonishingly voted against allowing Frei to leave the country. They acted under an anachronistic constitutional provision that requires the permission of the Congress before a Chilean chief of state can go abroad. The law dates back to 1833 and was written to protect against the possibility of the nation's leader hopping a ship to Europe and absenting himself from the country for months at a time. Ironically, it was one of several constitutional quirks that Frei was going to iron out when he put through a promised constitutional reform, but just hadn't gotten around to.

The vote marked the first time in Chilean history that the Congress had denied a President permission to go abroad to conduct international business. It was a calculated humiliation by Frei's opposition: the extreme-leftist Socialists (hewing to some kind of Peking line), the Moscow-lining Communists, the Ultra-Rightists and the more liberal Radicals. They demonstrated their scorn not so much for Frei personally—even his enemies respect him for his honesty and personal values—but for what they think he and his Christian Democratic Government are doing to them and to Chile, hand-in-hand with the United States.

Two days after the Senate vote Frei reacted in a way expected by almost no one. In a ringing speech from the balcony of the Moneda Presidential Palace in downtown Santiago, he called for the dissolution of the Congress and a new election. He claimed that he and his party faced a "conspiracy" of extremism and demanded a vote of confidence directly from the people. It appears now that he is going to get his new elections—perhaps by May or June—preceded by Congressional approval of a constitutional amendment that will make the extraordinary elections possible.

Frei is clearly taking a serious gamble. He is risking his party's present majority in the Chamber of Deputies (82 of 145 seats) for the opportunity of also getting a majority in the obstreperous Senate, where he now has only 13 out of 45 seats. Nobody is yet making any serious predictions that Frei will win this gamble, for if and when the election comes off the campaign before it is bound to be brutal. But there is no question that the Christian Democrats have some strong talking points—all the stronger considering what they have managed to accomplish in a country with such freakish geography and paucity of real riches.

Chile is an incredible 2,600 miles long and stretches from the parched nitrate sands of the Atacama Desert bordering Peru in the north to the desolate little point of Cape Horn in the Antarctic. To the East, Chile is walled in by the highest and most rugged peaks of the Andean cordillera; to the west is the Pacific.

In the 300-mile-long Central Valley live 76 per cent of the nation's people on 40 per cent of the arable land. There the top soil is at best six feet deep and crossed by fast-flowing rivers that start in the sterile mountain snows and leave little in the way of mineral deposits to revive the land as they rush by. Nonetheless, the valley does produce, when prompted hard, marvelous fruits and vegetables, grains and cattle—but today not enough.

Nothing in Chile is easy to get to or easy to exploit. The huge deposits of copper and iron in the mountains are perversely located where even eagles might find it difficult to go. The Kennecott Copper Company's gigantic El Teniente mine (the largest underground copper mine in the world) perches at 9,200 feet on the western slopes of the Andes, 110 miles by a most courageous railroad from the main copper port of San Antonio. The cattle, wheat and sheep areas are tied to distant markets by weaving roads over washboard terrain, and the fine timberlands of the far south are 1,000 or more miles from a good market (which means that almost everything Chile has to sell is expensive because of the cost of transportation).

In this strange and lovely land—broiled by the sun on one end, bitten by frost on the other, corrugated in between—live a people almost as unusual as they think they are.

Chileans are probably the least militaristic people in South America, though they have in fact won hands down almost every war they have fought. They have a fierce independence, perhaps in part due to their isolation, yet for a century they have been the most intensive seekers and users of foreign capital in Latin America. And they are, by and large, the most honest of Latins in their governmental dealing. Bribery, while certainly not unknown, is not a way of life as in most Latin countries, and when it is discovered, people actually go to jail.

Chile is one of the most politically sophisticated and mature nations in the world, and Chileans know it. Chile is also woefully underdeveloped, and Chileans know that, too. Today, on the shoulders of Eduardo Frei, the paradox of Chile's sophistication and its simultaneous underdevelopment is carried like a personal cross.

Tall and gaunt with straight graying hair and a nose to rival his friend de Gaulle's, President Frei projects an image of lean, quiet sternness that Chileans like because it suits their conception of the country. Frei is also a master politician and the ideologist-in-chief of his Christian Democratic party—a combination that further endears him to Chileans, who love politics and are highly proud of the nation's intellectual reputation.

Frei was born in Santiago on Jan. 16, 1911, the son of young Swiss parents just arrived from Europe. His father soon moved the family to the village of Lontué to the south, where he became the administrator of the wine cellars. There young Frei attended a one-room schoolhouse where he was, as he would be throughout his academic career, the best pupil; he ultimately was graduated from the Catholic University of Chile in Santiago as a lawyer, first in his class.

During Frei's university days many of the leaders of today's Christian Democrats got to know each other, and to respect Frei as a kind of born leader. He was president of the Catholic Youth of Chile and founder and ramrod of a lot of things. In 1935, Frei, then 24, and the present Interior Minister, Bernardo Leighton, founded the National Movement of the Youth of the Conservative party, which four years later became the National Falange party and 20 years after that, in 1959, became the Christian Democratic party of Chile.

The steel in Frei's political backbone was tempered during years of excellent government experience: as Minister of Public Works in 1945, Senator from the far-away Coquimbo and Atacama provinces in 1949, and Senator for Santiago, his major victory, in 1957. There are old photographs of Frei during these years, in shirtsleeves, in swimming pools, in large groups. His face always stands out, his deep-set eyes are always looking hard into the lens, he is almost always in the center. Frei was never lost in the crowd. Nor is he now.

The rich of Chile are very, very rich—and very, very conservative. The poor are dreadfully poor. The rich, who owned about 50 per cent of the useful land when Chile was a Spanish colony, own about that much today. The poor, the *mestizos* and the factory workers, live today in grinding poverty (the slum-covered mountainsides in Valparaiso are no better, and perhaps worse, than the *favela*-covered mountains in Rio) and they outnumber the rich and the middle class by a good sum. Bernardo O'Higgins, Chile's great "Liberator," recognized and even then tried to come to grips with these social problems following independence 149 years ago. He was overthrown by an oligarchy-led coup for his efforts. And the battle between the rich and the poor goes on today in much the same fashion.

From the nineteen-twenties onward the growth and organization of the Socialist and Communist parties was rapid and sometimes frightening. Both are now the best-organized (though financially not very sound) Marxist parties in the hemisphere. For 13 years their coalition, the *Frente Popular,* ran Chile—from 1938 to

1951. It finally faded when the Communist coalition partners made a naked, though abortive, grab for power.

In 1952, Gen. Carlos Ibáñez was elected, and with his weird Peasants Workers party proceeded to emulate Argentina's Juan Perón and to promote a kind of socialism-fascism that only served to get the cauldron of social restlessness boiling faster. In 1958, with the election of Jorge Alessandri as President, the conservative Old Guard finally got back into power. It was clear, however, that in Chile the days of oligarchic presidents were numbered.

For one thing, the Socialists and the Communists had formed a new coalition called *Frente de Acción Popular,* the Popular Action Front, better known as the FRAP. It was led by Dr. Salvador Allende, a well-to-do Santiago physician with a deep belief in Marxism, who was also the leader of the Socialist party. Allende yearned to be President of Chile and in the 1958 elections was beaten by only 33,000 votes.

The radicalized Chilean left grew enormously during the next three years. It was clear that Allende was heading toward his dream of the presidency. His slogans were working, his opposition was split and bankrupt of ideas and ideology. The State Department was rattled; Western Europe was jittery; businessmen were all but panic-stricken. Chile seemed destined to become the first country in the Americas to elect freely a Communist-controlled government.

Enter, not at all inconspicuously, Eduardo Frei and his Christian Democrats. In 1961, the Christian Democrats won for the first time a small but useful number of seats in the Chilean Congress: 23 out of 147 deputies, 3 out of 45 Senators. But this was enough to give Frei a platform (while tiny, the party was suddenly the third largest in the country), and he used it with great skill and no lack of demagoguery.

Frei grabbed the banner of reformism from the FRAP. He proposed massive social reforms, harangued about the crying need of agrarian reform and promised labor unions more bargaining freedom. He sounded, to many unhappy conservatives, more outrageous than the Communists. In fact, Frei and his fledgling party were proposing real revolution in Chile, albeit a peaceful one. As their slogan put it, "Revolution in Liberty."

To this day nobody can really say, although Christian Democrats write about it *ad infinitum,* what Christian Democracy really is. But it does seem to be an exceedingly flexible middle road between classical Marxism and progressive capitalism—a leftist Catholicism that spurns communism but does not mind toying around with Communist and Socialist economic theories if they suit the occasion. Or, as some of the Christian Democrats express it: a Third Force alternative to communism, and the only one.

When the 1964 Presidential elections came, the choice for Chileans was highly complex and frustrating. They could cast their ballots for FRAP and Allende and hope for the best, even if the United States and the West in general would be sick and furious. They could vote for the conservative-rightist-liberal coalition, which was certain to lose—a wasted ballot in a country that does not like political wastefulness. Or they could vote for Frei and the Christian Democrats, the Third Force, which would mean putting a new, untested, unknown team with who-knew-what-kind of philosophy in the Moneda Palace.

Frei played his hand with the skill and cunning of a professional Latin gambler. He played his best card—the one that said "The Only Alternative"—both inside and outside the country. And with equal success.

In Washington he convinced the White House and the State Department that the United States must back him; on Wall Street he convinced the businessmen. No, he kept arguing, we will not nationalize the copper mines (almost all American-owned), but we do want them turned into partnerships. No, we will not expropriate all the land, but we are going to take and redistribute what is being left fallow and we will damned well see to it that what we don't take produces food. Yes, we are going to increase taxes, but you of course realize that taxes are now ridiculously low, so no right-thinking man can mind that.

Backing he finally got. By mysterious ways, not talked about and always officially denied, Frei's campaign was bolstered by Yankee dollars and piles of Chilean pesos. A reasonable estimate is that the Christian Democrats got about $1-million a month, for many months, from American sources, and an estimated $18- to $20-million more from the Christian Democrats in West Germany, Italy and Belgium. At the same time, of course, Allende and the FRAP were known to be getting cash from sources of their own, including Cuba and the Soviet Union.

If the campaign financing favored Frei, so did the Christian Democrats' ability to grab and hold votes. Frei hammered away at Allende's association with the Communists, blaming Allende personally for the Berlin Wall, the Hungarian bloodshed, the missile crisis, and any other Eastern bloc sin he could think of.

Frei won in a landslide, and the Christian Democrats became the first party in 124 years to have an absolute majority in the Chamber of Deputies. (It fared less well in the Senate because only half that chamber is elected every eight years, but even there it won more than half of the seats contested.)

Washington turned handsprings. Not that there still weren't reservations about Frei in the State Department, but he *had* preserved the keystone of United States cold-war diplomacy: no Communist ever gets elected head of a nation in free elections in the free world. President Johnson named Ralph Anthony Dungan, a former White House Latin American adviser to President Kennedy and a practicing Catholic, as U.S. Ambassador to Chile.

The accomplishments of Frei and the Christian Democrats in the two and a half years since the election do not knock one's eye out. The Frei Government has built its share of roads (1,500 miles) and bridges (25) and dams and ditches. But the real progress made by Frei is best measured, as an American economist put it, by the "shrieks and moans of Chileans who are finding out for the first time what it is to have a government that is serious about deep changes in the old feudal order."

What Chileans are screaming loudest about today is, not surprisingly, taxation. The last nationwide assessment survey in Chile was in 1932, when the Chilean peso was worth about 4,000 times more than it is now. On that tax base levies were absurdly low. Since a new assessment survey, two years ago, property taxes have risen two or three times what they were before Frei (though by modern-nation standards they are still laughably low). The Government has rigidly applied a "wealth tax" on automobiles, stocks and assets held abroad, and real tax income to the Government has risen by 25 per cent a year. The treasury expects to reap a higher percentage in the years to come.

In the meantime, Frei has launched a full-scale attack on inflation. With price controls and firm import regulations, he has managed to bring down the increase in the cost-of-living index from 38.9 per cent in 1964, to 25.6 per cent in 1965, to somewhere around 20 to 25 per cent last year.

At the same time the world price of Chile's major export, copper, has risen to record heights and is now about 50–55 cents a pound. And within the last month the Government has signed agreements with all of the major copper companies that give Chile, for the first time, a major interest in its largest industry and still keep American know-how. The pacts provide for a 100 per cent increase in the production of copper (from 600,000 metric tons annually to 1.2-million metric tons by the early nineteen-seventies), and also the "Chileanization" of the mines. Chile, for example, will take over 51 per cent of the Kennecott mine, and for its share the country will put up 51 per cent of the new expansion capital—an amount close to $200-million. The Government will also become a 25-per-cent partner in a new Anaconda mine, while Anaconda will invest about $300-million for expanded production over the next five years. The American copper companies, it should be noted, are well pleased with the agreements: with tax-bracket advantages and other complicated legal largess, they may well profit more than when they owned the mines outright.

The Frei Government is investing vast sums in the nation's impoverished majority. In the past two years 87,000 permanent houses and 48,000 "emergency" dwellings were built as part of a slum-clearance program. An eighth year of free and compulsory education was approved, and teachers were hired to man 2,000 new schools. Dozens of new hospitals and clinics were built, and free medical care was increased.

The Chilean poor are getting the idea that the Christian Democrats are at least trying. But serious social reform in Chile has always run up against the same problem: the right insists that almost any reform is too leftist, and the left cries that all the reforms are not leftist enough. Frei's attempts at agrarian reform have bogged down in the face of precisely that age-old problem.

Agrarian reform is his most pressing problem, just now. Chile's large farmers, with the threat of possible expropriation over their heads, have all but given up worrying about producing. Once a net exporter of food, Chile now spends nearly $200-million yearly importing milk, meat, wheat and potatoes—all of which could be grown in surplus were it not for this to-hell-with-it attitude.

Government proposals still have not taken final shape and much of the legislation to make a full reform possible is bottled up in the Congress. But in rough outline they would allow the Government to decide if a landowner were producing enough, and if not, his property would be confiscated and the land collectivized, to be worked from three to five years by the landowner's former employes. At the end of that time title to the land would be granted to the peasants, in return for some nominal payment.

In all, somewhere in the neighborhood of 3,000 big landowners are expected to lose their property, according to some Government estimates. But both the right and the left have so far successfully helped to delay agrarian-reform bills in the Congress.

The left—Socialists, Communists and even the militant young left wing of Frei's own party—has argued that Frei's reform approaches a fraud because it does not allow for the collectivization of *every* farm in the nation. The right points out with horror that the Government will have to spend at least $55-million a year on its program, in compensation, resettlement grants and food import payments, to cover the inevitable decline in farm production; and that is more than double what the country invested in profitable mining and industry in 1965. Meanwhile, as the debate rages on, the *campesinos* are again growing restive, and therefore more responsive to the Communists' new campaigns in the rural areas.

The rising Chilean discontent, only part of which can be attributed to mid-term doldrums, is now deeply disturbing for Frei and his friends. He is spending a great deal of time trying to rein in the noisy left wing in his own party, fighting "secret cartel" charges leveled against him by the right, and running hard to out-think and outmaneuver the FRAP on the other extreme.

His political fortunes suffered a nasty blow last December when Allende, in a deal with the Radicals that can only be described as ultra-cynical, was voted president of the Senate. Already he has given Frei headaches because of his expert manipulation of the Senate's rules and regulations, and Allende will give Frei many sleepless nights to come.

The Christian Democrats and Frei may finally fail in Chile. Yet, somehow, one gets the feeling that they are going to succeed, against the odds, in changing the political and social character of the country. "How difficult it is to criticize when finally, after so many years of so little progress, there come a man and a party that look so promising," wrote an American political scientist recently.

But it cannot be forgotten that Frei and his party are attempting to work a bona fide revolution—"a revolution without the execution wall," Frei said in a speech last September—and revolution is not an easy business.

Suggested Reading

Clarence Ayres, *Theory of Economic Progress,* New York, Schocken Books, 1962 (Schocken paperback).

Robert E. Baldwin, *Economic Development and Growth,* New York, John Wiley & Sons, 1966 (Wiley paperback).

Paul A. Baran, *The Political Economy of Growth,* New York, Monthly Review Press, 1957 (Modern Reader paperback).

J. Bronowski, *Science and Human Values,* New York, Harper & Row, 1965 (Harper Torchbook paperback).

Thomas R. De Gregori and O. Pisunyar, *Economic Development,* New York, John Wiley & Sons, 1969 (Wiley paperback).

Celso Furtado, *The Economic Growth of Brazil,* Berkeley, University of California Press, 1968 (paperback).

John Kenneth Galbraith, *Economic Development,* Cambridge, Mass., Harvard University Press, 1964 (Houghton Mifflin Sentry paperback).

Clifford Geertz, *Peddlers and Princes,* Chicago, University of Chicago Press, 1968.

Wendell Gordon, *The Political Economy of Latin America,* New York, Columbia University Press, 1965 (Columbia paperback).

Robert L. Heilbroner, *The Great Ascent,* New York, Harper & Row, 1963 (Harper Torchbook paperback).

Albert O. Hirschman, *The Strategy of Economic Development,* New Haven, Yale University Press, 1958 (Yale paperback).

Irving Louis Horowitz, *Three Worlds of Development,* New York, Oxford University Press, 1966 (Oxford paperback).

Gunnar Myrdal, *An Approach to the Asian Drama,* New York, Random House, 1970 (Vintage paperback).

Jacob Oser, *Promoting Economic Development,* Evanston, Ill., Northwestern University Press, 1967.

Walter W. Rostow, *The Stages of Economic Growth,* Cambridge, Cambridge University Press, 1960 (Cambridge paperback, 1962).

Barbara Ward, *The Rich Nations and the Poor Nations,* New York, W. W. Norton, 1962 (Norton paperback).

Jack Woddis, *Introduction to Neo-Colonialism,* London, Lawrence & Wishart, 1967 (paperback).

Index

A Note on the Editor

James Cornehls was born in Dallas, Texas, and studied at the University of the Americas, Mexico City, and the University of Texas, Austin. He is co-author of *Manpower and Economic Development in Peru* and the author of articles on Latin-American development. He is now Associate Professor of Economics and Urban Affairs at the University of Texas, Arlington.

NEW YORK TIMES BOOKS published by QUADRANGLE BOOKS

AMERICAN FISCAL AND MONETARY POLICY
edited with an Introduction by Harold Wolozin
AMERICAN FOREIGN POLICY SINCE 1945
edited with an Introduction by Robert A. Divine
AMERICAN LABOR SINCE THE NEW DEAL
edited with an Introduction by Melvyn Dubofsky
AMERICAN POLITICS SINCE 1945
edited with an Introduction by Richard M. Dalfiume
AMERICAN SOCIETY SINCE 1945
edited with an Introduction by William L. O'Neill
BLACK PROTEST IN THE SIXTIES
edited with an Introduction by August Meier and Elliott Rudwick
BRITAIN, 1919—1970
edited with an Introduction by John F. Naylor
CITIES IN TROUBLE
edited with an Introducton by Nathan Glazer
THE CONTEMPORARY AMERICAN FAMILY
edited with an Introduction by William J. Goode
THE CORPORATION IN THE AMERICAN ECONOMY
edited with an Introduction by Harry M. Trebing
CRIME AND CRIMINAL JUSTICE
edited with an Introduction by Donald R. Cressey
ECONOMIC DEVELOPMENT AND ECONOMIC GROWTH
edited with an Introduction by James V. Cornehls
EUROPEAN SOCIALISM SINCE WORLD WAR I
edited with an Introduction by Nathanael Greene
THE MEANING OF THE AMERICAN REVOLUTION
edited with an Introduction by Lawrenoc H. Leder
MODERN AMERICAN CITIES
edited with an Introduction by Ray Ginger
MOLDERS OF MODERN THOUGHT
edited with an Introduction by Ben B. Seligman
NAZIS AND FASCISTS IN EUROPE, 1918—1945
edited with an Introduction by John Weiss
THE NEW DEAL
edited with an Introduction by Carl N. Degler
POP CULTURE IN AMERICA
edited with an Introduction by David Manning White
POVERTY AND WEALTH IN AMERICA
edited with an Introduction by Harold L. Sheppard
PREJUDICE AND RACE RELATIONS
edited with an Introduction by Raymond W. Mack
TECHNOLOGY AND SOCIAL CHANGE
edited with an Introduction by Wilbert E. Moore